The
Blackmore
Country

Also from Westphalia Press

westphaliapress.org

The
Blackmore
Country

A Pedigree of the
Blackmore Family

by F. J. Snell

WESTPHALIA PRESS
An imprint of Policy Studies Organization

Westphalia Press
An imprint of Policy Studies Organization
1527 New Hampshire Ave., NW
Washington, D.C. 20036
info@ipsonet.org

ISBN-13: 978-1-63391-386-8
ISBN-10: 1-63391-386-4

Cover design by Taillefer Long at Illuminated Stories:
www.illuminatedstories.com

Daniel Gutierrez-Sandoval, Executive Director
PSO and Westphalia Press

Updated material and comments on this edition
can be found at the Westphalia Press website:
www.westphaliapress.org

The Pilgrimage Series

THE BLACKMORE COUNTRY

ON THE LYN, BELOW BRENDON (page 162).

THE
BLACKMORE COUNTRY

BY

F. J. SNELL

AUTHOR OF "A BOOK OF EXMOOR," ETC.

SECOND EDITION
WITH 32 FULL-PAGE ILLUSTRATIONS
FROM PHOTOGRAPHS BY
CATHARINE W. BARNES WARD

LONDON
ADAM AND CHARLES BLACK

"So holy and so perfect is my love,

.   .   .   .   .   .

That I shall think it a most plenteous crop
To glean the broken ears after the man
That the main harvest reaps."
—Sir PHILIP SIDNEY.

First Edition, containing 50 *illustrations, published* 1906
This Edition published 1911

PREFACE TO THE SECOND EDITION

THE *Blackmore Country* having achieved a second edition, it is proper to state that it is now presented to the public substantially in the same form as in the original issue. Advantage, however, has been taken of a friendly critique by Mr Arthur Smyth to effect some revision. Mr Smyth, who was well acquainted with the Blackmore family, and indeed a distant relation, is rather perplexed at the assertion that the novelist's father was a poor man; but he certainly passed for such at Culmstock, and the fact that he took pupils, in addition to serving his poor cure, tends to show that he was by no means too well off.

In my *Early Associations of Archbishop Temple* it is stated with reference to the restoration of Culmstock Church : "Nobody knew from what source Mr Blackmore obtained the necessary funds, but it was supposed that his wife's relations were rich." This is, in a sense, confirmed by Mr Smyth, who says that Mr Turberville, R. D. Blackmore's elder brother, inherited considerable property from his mother; but, when I wrote the passage above quoted, I was not aware that John Blackmore was married twice. His first wife, who died three years after their

v

marriage, and before John Blackmore set foot in
Culmstock, may not have been in possession of
means, although Turberville's estate—Mr Smyth
says, "his will was proved for (I believe)
£20,000"—may have been derived from his
maternal connections.   Mr Snowden Ward, in
his Introduction to the Doone-land edition of
Lorna Doone, informs us regarding R. D. Blackmore, also a son of this lady : "A bequest from
the Rev. H. Hay Knight, his mother's brother,
put an end to his financial worries."

Nevertheless, it may be doubted whether the
novelist was ever in even "comparative affluence."
He himself publicly declared that he lost more
than he gained from market-gardening—he was,
by the way, a F.R.H.S.—and the late Rev. D.
M. Owen, Blackmore's old schoolfellow, with
whom he maintained a lifelong correspondence,
told me that he was constantly complaining of
his pecuniary limitations.   Mr Owen's reply was
that he had no excuse ; he had only to write
another *Lorna Doone* to replenish his treasury
to the brim.   When, also, he was asked for a
subscription to the Culmstock flower show,
Blackmore declined, assigning as the reason
that he "couldn't afford it."   This does not look
like "comparative affluence."

Mr Smyth says that he never saw or heard
of any daughters of the Rev. John Blackmore.
If he implies that there were none, he is certainly
mistaken (see Prologue), but he raises a problem
which, I confess, I am not able to solve.   "In
Charles Church there is a marble slab erected to
the memory of the Rev. John Blackmore by his
children, J. B., R. B., M. A. B.   No allusion is

made to M. A. B. in the pedigree either by the Rev. J. F. Chanter or Mr Snell." The only explanation which occurs to me is that M. A. B. may represent the initials of their full sister, who died in infancy. The Rev. John Blackmore married in 1822. Three years later he sustained a terrible trial. "The novelist's father," says Mr Ward, "was a 'coach' for Oxford pupils, until, in 1825, a great outbreak of typhus fever swept away his wife, daughter, two pupils, the family physician, and all the servants, and almost broke John Blackmore's heart." R. D. Blackmore's mother's maiden name was Anne Basset Knight; and the A. in M. A. B. suggests that her daughter may have been called Anne—perhaps Mary Anne, if M. A. B. indicates that daughter. She had long been dead, but the brothers, as an act of piety, may have chosen to commemorate her in this way, whilst ignoring the daughters of the second family, whom Mr Smyth never saw or heard of.

In conclusion, the demand for a second edition of this work is a satisfactory answer to the disparaging remarks of the late Mr F. T. Elworthy in a presidential address to the members of the Devonshire Association for the Promotion of Literature, Science, and Art. It is a bad precedent that the title and contents of a new work should be officially censured on an occasion when it was by an accident that the author was not present to be lectured for his shortcomings, just as it was a pure accident that Mr Elworthy was not named in the book as accompanying Dr Murray and Professor Rhys in their visit to the Caractacus stone on Winsford Hill (p. 109)! I now repair this omission, and at the same time express regret that the secretaries did not take steps to delete from the reports of a learned and very useful association criticism which, to say the least, was beside the mark.

F. J. SNELL.

January 30, 1911.

PROLOGUE

THE "Blackmore Country" is an expression requiring some amount of definition, as it clearly will not do to make it embrace the whole of the territory which he annexed, from time to time, in his various works of fiction, nor even every part of Devon in which he has laid the scenes of a romance. The latter point may perhaps be open to discussion in the sense that, ideally, the glamour of his writing ought to rest with its full might of memory on all the neighbourhoods of the West around which he drew his magic circle. As a fact, however, it is North Devon and a slice of the sister county that form his literary patrimony, while Dartmoor is a more general possession, which he failed to seal with the same staunch and archetypal impression. There have been many good Dartmoor stories, and one instinctively associates that region with the names of Baring-Gould and Eden Phillpotts; with Blackmore, hardly at all. But from Exmoor to Barnstaple, and from Lynton to Tiverton, he reigns supreme — and naturally, for this was his homeland, which, through all its length and breadth, he knew with an intimacy,

b

and loved with a devotion, and portrayed with a skill, that will surely never again be the portion of any child of Devon.

Richard Doddridge Blackmore was born on June 7, 1825, at Longworth, in Berkshire — a circumstance which raises the delicate and important question whether, after all, he can be justly claimed as a Devonshire man. On the whole, I think, the question may be answered affirmatively, although it is evident that he cannot possibly be described as a native of the county. Who, however, would dream of depriving an Englishman of his nationality merely for the accident of his being born abroad, unless indeed he deliberately abandoned that proud title and threw in his lot with the country of his birth, to the exclusion of his ancestral home? And this practically represents the state of affairs as regards Blackmore. In one sense it must be admitted he did not remain constant to his Devonshire connections, inasmuch as he resided through a great part of his life, and to the day of his death, at Teddington, in Middlesex. But as against this must be set the facts that he descended from an old North Devon stock, a stock so old that it may fairly be termed indigenous, and that his boyish experiences were almost entirely confined within the county. To these weighty considerations may be added that he eventually became possessor of the ancient residence of his race, that he always manifested the warmest interest in county concerns, and that his great achievement in literature was inspired by West-country legend. That well-known authority, the Rev. J. F. Chanter, worthy son of a worthy sire, would like to say "Devon" legend, and much may be urged in favour of his contention, notwithstanding that modern Exmoor is altogether in Somerset. He points out, for instance, that Bagworthy (or "Badgery") Wood, the centre of the Doone traditions, is in Devon. Still it were better, perhaps, to consider *Lorna Doone* in the light of a border romance. Indeed, on an impartial survey, it seems almost necessary to adopt this view ; and Blackmore himself was anything but unwilling to recognise, and even to emphasise, the Somerset element in his story.

Not long before the novelist's death, a gentleman wrote to him from Taunton, calling attention to the widely prevalent idea that in the course of the tale he conveyed the impression of allocating this charming country to North Devon rather than West Somerset ; and Mr Blackmore's correspondent went on to mention that recently strenuous efforts had been made to procure the inclusion of Exmoor in Devon, but that the policy of plunder had been defeated by the vigilant action of the Somerset County Council. In reply to this communication the following letter was received :—

"My dear Sir,—Nowhere, to the best of my remembrance, have I said, or even implied, that Exmoor lies mainly in Devonshire. Having known that country from my boyhood—for my grandfather was the incumbent of Oare as well as of Combe Martin—I have always borne in mind the truth that by far the larger part of the moor is within the county of Somerset, and the very first sentence in *Lorna Doone* shows that

John Ridd lived in the latter county. Moreover, when application is made to Devon J.P.'s for a warrant against the Doones, does not one of them say that the crime was committed in Somerset, and therefore he cannot deal with it? See also p. 179 (6d. edition), which seems to me clear enough for anything. Moreover, the rivalry of the militia, both in *Lorna Doone* and *Slain by the Doones*—which title I dislike, and did not choose freely—shows that the Doone Valley was upon the county border. I think also that Cosgate, supposed to be 'County's Gate,' is referred to in *Lorna Doone*, but I cannot stop to look.[1] The Warren where the Squire lived is on the westward of the line, as Lynmouth is—or, at least, I think so—and therefore North Devon is spoken of the heroine who lives there. All this being so very clear to me, I have been surprised more than once at finding myself accused in Somerset papers of describing Exmoor as mainly a district of Devonshire—a thing which I never did, even in haste of thought. And if you should hear such a charge repeated, I trust that your courtesy will induce you to contradict it, which I have never done publicly, as I thought the refutation was self-evident."

It is certainly true that at Dulverton, which, if not Exmoor, is next door to it, visitors frequently imagine that they are in Devonshire, as I have myself proved, but, for my own part, I have never attributed this delusion to the influence of *Lorna Doone*. On the contrary, it

---

[1] Cosgate is mentioned in chapter xlviii., where the county boundary is defined.—F. J. S.

has seemed to me that a river is the culprit.
The Exe is universally esteemed a Devon stream,
and lends its name to the metropolis of the West.
That in these circumstances Exmoor should be
anywhere but in Devonshire, may well appear a
violation of the fitness of things, and as coloured
maps seldom perhaps emerge from their impedimenta, these visitors revenge themselves on the
makers of England by substituting for artificial
delimitations their own easy beliefs and natural
assumptions.

This, however, is somewhat of a digression.
I return to the probably more interesting topic
of Mr Blackmore's Devonshire "havage," which
good old West-country term I once heard a good
old West-country clergyman derive from the
Latin *avus*—needless to say, a most unlikely
etymon. In the above-quoted letter reference is
made to the novelist's grandfather as incumbent
of Oare and Combe Martin, but, had the occasion
required it, Blackmore could no doubt have
furnished a much fuller account of his North
Devon pedigree. It is extremely probable, but
not absolutely certain, that one of his remote
ancestors, sharing the same Christian name
Richard, married a Wichehalse of Lynton. To
have read *Lorna Doone* is to remember how John
Ridd rudely disturbed young Squire Wichehalse
in the act of kissing his sister Annie ; and I shall
have more to say of this half-foreign clan, their
fortunes, and their eyry in a subsequent chapter.
Meanwhile one may note that the first entry in
the parish register of Parracombe relates to the
marriage of Richard Blackmore and Margaret,
daughter of Hugh Wichehalse, of Ley, Esq. ;

and, further, that the bride's father died on
Christide, 1653, and the bride herself thirty years
later. These dates are important, as they seem
to preclude the possibility of the Richard Blackmore who wedded the Lady of Ley being the
direct progenitor of the Richard Blackmore who
wrote *Lorna Doone*, though it can scarcely be
questioned that he was of the same kith and kin,
and so, in the larger sense, an ancestor. In any
case, the match cannot be accepted as a criterion
of the standing of the family. *Mésalliances* are
not unknown in North Devon, one such romantic
union of erstwhile celebrity being the marriage
of a small farmer's son with a daughter of the
resident rector, a gentleman of good descent and
prebendary of Exeter Cathedral. From the time
of John Ridd, and who shall say for how many
ages antecedent thereto, love has laughed at lock-
smiths and gone its own wilful way.

Small farmers, however, the Blackmores were
not. They were freeholders settled at East
Bodley and Barton in the parish of Parracombe,
and leaseholders of the neighbouring farm of
Killington, or Kinwelton, in the parish of
Martinhoe. Over the porch of the old farm-
stead at Parracombe may still be read the
inscription, "R.B., J.B., 1638"; and as the
Subsidy Rolls of 16 Charles I. for Parracombe
and Martinhoe contain the names of Richard
and John Blackmore, we may conjecture without
difficulty to whom the initials belonged. The
first of the yeomen on whom we can fasten as a
certain ancestor of the novelist was a John
Blackmore who died in 1689. His son Richard,
and grandson John, and great-grandson John—

not to mention other members of the family
whose names are duly recorded—suffered themselves to be absorbed with the peaceful and
healthful pursuit of husbandry, which they
practised, generation after generation, on their
estate at Bodley.   Then, towards the end of the
eighteenth century there occurred a change ; and
the Blackmore name, in the person of another
John, took what may be termed an upward turn.
This John Blackmore, born in 1764, betrayed a
taste for learning, and through Tiverton School
found his way to Exeter College, Oxford, where
he won the degree of B.A.   He was soon after
ordained, and entered on his duties as curate of
High Bray, on the outskirts of Exmoor, and in
his own country and county.   An antiquary and
a person of general cultivation, he was at the
pains of copying the parish register, and in the
new edition did what every parson should do, set
down items of current interest, together with an
informal history of the parish, so far as it could
be learned.   He did also what few parsons should
attempt—adorned his copy of the register with
original Latin verses.   Such specimens of new
Latin poetry as I have disinterred from parochial
records are, for the most part, fearful and
wonderful lucubrations as to both sentiment and
technique, whereas it is frequently the case that
voluntary jottings in the vulgar tongue gild and
redeem, with their human touches, whole conti-
nents of inky wilderness.

Not long after his advent at High Bray Mr
Blackmore appears to have married, and in
process of time his wife bore him a first-born
son, whom he named John.   He was, however,

not quite content with his position as curate;
and accordingly he bought the advowson of the
adjacent living of Charles, in the confident
expectation that it would shortly become void,
pending which happy consummation he agreed to
serve as curate-in-charge.   No speculation could
have been more disastrous, since, in point of fact,
the hoped-for vacancy did not occur till quite
half a century had passed over his head, and at
that advanced age he did not think proper to
enter upon possession.   Instead of doing so, he
presented his second son Richard to the rectory.
During this protracted era of suspense John
Blackmore, senior, as he must now be designated,
did not lack preferment.   In 1809 he was
appointed rector of Oare, and in 1833 (pluralities
being still admissible) he received in addition the
valuable living of Combe Martin ; and both these
appointments he continued to hold till his death
in 1842.

As has been intimated, the original Parson
Blackmore had two sons, John and Richard,
each of whom, following in his footsteps, entered
the Church ; and the elder at all events met
with considerably worse luck than his father.
Curiously enough, his early life was full of
promise, for in 1816 he was elected Fellow of
Exeter, his father's old college, and this might
well have proved the inception of a long and
successful academic career, either in Oxford or at
one of our public schools.   But in 1822 he
vacated his fellowship on his marriage with Anne
Basset, daughter of the Rev. J. Knight, of
Newton Nottage.   Thirteen years later he had
attained to no higher position than that of

curate-in-charge of Culmstock, near Tiverton;
and when he retired from that, it was only to
proceed in a similar capacity to Ashford, near
Barnstaple. He was always poor, but deserved
a happier fate, since he was always good (see
Maid of Sker, chapter xxxix.). He died in
1858.

By his wife Anne the Rev. John Blackmore
had one daughter and two sons, Henry John,
who afterwards took the name of Turberville,
and Richard Doddridge. The former produced
a bizarre poem entitled "The Two Colonels,"
and was proficient in a number of sciences,
notably in astronomy, but he was eccentric to
such a degree that there was grave doubt, in
spite of all his attainments, whether he was quite
compos mentis. He resided at Bradiford, near
Barnstaple, died at Yeovil under distressing
circumstances, and was buried at Charles (in
1875). He assumed the name Turberville, so it
is said, out of resentment at the sale of the
family estates for the benefit of a half-brother,
Frederick Platt Blackmore, an officer in the army
and a spendthrift; and he notified his intention,
as well as his reason, to all whom it might
concern in a printed handbill. Anger was also
the motive for his writing "The Two Colonels";
he conceived there had been discourtesy on the
part of the members of the Ilfracombe Highway
Board and others. The publication caused much
excitement, and at one time an action for libel
seemed imminent. Eventually, it is believed, the
book was withdrawn.

Besides the son already mentioned, the Rev.
John Blackmore had by his second wife two

daughters, Charlotte Ellen, who married the Rev. J. P. Faunthorpe, of Whitelands College, Chelsea, and Jane Elizabeth, who was the wife of the Rev. Samuel Davis, for many years vicar of Barrington, Devon. He was for a year or two at Bude Haven, and won some reputation there as a preacher. Hence, his son, Mr A. H. Davis, thought he might possibly be the "Bude Light" of *Tales from the Telling House*, but my friend, the late Rev. D. M. Owen, who probably knew, gave me to understand that the "Bude Light" was the Rev. Goldsworthy Gurney.

Returning to the first family—the second son was Richard Doddridge Blackmore, the novelist. In his case, although great wit is proverbially allied to madness, the question of sanity is not likely to be raised; and probably the worst fault that the world will lay to his charge is that of undue secretiveness. It is common knowledge that he interdicted anything in the shape of a biography, and doubtless he took measures to prevent the survival of private papers and letters which might be used as material for the purpose. Whether or not he did this, his wish will assuredly be held sacred by his more intimate friends, who alone are qualified to undertake such a work. Meanwhile the novelist has to pay for his prohibition of an authentic Life, by the unrestricted play of *ben trovare*. Having myself been victimised by this insidious enemy of truth, I seize the opportunity to protest that any statements regarding the late Mr Blackmore to be found in the present work are made without prejudice and with all reserve,

as being, conceivably, the inventions of the
Father of Lies. At the same time, as due
caution has been observed and the evidence has,
in various instances, been drawn from reputable
and independent witnesses who, without knowing
it, acted as a check on each other, I cannot
seriously believe that these contributions to
history are either gratuitous or garbled.

An illustration, pointed and germane, is not
far to seek. I always understood from my late
kind friend, the Rev. C. St Barbe, Sydenham,
rector of Brushford, who, to the deep regret of a
wide circle of acquaintance, passed away in the
spring of 1904 at the age of 81, that R. D.
Blackmore, as a boy, spent many of his vacations
at the moorland village of Charles, to the rectory
of which his uncle Richard had, as we have seen,
been presented by his grandfather. Mr Sydenham
even went so far as to use the expression
" brought up " in this connection, which indicates
at least the length and frequency of young
Blackmore's visits. Now the Rev. J. F. Chanter,
in a paper written in 1903, shows that he also
has gained a knowledge of the circumstance—
certainly by some other means. As the rector
of Charles did not die till 1880, and so lived to
see his nephew and guest grown famous, it is not
to be supposed that he allowed his share in the
hero's tirocinium to remain obscure. What more
natural than that he should communicate it freely
to his neighbours, with all the pride of a fond
uncle with no children of his own? Would he
not have related also, as the harvest of imparted
wisdom, that in the rectory parlour, the scene of
former instruction, great part of *Lorna Doone* was

written ? Nor must we forget the old Blackmore
property at Bodley, where the novelist's grandfather, in order to adapt it to his requirements
as an occasional residence, had added to the
venerable homestead a new wing ; and where,
or at Oare rectory, the future romancer passed
blissful holidays, roaming at will in the North
Devon fields and lanes, and drinking in quaint
lore, conveyed in the broad, kindly accents of the
North Devon country-folk.   The Bodley estates,
consisting of East Bodley, West Hill, and
Burnsley Mill, passed to the novelist's father, by
whom they were sold a few years before his
death.   Mr Arthur Smyth, referring to R. D.
Blackmore's college days, avers that even then
he was very reserved.   Mr Smyth's father often
went shooting with him.   About this time a
white hare was caught at Bodley, and, having
been stuffed, was treasured by the Rev. R. Blackmore in his dining-room at Charles.

Thus the limits of the Blackmore country are
definitely staked out by family tradition, as well
as by literary interest, running from Culmstock to
Ashford, and from Oare to Combe Martin, with
the commons appurtenant.   The confines are
somewhat vague and irregular, and I must crave
some indulgence for my method of configuration.
Obviously, the novelist's recollections of his youth
with their accompanying sentiments and inspira-
tions, cannot be taken as an absolute guide, for
then it would be requisite to cross the Bristol
Channel to Newton Nottage, his mother's home,
in the vicinity of which are laid the opening
scenes of the charming *Maid of Sker.*   Such a
course would infringe too much on the popular

conception of the phrase, and the attempt to link localities without any natural connection, and severed by an arm of the sea, however successfully accomplished in the romance, would in our case involve needless confusion. What little is said about Newton Nottage, therefore, may as well be said here.

A village in Glamorganshire, it had peculiarly sacred and solemn associations for R. D. Blackmore. Nottage Court, the seat of the Knight family, was his mother's ancestral home, and it was also one of the homes of his own childhood. Here he wrote his first book, the above-named romance, which was ever his favourite, but the story was re-written, and not published till a later date. For Blackmore, however, the place had sad as well as pleasant memories, for it was here that his father, then curate of Ashford, was found dead in his bed on the morning of September 24, 1858, whilst on a visit to his wife's people, and at Newton Nottage he lies buried.

If this is crossing the Bristol Channel, so be it ; we are soon back again, and ready to discourse of Tiverton, and Southmolton, and Lynton, and Barnstaple, and their smaller neighbours, with the moors and commons appurtenant.[1]

---

[1] This term recurs to me almost as often as I think of moors and commons, and for the following reason. An old friend of mine, who lived to be nearly ninety, a lawyer by profession and a wit by practice, once told me how he attended an inquiry held in West Somerset by a certain Government Commission, concerning a well-known tract adjacent to his property. To his surprise, a fussy solicitor, who did not know that he was addressing another "limb of the law," rushed up to him, and after expatiating volubly on the difference between a claim in gross, a claim appendant,

and a claim appurtenant, begged to be informed what was
the nature of his claim.   "*Im*pertinent, if any," replied my
friend, delighted at the opportunity, "as I am not here on
business."

PEDIGREE OF THE BLACKMORE FAMILY

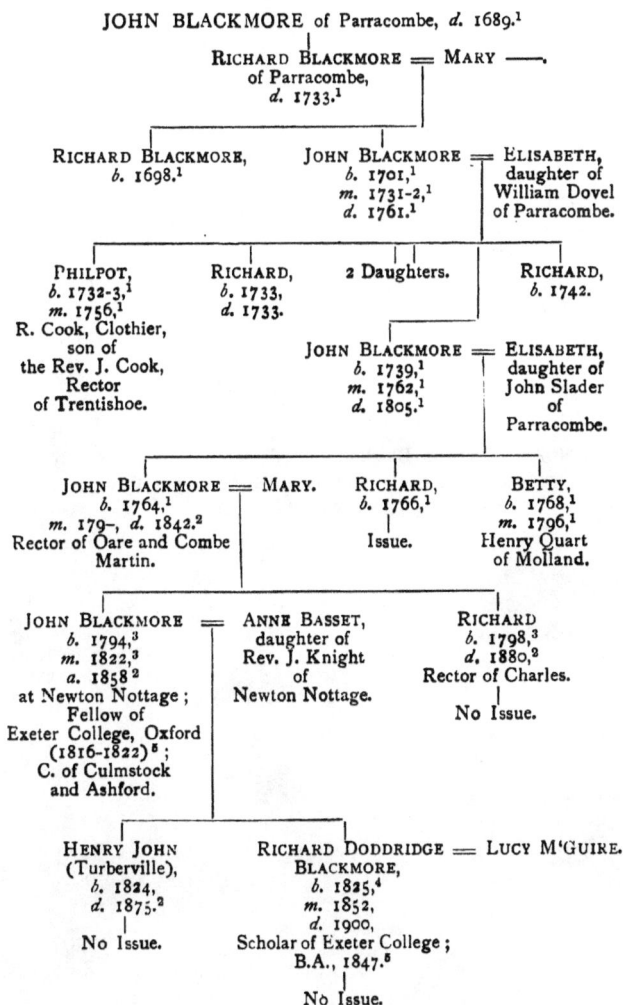

JOHN BLACKMORE of Parracombe, *d.* 1689.[1]

RICHARD BLACKMORE = MARY ——.
of Parracombe,
d. 1733.[1]

RICHARD BLACKMORE,
b. 1698.[1]

JOHN BLACKMORE = ELISABETH,
b. 1701,[1] daughter of
m. 1731-2,[1] William Dovel
d. 1761.[1] of Parracombe.

PHILPOT,
b. 1732-3,[1]
m. 1756,[1]
R. Cook, Clothier,
son of
the Rev. J. Cook,
Rector
of Trentishoe.

RICHARD,
b. 1733,
d. 1733.

2 Daughters.

RICHARD,
b. 1742.

JOHN BLACKMORE = ELISABETH,
b. 1739,[1] daughter of
m. 1762,[1] John Slader
d. 1805.[1] of
Parracombe.

JOHN BLACKMORE = MARY.
b. 1764,[1]
m. 179-, *d.* 1842.[2]
Rector of Oare and Combe
Martin.

RICHARD,
b. 1766,[1]
Issue.

BETTY,
b. 1768,[1]
m. 1796,[1]
Henry Quart
of Molland.

JOHN BLACKMORE =
b. 1794,[3]
m. 1822,[3]
a. 1858[2]
at Newton Nottage ;
Fellow of
Exeter College, Oxford
(1816–1822)[5] ;
C. of Culmstock
and Ashford.

ANNE BASSET,
daughter of
Rev. J. Knight
of
Newton Nottage.

RICHARD
b. 1798,[3]
d. 1880,[2]
Rector of Charles.

No Issue.

HENRY JOHN
(Turberville),
b. 1824,
d. 1875.[2]

No Issue.

RICHARD DODDRIDGE = LUCY M'GUIRE.
BLACKMORE,
b. 1825,[4]
m. 1852,
d. 1900,
Scholar of Exeter College ;
B.A., 1847.[5]

No Issue.

---

[1] Parracombe Registers. [2] Charles Registers. [3] High Bray Registers.
[4] *Dict. Nat. Biog.* [5] Register Exeter College.

NOTE.—For the Blackmore pedigree and other kindly assistance, the author is indebted to the Rev. J. F. CHANTER, of Parracombe.

CONTENTS

LIST OF ILLUSTRATIONS

FROM PHOTOGRAPHS BY CATHARINE W. BARNES WARD.

THE BLACKMORE COUNTRY

CHAPTER I

THE APPROACH

R. D. BLACKMORE was about ten years of age when his father took up his abode at Culmstock, a village in East Devon, at the foot of the Blackdowns. Notwithstanding an inclination to wander, evidence of which has been adduced in the previous section, the boy must have passed a fair amount of time at home; and wherever Blackmore tarried, he became imbued with the spirit of the place, wrested all its secrets, and acquired an intimate acquaintance with its arts and crafts such as would do credit to a committee of experts. Above all, he had the enviable gift of being able to distil from the rude realities their poetic essence—the prize of loving intelligence.

So far as Culmstock and the neighbourhood are concerned, the fruits of his observation are to be seen in *Perlycross*, and in a much lesser degree in *Tales from the Telling House*. The former, by no means so *répandu* as *Lorna Doone*, labours under the disadvantage, which is yet not all disadvantage, of fictitious names; consequently but few are aware that Perliton, Perlycross, and

A

Perlycombe are pretty, but deceptive aliases of
Uffculme, Culmstock, and Hemyock.   These
little places—Uffculme, however, claims to be a
town—are tapped by a light railway of serpentine
construction, which branches from the main line
at Tiverton Junction.   The trains are appallingly
slow, chiefly on account of the curves ; and just
outside the junction is a stiff gradient, the ascent
of which, especially in frosty weather, is proble-
matical.   Often there is nothing for it but to drop
back to the station and try again, or, as the
French have it, *se reculer pour mieux sauter.*

The level champaign traversed by the
caricature of locomotion is remarkable for its
fertility, and for many other things redolent, I
wot, to the ordinary resident of nothing but the
meanest bathos—so deadly in use! It is otherwise with the stranger within the gates, to whom
these items of every day unfold themselves as
precious boons, creating a joyous sense of novelty
and possession.   A rapid but happy and accurate
description of the vale by Mr Henry, who, I believe,
is an Irishman, points the common lesson how
much of beauty and wonder lies around us, had
we but eyes to see.   Impatient for the hills,
and doubtless as purblind as my neighbours, I
should scarce have lingered amid these pastoral
scenes but for his restraining touch, so that I
rest doubly indebted to his sage and kindly
interpretation.

"I live in Uffculme.   Its name might appro-
priately be Coleraine, for it is indeed a corner of
ferns ; every lane abounds with them, the hart's
tongue being specially abundant.   Uffculme takes
its name from the river Culm, and means simply

up Culm. It is noted for 'zider' and its grammar school. It is a quaint and quiet village. I love its charming thatched cottages, with their niched eaves, each niche the eyebrow of a little window. The inns too are quaint, with their suspended signs, each a symbolic gem. Some in the country around here bear such names as the 'Merry Harriers,' the 'Honest Heart,' the 'Rising Sun,' the 'Half Moon,' the 'Hare and Hounds,' etc.

"There are four streets in Uffculme, and a triangular 'square,' on which a market is held every two months. In the interval the grass has its own sweet will. Everything is still; the smoke rises like incense in the air. Here, as I write, looking into a garden, which even now, in October, has many flowers in bloom, I hear no sounds but the song of the robin enjoying the glory of the morning sun, a chanticleer crowing in the distance, and the clanging anvil of the village blacksmith.

"The narrowness of the lanes around adds greatly to the country's charms, their high hedgerows being a mass of many kinds of flowers. Thoroughly to enjoy the beauties of the neighbourhood, however, it must be viewed from one of the hills or downs. Embowered in a wealth of greenery, Uffculme sleeps on a slope of the Culm valley. As far as the eye can reach, lies a most beautiful panorama of diversified hill and dale with rounded trees, every field hedged with them. The quiet herds of Devon cattle lie ruminating and adorning the green bosom of the country. The whole scene has a charming cultured aspect, as if some giant landscape-gardener had laid it

out. What peacefulness! How beautiful the
cattle!

> 'Aren't they innocent things, them bas'es,
> And haven't they got old innocent faces?
> A-strooghin' their legs that lazy way,
> Or a-standin' as if they meant to pray.
> They're that sollum an' lovin' an' steady an' wise,
> And the butter meltin' in their big eyes,
> Eh, what do you think about it, John?
> Is it the stuff they're feedin' on?
> The clover, and meadow grass, and rushes,
> And then goin' pickin' among the bushes,
> And sniffin' the dew when its fresh and fine,
> The sweetest brew of God's own wine.'

"And then the Devonshire clotted cream!
It is delicious, yet simply made. The milk
stands on the hob till the cream rises and
attains almost the consistency of dough. Every
son of Devon, native and adopted, enjoys this
luxury to the full.

"The Culm is a little wandering river,
abounding in trout. Otters are hunted at
Hemyock. Foxes also are found in the neighbourhood, and on one occasion the noble wild
red deer approached within five miles of us.
Birds of all kinds are plentiful, and flowers
abound. Bullfinches are a pest, even among
the apple-trees. In my first walk, I saw a king-
fisher and a jay. The country exudes vegetation
at every pore. The mildness of the climate is
evidenced by the fact that on Saturday last
(October 17) I saw in bloom the foxglove,
poppy, primrose, wild anthernum, and many
other flowers. I ate a strawberry grown in the
open; watched the bees on the mignonette beds,
and saw a wood-pigeon's nest with young. The

climax is reached when I say that a man of great agricultural faith, in the neighbouring parish of Halberton, is attempting a second crop of potatoes.

"The country is well-watered; little rills gush from every quarter. The natives reckon by the flowers—*e.g.*, 'He went to Canada last hyacinth time.' The gentlemen's seats are lovely in the extreme, and are surrounded by trees that would not grow 'in the cold North's unhallowed ground.' Within a stone's throw of the 'square,' and in a former Coleraine gentleman's seat, grow Wellingtonia pines, the cypress, the breadfruit tree, the Spanish chestnut, and other exotic beauties. A house in the village has its walls adorned with passion-flowers, now in bloom.

"We are out of the tourist's track here. The motor rarely invades our quiet life; indeed, the roads are not suited for motoring, as the streams cross them in several places, and a foot-bridge affords the only means of dry transit for the passengers.

"I need not dwell on the Devon dialect. It is familiar to every reader of *Lorna Doone.* Suffice it to say that it slides out with the maximum ease, and in defiance of every rule of grammar. Have I exhausted Devonian joys? Nay, I could mention the melodious church-bells, the beauty of the children, and many other matters; but I have fulfilled my intention, if I have conveyed the quaintness, the peace, and the good living of this part of rural Devon—a land 'where the plain old men have rosy faces, and the simple maidens quiet eyes.'"

Hence it appears that all the glory did not

depart from Devon with fustian coats and brass buttons.

Mr Henry, it will be observed, speaks admiringly, as well he may, of the extreme loveliness of the country-seats. So far as the Culm valley is concerned, none will compare with Bradfield, the immemorial home of the Walrond family. Readers of *Perlycross* will recollect the brave veteran, Sir Thomas Waldron, and the wrong done to his honoured remains; and they may perchance note the different modes of spelling the name. Blackmore follows the local pronunciation, and the precedent of good old John Waldron, founder of an almshouse at Tiverton, of whom Harding remarks, "By his arms I judge his ancestors were branched from the ancient family at Bradfield, near Cullompton, where they were located in Henry II.'s time."

According to Hutchins, the family of Walrond is descended from Walran Venator, to whom William I. gave eight manors in Dorsetshire. The name is indubitably of French origin, and apparently represents the old Latin patronymic Valerian.

To turn from names to things, an authentic note attests that, in 1332, John Walrond had a licence for an oratory. Presumably this was the ancient chapel of which Lysons speaks, and which probably stood on a site still known as the Chapel Yard, on the north side of the mansion. The present house does not go back to so remote a time. On the north wall are the words, "Vivat E. Rex"; and elsewhere may be seen the dates 1592 and 1604. It is considered that the house was rebuilt in sections

and at intervals, during the short reign of
Edward VI., and towards the close of that of
Elizabeth.

Apart from inevitable decay, the mansion
remained practically unaltered until about the
middle of the last century, when it was thoroughly
restored by the late Sir John Walrond, who
planted the fine avenues of oak and cedar. Sir
John did nothing to destroy or impair the
character of the place, and the changes he introduced were extremely judicious, as indeed was to
be expected from a gentleman of his refined taste.
Son of Mr Benjamin Bowden Dickinson, of
Tiverton, who assumed his wife's name on his
marriage with the heiress of the last of the
Bradfield line, he came into possession in 1845.
At that time the house consisted of north and
south gabled wings, united by the old hall, and
in ruinous repair, roughcast and whitewashed.
Low offices disfigured the west side, and the
south wall was propped with timber. A farmyard and other buildings occupied the site of the
present entrance.

Such was Bradfield. To-day it is one of the
most charming and beautiful homes in the West.
The most ancient and characteristic portion is
the noble hall, which is forty-four feet long by
twenty-one feet wide, and glories in a magnificent
hammer-beam roof, adorned with carved angels,
a rich cornice, carved pendants, and old oak
plenishings. The napkin panelling is in excellent
preservation, and the fine woodwork, once covered
with many coats of paint, is now fully exposed.
Quaint and delightful features of the apartment
are the open fireplace, the minstrel gallery, and

a dog-gate which kept canine favourites below stairs. Just off the minstrel gallery is the state bedroom, containing a good sketch of the hall and gallery in days of yore, which gives one to see how rich the colouring must have been. Below the gallery is the "buttery hatch," and beyond the "buttery hatch," the old kitchen, now the library.

The drawing-room, communicating by a door-way with the hall dais, and one of the last rooms to be restored, has, in lieu of paint and white-wash, walls of moulded oakwork, a richly panelled and decorated ceiling, and a Jacobean mantelpiece. On the screen over the doorway are coloured figures of Adam and Eve; and among other curios are an embroidered silk sachet, in which is enclosed a love letter from Mr Walrond to Anne Courtenay, written on parchment, and dated October 27, 1659, and a prayer-book belonging to the old family chapel. Many other charming sights the interior affords, such as the oak panelling of the dining-room, its old chimney-piece, its pictures. And outside is a rare plesaunce, with clipped box-trees, and great clipped yews, and a lake, and an old bowling-green. Truly, an ideal country-house!

Another branch of the Walronds lived at Dulford House, which is also in the neighbour-hood. Neither of these mansions can be exactly identified with the "Walderscourt" of the romance, which is represented as standing on a spot roughly indicated by Pitt Farm, in the parish of Culmstock, and not far from the village.

CULMSTOCK VICARAGE AND CHURCH (page 33).

There are coloured effigies of the Cavalier period in Uffculme Church, which, by the way, has a magnificent screen, sixty-seven feet in length, probably the longest in the county. Nothing authentic is known about the effigies, but many have the impression that they represent members of the Walrond family. It is possible, however, that the originals of the busts were Holways, of Leigh, since the oldest monuments in the church were erected in memory of their dead. Leigh Court is the name of the present mansion, but Goodleigh, as is shown by old deeds, was the description of the more ancient manorial residence, which did not stand on the same site. And thereby hangs a tale.

The late Mr William Wood, father of my kind friend, Mr William Taylor Wood, of Gaddon, owned and lived at Leigh, and, being of an economical turn of mind, he thought he would clear away the few mouldering ruins of the old manor house, which only cumbered the ground, and thus extend the area of one of his fields. Men were engaged for the work, and had already proceeded some way with their task, when suddenly a workman threw down his tools and vanished clean out of the neighbourhood. For years there were no tidings of him. Eventually he returned, but never vouchsafed the least explanation of his extraordinary conduct. The people of the place, by whom a new coat or pair of boots would have been scrutinised with suspicion, all decided that he had found a "pot of treasure," whilst Mr Wood, who, with all his good qualities, was somewhat touched with

B

superstition, commanded the operation to be stayed.

Wandering about in this pleasant and hospitable region one gathers many a charming idyll of bygone times. Such, for instance, is the story of the young lady who arrived at Gaddon on a short visit and remained fourteen years. It seems that the old housekeeper was sitting on a box before the kitchen fire, preparing lamb's tails for a pie (by dipping them in water brought to a certain temperature, in order to facilitate the removal of the wool), when all at once she fell back—dead.

The master of the house, Mr Richard Hurley, had relations living in another part of the parish, and, on learning the sad news, sent off to them for assistance. There were a lot of girls in the family, and they and their mother were sitting cosily round the hearth, when there came a knock at the door. In those days a knock at the door was enough to throw any country household into a ferment of excitement, which, in this instance, was not diminished when the messenger announced his errand.

" Please, master wants one of the young ladies to come over, because old Betty has dropped dead."

Upon this a family council was held, and the following morning Mary Garnsey, a pretty, rosy-cheeked maiden of fourteen, mounted her horse, and with her impedimenta slung from the saddle-bow—there were no Gladstone bags in those days—rode over to Gaddon to aid her uncle in his difficulty. Pleased with her agreeable company, and more than satisfied with her efficient services, Mr Hurley became loth to part with her, and, in fact, coaxed her to remain till she was twenty-eight, when she left to be married. Old inhabitants may, perchance, remember Mrs Pocock, of Rock House, Halberton. She was the lady.

CHAPTER II

BLACKMORE'S VILLAGE

AT Culmstock one finds oneself in a village of considerable beauty, to which the little stream with its border of aspens, and the fine old church on the knoll, are the principal contributors. Hence also are avenues leading up to the witching prospects of the Blackdown Hills, Culmstock Beacon, in particular, being a favourite spot for picnics. So far so good. But there are drawbacks. When one sets foot in any of these West-country villages, one is apt to be affected with a sense of half-melancholy. Stillness is, of course, to be expected ; stillness, indeed, is one of the great charms of the country, and a happy contrast to the bustle and confusion of the town. But stillness, to be entirely welcome, must not be emblematic of decay.

Not that Culmstock is altogether in that parlous state ; there are many signs of enterprise and activity. Witness the erection of tidy brick houses in lieu of crumbling, thatched cottages, so sweet to look upon, but not specially comfortable to live in. That, however, is not all. One reason why cob-cottages are no longer built is that this is, to a great extent, a lost art. A friend of mine, who is not an architect, but is a pretty shrewd observer of things in general, has explained to me what he believes to have been the process. The angle of a roof is formed by "half-couples," and in the case of cob-cottages my friend thinks that underneath the "half-couples," at tolerably close intervals, were set upright posts. The whole of this scaffolding constituted the permanent frame of the building, and as soon as it was completed by the addition of horizontal timbers, the roof was thatched. Then the "cob," which resembled mortar with a thickening of hair, etc., was erected in sections about two or three feet high, so as to envelop the posts, and each section was allowed to dry before the mud-wall was carried higher. This was a necessity, but, as the result, the work was slow and tedious, and nowadays would be more expensive than building with brick or stone.

Be that as it may, the fact cannot be gainsaid that at Culmstock, and not at Culmstock alone, the advent of the railway and the newspaper, and the general opening-up of communications with the outer world, have made a difference. So great indeed is the revolution that one is constrained to admit that here, though one is in Blackmore's village, one is yet not properly in the village that Blackmore knew. True, there is the old church tower, the stone-screen (Mr Penniloe's glorious "find"), and even the old yew-tree springing from the ledge below the battlements. The bridge, too, is much the same, save for a tasteless, if necessary, addition. The vicarage also stands, its back turned discourteously on the wayfarer; and I certify that it is the identical structure which sheltered Blackmore as a boy, though his father was never the vicar, only curate-in-charge.

All this may be granted, but the man of feeling still mourns the loss—for loss he knows there has been—of local life and colour. As Pericles observed many centuries ago, a city is not an affair of walls only ; and were the material village of seventy years since more intact than it is, the change in its social conditions would be none the less. In the old days, Culmstock was no mere geographical expression ; it was a distinct entity, a separate organism, fully equipped for its own needs, and harbouring, as *Perlycross* testifies, a spirit of pride and independence. The warlike rivalry between rustic communities like Culmstock and Hemyock, though almost universal, may strike one as a trifle ridiculous ; but if a "bold peasantry" could be retained at the cost of occasional horseplay, it was worth the price. What can be conceived more admirable than a strong and healthy, and in its heart of hearts, contented population, grouped into parishes, living on the land ?

Old inhabitants with a tincture of education do not, I admit, see things quite in this light. They are all for modern improvements, and refer with bitter cynicism to the hardships experienced, and the low wages earned, in days of yore, for which they have usually not a particle of regret. But such people are not always right, and now and then one meets with a pleasing appreciation of the olden times. Not long ago there might have been seen, tottering about the village, a Culmstock veteran, who had been wont to ply the flail. The staccato of the "broken stick," however, had yielded place to the drone of the threshing-machine, which was not so agreeable. Suddenly he paused and cocked his ear—what was that? From the interior of a yeoman's barn came a familiar sound. Bang! bang! bang! bang! 'Twas the flail; and the wrinkled old face beamed with delight as Hodge exclaimed, rubbing his hands, "Blest if Culmstock be dead yet!"

(Which demonstrates, by the way, the truth of Blackmore's dictum — "There are very few noises that cannot find some ear to which they are congenial.")

The task will not be easy, but let us endeavour to form some idea of Culmstock parish as it appeared to the veteran in his long-past youth. Most likely he was a parish apprentice, bound out at one of the triennial meetings of the local magistrates held for that purpose in a cottage near the church. Farmers generally appreciated the privilege of having poor boys assigned to them as apprentices, especially as they were not compelled to take any particular boy; but this was not invariably so, and sometimes they would pay a tailor or a shoemaker (say) five pounds to relieve them of the distasteful duty. We will suppose, however, that the farmer is willing to stand *in loco parentis* to the trembling little mortal —not more than ten years old, perhaps—and accordingly signs his name and sets his seal to the indenture.

Have you ever seen such a document? A more portentous agreement than "these presents," seeing that the business itself was so simple, was

surely never devised by misplaced ingenuity.   No
less than six officials—to say nothing of the
master — were parties to the deed, viz., two
justices, two overseers, and two churchwardens;
and their names were entered in the blank spaces
of the form reserved for them.   I will not inflict
the whole of the rigmarole on the reader, but
here is the cream of it :—

The instrument conveys that the churchwardens and overseers between them do put and
place M. or N., a poor child of the parish,
apprentice to John Doe or Richard Roe, yeoman,
with him to dwell and serve until the said
apprentice shall accomplish his full age of twenty-
one years, according to the statute made and provided, during all which term the said apprentice
the said master faithfully shall serve in all lawful
business according to his power, wit, and ability;
and honestly, orderly, and obediently, in all things
demean and behave himself towards him.   On
the contrary part, the said master the said
apprentice in husbandry work shall and will
teach and instruct, and cause to be taught and
instructed, in the best way and manner he can,
during the said term; and shall and will, during
all the term aforesaid, find, provide, and allow
unto the said apprentice, meet, competent, and
sufficient meat, drink, and apparel, lodging,
washing, and all other things necessary and fit
for an apprentice.

With such tautological, though no doubt
impressive verbiage, was the poor child of the
parish launched on the sea of life.   Conducted to
the farmhouse, he was speedily initiated into the
habits of the occupants— rough people, but some-

RECTORY HOUSE AT CHARLES (page 225).

times not unkindly. At dinner the "missus" usually presided, with the master on one side and the family on the other, and the servants in the lowest places. For the broth, which was an important item in the menu, wooden spoons were in favour, although an old fellow called Tinker Toogood came round from time to time and cast the lead that had been saved for him into a pewter spoon. In some farmhouses no real plates of any description were employed; instead of that, the table was carved throughout its length into a series of mock plates, and on these spaces the meat was placed. Every day the table was washed with hot water, and covers were set over the imitation plates to keep the dust off. It was the custom to serve the pudding and treacle first, so as to lessen the appetite and effect a saving in the meat—salt pork as a rule. Wheaten bread was unknown. It was always barley bread, nearly black, and cut up into chunks. These were placed in a wooden bowl.

In addition to Tinker Toogood, itinerant tailors, shoemakers, and harness-makers were regular visitors at the farmhouses, where they performed their tasks and were allowed free commons. Harness-menders were the best paid; they received two shillings a day. Commons, although free, were not always abundant; and a Mr Snip once complained, in the bitterness of his heart, that he had tea and fried potatoes for breakfast, fried potatoes and tea for dinner, and tea and fried potatoes for supper. With the blacksmith the farmer made a contract, agreeing to pay so much for the shoeing of horses, repairing of ploughshares, etc., and, as in the ploughing season coulter and share required to be sharpened every night, the smithy on the hill was generally crowded.

At least fifty oxen were kept on the different farms for ploughing ; and, in the opinion of some, these animals were better than horses. Young bullocks were stationed between the wheelers and the front oxen, but soon became used to the work, and placed themselves in the furrow as a matter of course. All the time a boy, armed with a goad, used to sing to them :

> "Up along, jump along,
> Pretty, Spark, and Tender " [*i.e.*, the near bullocks].[1]

Wishing to encourage his team, the boy would say, not " Woog up!" as in the case of horses, but " Ur up!" Other cries were, " Broad, hither !" " Tender, hither !" and the like.

In reaping, when the time came for sharpening hooks, the foreman sang out :

> "A sheave or two further, and then—

whereupon the catchpoll asked,

> " What then ?

To this the foreman replied,

> " A fresh edge, a merry look, and along agen,

---

[1] Vancouver, referring to this custom, observes: " Their day's work at plough or harrow is usually performed in a journey of about eight hours, during which time the plough-boy has a peculiar mode of cheering them on with a song he continually chaunts in low notes, suddenly broken and rising a whole octave. The ceasing of the song is said to occasion the stopping of the team, which is either followed by a man holding the plough, or as occasion may require, in attending the drag or harrows."

and the catchpoll rejoined,

"Well done, Mr Foreman!"

As the finale, all drank out of a horn cup.

In the first verse of an old Devonshire harvest-home song, convivial spirits were thus addressed:

"Here's a health to the barley mow, my brave boys;
Here's a health to the barley mow!
We'll drink it out of the jolly brown bowli;
Here's a health to the barley mow!"

In successive verses they were adjured to drink it out of the nipperkin, the quarter-pint, the half-pint, the quart, the pottle, the gallon, the half-anker, the anker, the half-hogshead, the hogs-head, the pipe, the well, the river, and, finally, the ocean.

In the direction of Nicolashayne were three large barns (since converted into six cottages) in front of which was a broad area of road for the wagons to halt upon. The "Church of Exeter" has proprietary rights in the parish; and a proctor came up from Thorverton to receive tithes on behalf of the Dean and Chapter. Only the small tithes went to the vicar.

The grandson of Clerk Channing of *Perlycross*, a man over seventy, tells me that he can remember the introduction of the first wagon and the first spring-cart at Culmstock, pack-horses being used always before. This circumstance can be accounted for in two ways, partly from the intense conservation of rural Devonshire—at last, perhaps, broken up—and partly from the pose of the village, with its face towards the valley of the Culm and its back against the hills. In a rough country like the Blackdowns the pack-horse

would be certain to tarry longer than in more
cultivated regions, and a large portion of the
parish of Culmstock, though, according to Blackmore, it comprises some of the best land in East
Devon, consists of hills and commons.

The wildest tract of all is Maidendown—a
dreary waste compact of bog and scrub in the
vicinity of the late Archbishop Temple's paternal
home, Axon, and reaching out to the main road
between Wellington and Exeter. Its situation
does not agree with that of the Black Marsh, or
Forbidden Land, of *Perlycross*, which is described
as lying a long way back among the Blackdown
Hills, and " nobody knows in what parish " ; otherwise one might have guessed that Maidendown
was the prototype of that barren stretch with a
curse upon it.

In the West country pack-horses are equally
associated with moors and lanes. Nowadays a
Devonshire lane—love is compared to a Devonshire lane—is regarded as essentially beautiful,
with its beds of wild flowers and tracery of briars ;
but Vancouver's impartial testimony compels one
to think that in former days this domain of the
pack-horse was not so attractive.   He says :

" The height of the hedge-banks, often
covered with a rank growth of coppice-wood,
uniting and interlocking with each other overhead,
completes the idea of exploring a labyrinth rather
than that of passing through a much-frequented
country. This first impression, however, will be
at once removed on tнe traveller's meeting with,
or being overtaken by, a gang of pack-horses.
The rapidity with which these animals descend
the hills, when not loaded, and the utter impossi-

bility of passing loaded ones, require that the
utmost caution should be used in keeping out of
the way of the one, and exertion in keeping ahead
of the other. A cross-way in the road or gateway
is eagerly looked for as a retiring spot to the
traveller, until the pursuing squadron, or heavily-
loaded brigade, may have passed by. . . . As
:here are but few wheel-carriages to pass along
them, the channel for the water and the path for
the pack-horse are equally in the middle of the
way, which is altogether occupied by an assemblage
of such large and loose stones only as the force of
the descending torrents have not been able to
sweep away or remove."

This was certainly not pleasant, although in
most other respects Culmstock was then a more
interesting place than now. I do not assert that
it was more moral. About seventy years ago, a
native of the village, one Tom Musgrove, was
hanged for sheep-stealing, being the last man, it
is said, to experience that fate in the county of
Devon. We stand aghast at the barbarity of our
forefathers ; but if ever the penalty could be made
to fit the crime, then it must be owned, Tom
deserved the rope. He was a notorious thief,
whose depredations were the common talk of the
village, and, to make matters worse, his evil deeds
were performed under the cloak of religion. Once
a couple of ducks were missed, and, whilst every
cottage was being searched in the hope of
regaining the stolen property, Tom, secure in his
pretensions to piety, stood complacently in his
doorway, and the party of inquisitors passed on.
Just inside were the ducks, feeding out of his
platter.

One night a huckster's shop, kept by Betsy Collins, at Millmoor, was feloniously entered and robbed. Next morning, Tom, apprised of the event, ran off in his night-cap to condole with the poor woman in her misfortune, and succeeded so well as to be invited to share her morning repast. "There!" said he, "her've a-gied the old rogue a good breakfast."

As a professor of religion Tom contracted a warm friendship with a baker named Potter, who was an ardent Methodist. Neither friendship nor religion, however, prevented Mr Musgrove from enriching himself at his neighbour's expense. Profiting by an opportunity when Potter was at chapel, and closely engaged with pious exercises, Tom and his one-armed daughter broke into the bakehouse and carried off Potter's bacon, the lady burglar aiding herself with her teeth.

These breaches of morality appear to have been condoned—at any rate, they did not land the culprit in any serious trouble. But at last Tom went a step too far. Down in the hams, or water-meadows, between Culmstock and Uffculme, he seized a large ram, which he slew, brought home, and buried in his garden. The crime was traced to his door, professions and protestations proved unavailing, and Musgrove, tried and convicted at the following Assizes, was publicly executed at Exeter Gaol. It will be remembered that Mrs Tremlett's "dree buys was hanged, back in the time of Jarge the Third, to Exeter Jail for ship-staling" (*Perlycross*, chapter xxvi.)

Sheep-stealing was not the only excitement.

In Blackmore's youth—and *Perlycross* is built
on the circumstance—smuggling was carried on
with spirit (in both senses) over the Blackdowns,
and queer stories are told of fortunes made by
"fair   trade,"   in   the   conduct   of   which   a
mysterious tower, out on the hills, is said to
have   played   an   important   part.   An   octo-
genarian of my acquaintance admits that, as a
boy,   he   shared   in   these   illegal   adventures,
which did not receive that amount of social
reprobation they may have deserved.   He does
not deny that he slept in a friend's house over
kegs of brandy which he knew to be contraband,
nor does he disguise the fact that he was not a
mere sleeping partner.   He acknowledges being
sent with a keg to meet a fellow-conspirator,
who for the sake of appearances toiled in the
local woollen factory, but out of business hours
drove a lucrative trade with the farmers in the
forbidden thing.   Worst of all, on one occasion,
when an excise officer was reported to be in the
village, a cask was hastily transferred to his
shoulders, which, as being youthful, were less
likely to attract suspicion, and he actually walked
past the Government man—barrel and brandy
and all!   Horses laden with the foreign stuff
came up from Seaton.   They had no halters,
and were guided, says my friend, by the scent,
the   journey   being   naturally   performed   in   the
dark.
    Smuggling,   however,   took   various   forms.
Men from Upottery, Clayhidon, and elsewhere
would halt a cart on the outskirts of the village,
and go round with brandy or gin in bladders,
which they carried in the pockets of their great-

coats.   One Giles, of Clayhidon, had a donkey
and cart with a keg of brandy concealed in a
furnace turned upside down.   A Culmstock man
called Townsend, landlord of the "Three Tuns,"
is said to have been ruined by a smuggler, who
sold him a gallon of brandy and demanded
accommodation, as usual.   The publican refused
it on the ground that the house was already full,
upon which the smuggler, stung with resentment,
informed the police, and Townsend was fined
£270.

By these instances, something, it may be
hoped, has been done towards reconstructing the
Culmstock in which Blackmore grew up, and
which helped to make him what he was—
essentially the prophet of the village and rural
life.   And here I must rectify a possible mis-
understanding,   Because stress has been laid on
changes in the social conditions of the parish, as
being of deeper significance, it must not be
inferred that there have been no alterations, or
none of any importance, in the face of things.
The contrary is the truth, and, on a reckoning,
one is tempted to say with Betty Muxworthy,
"arl gone into churchyard."

Culmstock churchyard has indeed swallowed
up, not only successive generations of the
inhabitants, but a goodly share of the village
itself.   This is the more regrettable, as the
portions absorbed are precisely those which, being
redolent of the olden times, one would have liked
preserved.   The shambles, a covered enclosure
for butchers attending the weekly market, has
gone the way of all flesh.   So also has the stock-
house, which was, rather inconsequently, an open

CULMSTOCK CHURCH AND RIVER (page 12).

space where the stocks were kept. Hard by stood an inn, called the " Red Lion," which either failed to draw sufficient custom, or having a handsome porch, was deemed too good for a common inn and metamorphosed into a school. A Mr Kelso arriving with wife and daughters three, accomplished the transformation, and, according to local tradition, he had the honour of instilling the rudiments of learning into the late Archbishop Temple. This, not the National School which was built in the Rev. John Blackmore's time and mainly through his exertions, was the academy of Sergeant Jakes, the position of which is plainly defined in chapter xxxvi.[1]

There was formerly a considerable trade at Culmstock in combing and spinning wool. Thirty hands are now employed at the mill (no longer an independent concern, but a branch establishment of Messrs Fox Brothers, of Wellington); once four hundred were busy at home. Soap also throve. It was made on the right shoulder of the hill, and the manufacturer, a Mr Hellings, kept seven pack-horses to transport it to Exeter. Culmstock soap had a great vogue in the cathedral city, and it was a common observation that no one had a chance till Hellings was "sold out." In the neighbouring village of Clayhidon was a silk factory, employing, I believe, a hundred hands, and run by a gentleman of the Methodist persuasion, whose house and chapel adjoined—the three together producing a combination of the earthly

[1] Here and elsewhere in the chapter these references are to Blackmore's local romance *Perlycross*, unless otherwise stated.

and the heavenly which impressed my informant as the acme of convenience.   A similar factory in Red Lion Court, Culmstock, met with speedy failure.

These industries are now extinct, and one is somewhat at a loss in seeking for "live" interests, although it is impossible to forget that Hemyock is a famous mart for pigs.   The whole district is piggy, and the sleek black animal with the curly tail is as highly respected, in life and in death, as his congener in that porcine paradise, Erin.   I was talking to an old fellow at Culmstock, it may have been two years ago, and the conversation turned on swine.   Rather to my surprise, he spoke of a certain female of the breed as having been "brought up in house," and with full appreciation of the fun, volunteered a local saw to the effect that "when a sow has had three litters, she is artful enough to open a door."

Culmstock, it is not too much to say, is redolent of Waterloo.   The beacon was often aflame during the Napoleonic wars, and, upon their conclusion, the famous Wellington Monument was erected at no great distance, in honour of the Iron Duke, who took his title from Wellington in Somerset, the Pumpington of *Perlycross*.

Thanks to the industry of Mr William Doble, who is, I believe, a descendant of more than one of the local heroes, it is possible to restore the atmosphere which brought about the creation, years afterwards, of Sir Thomas Waldron and Sergeant Jakes.   When R. D. Blackmore was a boy, many were still living who could remember the incessant din of the joy-bells on the

announcement of the victory—a din continued
for several days ; and the scene in the Fore-
street, the "grateful celebration," when high and
low, indiscriminately, turned out to share the feast.
Naturally, however, the festivities were dashed
with some amount of sorrow and anxiety, as it
was not yet known what had been the fortunes of
the gallant fellows who had gone forth to fight
England's battle. Two stanzas of a song, which
an old lady of Culmstock sang as a girl, reflect
with simple pathos the dreadful suspense of
relations and friends.

> " Mother is the battle over ?
> Thousands have been slain they say.
> Is my father coming ? Tell me,
> Have the English gained the day ?
>
> " Is he well, or is he wounded ?
> Mother, is he among the slain ?
> If you know, I pray you tell me,
> Will my father come again ? "

A rough list of the Culmstock warriors
comprises the following names :—

Major Octavius Temple,
(father of the late Arch-
bishop).
Dr Ayshford.
Sergt. J. Mapledorham.
Sergt. W. Doble.
Sergt. Gregory.
William Berry.
William Sheers.
Robert Wood.
Thomas Scadding.
Richard Fry.
Abram Lake.
William Gillard.
John Jordan.
Thomas Andrews.
John Nethercott.
John Tapscott.
"Urchard " Penny.
James Mapledorham, jun.
Betty Milton.
Betsy Mapledorham.

Mapledorham, was too much of a mouthful
for Culmstock people, so they consulted their own

convenience by calling the couple Maldrom. The excellent sergeant already possessed a long record of service when summoned to the final test of Waterloo, and in several campaigns he had been accompanied by his faithful Betsy. Equally adventurous, Betty Milton was full of reminiscences of her hard life in the Peninsula.

William Berry, too, was fond of story-telling. He related, with humorous glee, that he had once captured a mule with a sack of doubloons. Unfortunately a wine-shop proved seductive, and whilst he was regaling himself therein, an artful Spaniard made off with the booty. Robert, better known as " Robin," Wood was literary, and published a penny history of his exploits, of which, alas! not a single copy is known to exist. William Sheers, figuratively speaking, turned his spear into a ploughshare, as he took to shopkeeping and became a pronounced Methodist and zealous supporter of the Smallbrook Chapel. I can just remember this bearded veteran, who in his last days was a victim to a severe form of cardiac asthma. Tapscott and " Urchard" Penny were both ex-marines. The former had been present at the Battle of Trafalgar and rejoiced in the nicknames " John Glory " and " Blue my Shirt." As for Penny, he was sometimes called " Tenpenny Dick," the reason being that he would never accept more than tenpence as his day's wage. When his turn came to be buried, the bystanders observed that water had found its way into his last resting-place, so that, it was said, he remained constant to the element in which he had so long served.

The foremost of the group of veterans is claimed to have been Doble, who, after starting in life as a parish apprentice, at the age of seven, took part in seven pitched battles in the Peninsula, and ended his military career at Waterloo. He retired from the service on a pension of twelve shillings a week, and was the proud owner of two medals and nine clasps. As a civilian, he was the trusted foreman of the silk factory in Red Lion Court, which, despite his probity, soon came to grief; and at his funeral his old comrades assembled, some from considerable distances, to pay a last tribute to the brave soldier who had rallied the waverers at Waterloo.

Dr Ayshford used to say that he had three sources of income—his pension, his practice, and his property. On the strength of these resources he kept a pack of hounds. He was naturally very intimate with the Temples, and I have been told by a descendant that it was thanks to his generosity that the late Archbishop Temple was enabled to proceed to Oxford. *Mutatis mutandis*, it seems not improbable that by Frank Gilham, Blackmore may have intended his schoolmate. Think of it. Major Temple was not only an officer of the army, but a practical farmer, and the late primate could plough and thresh with the best. Gilham is described as no clodhopper: he "had been at a Latin school, founded by a great high priest of the Muses in the woollen line," *i.e.*, Blundell. Again, his farm adjoins the main turnpike road from London to Devonport, at the north-west end of the parish; and where is Axon, the Temples' old place? The name "White Post" is perhaps adapted from "Whitehall," a fine old-fashioned farmhouse between Culmstock and Hemyock.

Like Parson Penniloe (see *Perlycross*, chapter xxxiii.), Parson Blackmore kept pupils—a fact to which allusion is made in *Tales from the Telling House*. The Bude Light was the Rev. Goldsworthy Gurney. The existence of a wayside cross, from which and the fictitious description of the Culm was formed the name of both village and romance, is attributed to the public spirit of one Baker, who lived in the Commonwealth time, and usurped the manor ; but whether it was anything more than a tradition in Blackmore's youth, is perhaps doubtful. Priestwell is Prescott, Hagdon Hill Hackpen, and Susscott Northcott. Crang's forge, had any such institution existed, would have been at Craddock.

The reader, however, may rest assured that Blackmore did not select these fanciful appellations without excellent reason. He desired for himself a large freedom, which, as we have seen, he used in transporting mansions, and other feats of imagination. One more illustration of this spiritual liberty may be cited. By the Foxes he evidently means the Wellington family. The dialogue between Mrs Fox of Foxden and Parson Penniloe, in chapter xliv., is sufficient to settle that. The name Foxdown, too, is evidently based on that of Mr Elworthy's residence, Foxdene. Yet in chapter xii. Foxden is stated to be thirty miles from Perlycross by the nearest roads. On the other hand, Pumpington, as Wellington is called in *Perlycross*, is just where it should be (chapter xxiv.).

Turning to another matter, Blackmore has

idealised the bells, inasmuch as he states that
on the front of one of them—the passing bell—
was engraven,

> "Time is over for one more";

and on the back,

> "Soon shall thy own life be o'er."

The Culmstock set is an interesting collection
of bells, but not one of them is adorned with
mottoes such as those.   One bears the inscription
"Ave Maria Gracia Plena," and this was cast
by Roger Semson, a West-country founder of
repute, who was dwelling at Ash Priors, in
Somerset, in 1549, and who stamped his initials
on the bell.   Another of his bells, at Luppitt, is
at once more and less explicit on this point, since
the inscription runs "nosmes regoremib."   To
make sense, this must be read backwards.   Two
modern bells, placed in the Culmstock belfry in
1852 and 1853 respectively, awaken proud or
painful memories.   The former was cast in
memory of the Duke of Wellington, the cost
being defrayed by subscription, while the latter
was "the free gift of James Collier, of Furzehayes,
and John Collier, of Bowhayes."   John Collier,
who was killed by lightning at Bowhayes, was
the sporting yeoman with the otter hounds, to
whom Blackmore alludes.   The old house, by
the way, was reputed to be haunted, and for
years no one would live in it.

Blackmore's description of the vicarage is
literally correct, save that he calls it "the
rectory."   A long and rambling house it
certainly is, and the dark, narrow passage, like

a tunnel, beneath the first-floor rooms, is a feature explained by the higher level of the front of the house "facing southwards upon a grass-plot and a flower-garden, and as pretty as the back was ugly" (*Perlycross*, chapter vi.).

HEMYOCK (page 26).

CHAPTER III

Although Culmstock and its immediate vicinity is somewhat deficient in what I have ventured to term "live" interests, it must not be inferred that the neighbourhood has nothing further to show; and among the objects that deserve to be scheduled as worthy of attention are the colossal stone quarries at Westleigh, which, whether viewed from the parallel line of railway or from the opposite height on which stands Burlescombe Church, present an imposing spectacle. For ages they have been the principal source of supply for the district, huge quantities of limestone having been drawn from them for building and agricultural purposes. Much of it was formerly conveyed to Tiverton in barges towed along the canal, the terminus of which was fitted with a number of kilns. These, in my boyhood, I have often seen burning, and regarded with no little awe, owing to stories that were circulated of persons having gone to sleep on the margin, fallen over into the glowing furnace, and been consumed to powder. They are now a picturesque ruin. Older men can recall a yet earlier time when pack-horses came to Westleigh from Tiverton and fetched lime in boxes. In front was a man riding a pony, and the horses followed without compulsion.

The string of pack-horses mentioned in chapter ii. of *Lorna Doone*, as arriving from Sampford Peverell, may be a reminiscence of this traffic.

Not far from the entrance to the Whiteball tunnel, and in the neighbourhood of the great limestone quarries, in a pleasant meadow facing south, are the ruins of Canonsleigh Abbey. To a connoisseur like Mr F. T. Elworthy, these remains tell their own story, and it is thanks to that gentleman's investigations and researches that we are able to furnish a concise account of the ancient nunnery. A gateway yet stands, though unhappily disfigured by the desecrating touch of modern man, and near it is a doorway of red sandstone leading to a staircase doubtless belonging to the porter. In the upper storey, square-headed windows — wrought, we may believe, in the fourteenth century—command the approach in either direction ; other features are less easy to determine, since there are modern walls and a modern roof, which have been added for the purpose of turning the place into a shed, and incidentally obscure the older architecture.

Without spending more time here, let us pass to a quadrangular building of massive construction, and supported at two of its angles by solid buttresses. Situated at the east end of the convent, this is considered to have been a great flanking tower communicating, by means of strong walls (fragments of which yet remain), at the angles opposite to the buttresses, with the residential portions. The outer or enclosing wall of the abbey precincts started from the middle of

the east wall of the tower ; and under the middle
of the tower flowed a stream, which issued through
a covered exit and continued its course outside
the boundary wall, washing its base.   The reason
for this somewhat peculiar arrangement was a
good one—the supply of the abbey stews ; but
its effect was to throw the tower out of line with
the walls and the other buildings.

Inside the walls were two spaces, irregular in
shape, and clearly open courtyards, from one of
which a doorway led into the tower.   The chief
entrances seem to have been from the two or
more floors of the domestic quarters.   On the
side next the convent, approached by a massive
doorway, is a narrow chamber, conjectured to
have been a "guard-room" for refractory nuns.
Over this, but running the entire length of the
building, and not, like the lower floor, divided by
wall and doorway, is a floor supported by beams.

This tower, with the plaster clinging to its
walls—how can we explain its survival when the
rest of the once stately abbey has vanished?
Probably the reason lies partly in its strength
and partly in its plainness and the absence of
wrought stone tempting human greed.   As has
been well said, "it still stands a picturesque and
sturdy relic of an age of good lime-burners and
honest masons."   The wrought stone of one or
two windows in the adjacent walls has been
removed, but what indications remain suggest
the close of the twelfth century as that virtuous
age.

The Priory of Leigh was founded, Dr Oliver
says, in the latter half of the twelfth century, and
Prebendary Hingeston-Randolph opines, before

1173. In its infant days, it seems to have been a dependency of Plympton Priory—at any rate, in the estimation of the latter monastery, whose head claimed the right to appoint the superior of Leigh. This demand was resisted, and in 1219 the then Bishop of Exeter composed the quarrel by deciding, as a sort of compromise, that the Prior of Plympton might, if he chose, be present at the election.

In the second half of the thirteenth century there were scandals at Leigh calling for episcopal cognisance and visitation ; and these disorders proving incurable, Bishop Quivil went the length of ejecting the prior and canons, and transferring the monastery, with all its belongings, to a body of canonesses of the same rule of St Augustine. And Matilda de Tablere became the first Prioress of Leigh. Next year, Matilda de Clare, Countess of Gloucester and Hertford, presented the convent with the (then) great sum of six hundred marks, in acknowledgment of which Bishop Quivil erected the priory into an abbey, and appointed the countess its abbess.

The patron saints, under the old régime, had been the Blessed Virgin Mary and St John the Evangelist. St Ethelreda the Virgin was now added, and practically displaced St Mary, whose name is omitted in later descriptions. Another change affected the name of the place, "*Mynchen*" being often substituted for "*Canon*"-leigh. "Mynchen" is the old English feminine of "monk," and therefore equivalent to the modern "nun."

The indignant canons did not take their extrusion meekly. They appealed to the archbishop, and, through him, to the king, against the usurpation of the "little women," but they appealed in vain.

Sad to relate, the ladies do not appear to have behaved much better than their predecessors. In 1314 Bishop Stapledon, Quivil's successor, addressed a letter to his dear daughters in Christ, telling them in Norman-French that he had heard of many *deshonestetes*, and calling particular attention to the fact that there was an entrance into the cellar where a man brewed *le braes*, and another under the new chamber of the abbess! These he ordered to be closed by a stone wall before the following Easter.

The abbey was suppressed in February 1538, and at the end of the same year the king granted a lease of the site and precincts, with the tithes of sheaf and the rectories of Oakford and Burlescombe, to Thomas de Soulemont, of London. The inmates, however, were not turned adrift on the charity of the cold world. Each received a pension, and this, in the case of the abbess, Elisabeth Fowell, was considerable. There were eighteen sisters in all, and some of them, as is proved by their names—Fortescue, Coplestone, Sydenham, Carew, Pomeroy — were of good West-country extraction.

In course of time the property passed through various hands, and out of the spoils of the abbey a certain owner appears to have built a mansion, which was demolished in 1821.

From Canonsleigh let us away to Dunkeswell, about equidistant from Culmstock, but in another direction. On the journey we may look again at the grassy plateau which has Culmstock Beacon at one extremity and the Wellington Monument, set up in honour of the Iron Duke and his victories, at the other.   This stretch of moorland is yet in its primitive state, and the Dean and Chapter of Exeter, whose property it is, exercise zealous supervision over it.   Time was when the villagers depastured their donkeys thereon, but of late years the privilege seems to have been withdrawn.

The Blackdowns, generally, have been enclosed and turned into farms ; and although one sometimes stumbles on desolate fields with patches of gorse, mindful of their ancient savagery, this does not affect, to any appreciable extent, the character of the country.   On the whole, a ride or walk across the long level chines is not specially delightsome, save indeed for the wholesome air and an occasional glimpse of a fairy-like *mappa mundi* spread out at their base.   It is only when one descends into charming little villages, like Hemyock, or Dunkeswell, or Broadhembury, with their orchards fair and hollyhocks, that complete satisfaction is attained, and then it *is* attained.

Amidst so much that is bare (and on this subject we have not said our last word) the ivied ruins of Dunkeswell Abbey, nearer Hemyock than Dunkeswell village, and lending its name to a very respectable hamlet, assuredly deserve remark. Situated in a charmingly secluded spot, they consist merely of parts of the gatehouse and fragments of walls.   The latter have a blackened appearance as if the destruction of the buildings had been accelerated by fire ; more probably, however, this is due to the mould of age.   In its

heyday the abbey boasted an imposing range of
buildings, the outlines of which may still be traced
in the grass, when, in the drought of summer, it
withers, more rapidly than elsewhere, over the
foundations.

The history of the abbey is almost as scanty
as its remains. It was founded in 1201 by
William Lord Briwere or Bruere, on land that
had previously belonged to William Fitzwilliam,
who, having borrowed from one Amadio, a Jew,
was compelled to mortgage his manor of Dunkeswell. According to one version, Briwere redeemed
the land from the Hebrew, but a charter of King
John shows the vendor to have been Henry de la
Pomeroy. There is clearly a tangle. Possibly
Pomeroy bought Dunkeswell from the mortgagee
and resold it to Briwere, who, in any case,
bestowed it on the Cistercians of Ford.

Just outside the north wall of the modern
church may be seen a stone coffin, with depressions
for the head and heels. It is one of two that were
discovered some thirty years ago covered with
plain Purbeck slabs, and containing skeletons—a
man's and a woman's; in all likelihood, those of
the powerful Lord Briwere and his good lady.
The body of the founder, it is known, was laid to
rest in 1227 in the choir of the abbey church;
and it is only natural to suppose, though there is
no evidence to prove it, that husband and wife
shared a common tomb. The bones, placed
together in one of the coffins, were reinterred,
while the other coffin, as I said, has been suffered
to remain above-ground, a gazing-stock for
posterity.

The abbey was richly endowed by its founder

with lands and tenements, including the manor of Uffculme and the mill there; and his munificence was supplemented by liberal gifts from the monks of Ford and others. At the date of its surrender, February 14, 1539, the annual value of the property amounted to £300—a large income in those days.

Most of the notices relating to the abbey are drawn either from the Coroners' or De Banco Rolls, and, as they are concerned with actions for debt or trespass, are anything but entertaining. The one exception is the account or accounts of the storming of Hackpen Manor by John Cogan, of Uffculme, his son Philip, and others, in the year of grace 1299. Entering the buildings *vi et armis*, they ejected the monks and lay brethren, who, after the custom of their order, were carrying on farming operations there; and beat and wounded two of the abbot's servants to such purpose that he was deprived of their services for a year or longer. Moreover, they were said to have captured three score oxen and a score of cows, and driven them to Cogan's manor of Uffculme, whither also they bore certain *furcæ*, which were there burnt.

To this grave indictment Cogan replied, denying the trespass, and alleging that the two manors adjoined, and that the abbot desired to "lift" *furcæ*, etc., the property of Cogan, whereupon he instructed his men to prevent him, which they did. Now as to those *furcæ*. Writing aforetime on the subject, I fell into the pardonable error, if error it be, of supposing that the term, being employed in an agricultural or pastoral context, denoted "pitchforks." It is my present

CULMSTOCK BRIDGE (page 13).

belief that these *furcæ* were the kind of thing that
gave its name to Forches Corner, just over the
Somerset border—in other words, gallows. The
abbot, as lord of Broadhembury, had not only
assize of bread and beer in that manor, but, very
certainly, a gallows. The Lady Amicia, Countess
of Devon, had at least one gallows, and consider-
ing the extent of her domains, probably gallows
galore; and apparently John Cogan had one.
The Abbot of Dunkeswell, it seems to me, must
have had at least two. If this reading be correct,
the undignified squabble was all about that grisly
symbol of mortality and power.

It is possible that a distorted version of
this affair yet lingers in Culmstock tradition. I
have heard from a Methuselah of the place
that, according to an old tale, a band of freebooters named Sylvester made an eyry of Hackpen,
whence they descended to the more fertile regions
below, raiding the farms, and carrying off the
fleecy spoil to their hold on the hill.

On the break-up of the monastery the site
of the buildings, the home farm, and other lands
were assigned by letters patent to John, Lord
Russell, who showed himself an utter vandal.
The lead of the roofs and the bells, of which
there were four in the church tower, were the
special objects of his rapacity; but all was grist
that came to his mill, and, as the result, the
fabric was left in a condition in which it was
bound to become "to hastening ills a prey."
As there was never an abbey at Culmstock,
either Canonsleigh or Dunkeswell probably served
as a model for the ruins described in *Perlycross*.
The latter is the more likely, owing to the

F

presence of the "district" church built by Mrs Simcoe, close to the remains of the ancient abbey.

At the southern end of the Blackdowns is Hembury Fort, an old British encampment, of triple formation and considerable extent, which commands perhaps the finest view in the neigh-bourhood. It is believed by some to have been also a Roman station — the Moridunum (or Muridunum) of Antonine. On this point, how-ever, there is considerable doubt, there being other claimants, of which High Peak on the coast is one, and Honiton another. The very latest view of the matter is that given by Canon Raven in *The Antiquary* of December 1904, in which he inclines to the opinion that the legion divided the year between a winter at Honiton and a summer at Hembury, with the advantage of a strong fort to retire upon in case of Dumnonian risings.

In writing of these distant ages, I have often felt how remote they are in another sense. Such a term as "Dumnonian," for instance, though we know its geographical significance as referring to the inhabitants of south-west Britain—how little it conveys, and perhaps can be made to convey, to us of the life that people lived, even if we are sure that beneath their breasts beat human hearts like our own, with interests and affections strong and manifold! Much gratitude, there-fore, is due to the late Rev. William Barnes, author of the classic Dorset poems, for his bold attempt to reconstruct for us the mode of existence and surroundings of those ancient Britons, of whom all have heard from their childhood. This also may be poetry, but it is worth perusing only as such. The picture he describes is that of a little pastoral settlement occupying a valley, and finding refuge in time of war in a great camp that crowns a neighbouring hill; and the season is the end of summer, after the reaping of oats and rye and the mowing of lawns and meadows round the homesteads.

"The cattle are on the downs, or in the hollows of the hills. Here and there are wide beds of fern, or breadths of gorse and patches of wild raspberry, with gleaming sheets of flowers. The swine are roaming in the woods and shady oak-glades, the nuts are studding the brown-leaved bushes. On the sunny side of some cluster of trees is the herdsman's round wicker-house, with its brown conical roof and blue wreaths of smoke. In the meadows and basins of the sluggish streams stand clusters of tall elms waving with the nests of herons; the bittern, coot, and water-rail are busy among the rushes and flags of the reedy meres. Birds are 'charming' in the wood-girt clearings, wolves and foxes slinking to their covers, knots of maidens laughing at the water-spring, beating the white linen or flannel with their washing bats; the children play before the doors of the round straw-thatched houses of the homestead, the peaceful abode of the sons of the oaky vale. On the ridges of the downs rise the sharp cones of the barrows, some glistening in white chalk, or red, the mould of a new burial, and others green with the grass of long years."

Close to Hembury Fort is a house built by Admiral Samuel Graves, whose best title to fame is that he invented the lifeboat. The fort is in the parish of Payhembury. The adjacent parish of Broadhembury, a picturesque village among the hills, could ·vaunt in ancient days a cell of Cluniac monks belonging to Montacute Priory, Somerset; and from 1768 to 1775 the incumbent was none other than Augustus Toplady, author of " Rock of Ages." The Grange, a fine old Jacobean manor house, long the residence of the Drewes, was built in 1610 by an ancestor of theirs, who was sergeant-at-law to Queen Elizabeth—Edward Drewe. It was modernised about the middle of the last century.

At one time the Blackdowns must have presented a very different appearance from that which they do now, and the cause of the transformation may be found in a measure passed in the thirty-ninth year of His Majesty King George the Third, up to which time the commons of Church Staunton, Clayhidon, and Dunkeswell produced little but heath, fern, dwarf-furze,[1] and very coarse, tough and wiry herbage. At the beginning of the last century these lands were taken in hand with a view to cultivation or planting.

The Napoleon of the reclamation was General Simcoe, an officer who, having greatly distinguished himself in the American War, afterwards settled down on the Blackdowns. Altogether he enclosed about twelve thousand acres, and part

[1] Two species of furze are produced in Devonshire— the rank luxuriant sort flourishing in the spring, and the smaller dwarf or dale furze, which blooms in the autumn. The larger, which goes by the name of French furze, forms considerable brakes, and is usually cut at four years' growth. Its crane stems used to be burnt for charcoal, whereas the dwarf furze was cut and grubbed by farmers and labourers for fuel.

of his design was to build two or three farm-houses, assigning to each of them about three hundred acres. The remaining allotments he portioned out to adjacent farms belonging to him, or converted into plantations. At Wolford Lodge—the name of his residence—he carried out some interesting experiments in arboriculture.

One practice adopted at Wolford, and apparently with success, was that of pruning the young oak, the stem being left clean to a height of twenty feet, and a proportionate top being allowed. The wounds soon healed and became covered with bark, and the result is said to have been a notable increase in the strength and substance of the stock.

General Simcoe paid much attention also to the culture of exotic trees. The black spruce of Newfoundland, the red spruce of Norway, the Weymouth pine, pineaster, stone and cluster pine, the American sycamore or butterwood, the black walnut, red oak, hiccory, sassafras, red bud, together with many small trees and shrubs of the sorts which, in the Western hemisphere, compose the undergrowth of the forests—all these different species were introduced and found to flourish at Dunkeswell.

The soil of Dunkeswell Common consisted chiefly of a brown and black peaty earth on beds of brown and yellow clay and fox-mould, all resting ultimately on a deep stratum of chip sand. Wherever the chip sand and marl emerged, the more retentive stratum of the latter held up the water, which burst forth into springs or formed "weeping ground"—"zogs," as it is termed by the natives, who add that you must be careful where you plant your foot. Many of the morasses and peaty margins along the declivities and side-hills abounded with bog-timber. Out of a bed of peat near Wolford Lodge was raised an oak of this description, about twenty feet long and squaring thirteen inches at the butt. The whole of its sap was gone, and, to judge from its appearance, it might have been a fork of a much larger tree. Before it was taken up, General Simcoe received and refused an offer of five guineas for it. Local opinion favours Roughgrey Bottom, Dunkeswell, as the original of Blackmarsh or the Forbidden Land of *Perlycross*. The situation is fairly suitable; it was not far from the Blackborough quarries (see chapter xxxviii.).

There is probably still preserved at Wolford Lodge, which is a treasure-house of interesting curios, a specimen of the serpent stone, or *cornu ammonis*, found at the Blackborough quarries, which in their time have produced a large crop of fossilised shells, and delighted the geologist with instructive visions of the underworld. The specimen in question exceeded fourteen inches in diameter.

Once upon a time the Blackdowns were generally known as the Scythestone Hills, and travellers often digressed from the beaten track in order to pay a visit to the whetstone pits at Blackborough, which were justly regarded as a remarkable scene of industry, and, indeed, one of the sights of the West. These quarries were worked in the following way. A road or level about three feet wide and about five and a half feet high was driven from the side of the hill to a distance of three or four hundred yards. All the loose sandstones within eight or ten yards of the road were extracted, pillars being left to support the roof of the mine, until, having served their purpose, these also were gradually worked out and the whole excavation suffered to fall in. The size of the stones rarely exceeded that of a horse's head ; and all were more or less grooved and indented, their appearance suggesting that they had been subjected to the action of rills or running water. Many years have elapsed since the pits were in full working order. A little while ago there were two shafts remaining ; to-day there is only one, and, most probably, by the time this paragraph is in print, the doom of the mines will be irrevocably sealed, and Finis appended to their history. Dr Fox's strange adventure in this weird spot must be in the recollection of all readers of *Perlycross* (chapter xii.).

But there is another wonder at Blackborough besides the quarries, and that is Blackborough House—a great rambling mansion, with windows and doors innumerable. The building, which is rented by an aged lady and her daughter, is so utterly inconsequent as to inspire curiosity concerning its origin in this lonely out-of-the-way place. Well, a good many years ago, Dr Dickinson, of Uffculme, was in one of the eastern counties when he fell in with an old admiral who knew the spot, knew its former owner—the eccentric Lord Egremont—and told him all about it. Long before, the earl and the admiral were looking over the property, when the latter chanced to remark that it might be a good thing to erect a residence there. My lord was impressed with the notion, and the construction of this gigantic

tenement—in its way almost as extraordinary as
Silverton House, now demolished, which stamped
him as an *aedificator* that neither reckoned nor
finished—was his mode of giving effect to the
idea.

In the middle of the last century Blackborough
House was a warren of young students pro
fessedly reading with the Rev. William Cookesley
Thompson, most of whom were of Irish nationality.   They were a wild set, and enjoyed nothing
so much as sharing in one of the country revels,
which were then so common in Devonshire.   On
one occasion they made their way to Kentisbeare
Revel, where an old woman had a gingerbread
stall.   Evening came on, and to avoid a slight
sprinkling of rain, the dame took refuge in the
doorway of the inn.   At the same instant a
wagonette or some such vehicle emerged from the
adjoining passage, and turning a sharp corner,
overturned the old woman's stall, whose contents,
tilted into the roadway, were eagerly scrambled
for by children.   Of course there were profuse,
if not very sincere, apologies, and sympathetic
promises of compensation, but whether they were
ever honoured in the sequel my informant is
inclined to query.

One great feature of a revel was wrestling,
and this reminds me that at Kentisbeare there
are about fifty acres of common, which were once
the subject of debate between that parish and
Broadhembury.   After much bickering it was
agreed to settle the point by "fair shoe and
stocking," with the result that the men of
Kentisbeare were victorious, and acquired firm
possession of the disputed territory.

OLD BLUNDELL'S SCHOOL, TIVERTON.

CHAPTER IV

In 1837 R. D. Blackmore underwent a momentous experience, that being the year in which he entered, a trembling novice, the portals of the famous school, founded by Mr Peter Blundell, clothier. With all its many virtues as a place of learning, Tiverton School long maintained a reputation for roughness, and those days were among its roughest. It might have appeared, therefore, a providential circumstance that the boy had a sturdy sponsor in Frederick Temple, with whom he at first lodged in the simplicity of Copp's Court, though afterwards he became a boarder inside the gates. Nor can it be doubted · that Temple, ever "justissimus unus," must sometimes have interposed to prevent any unconscionable bullying of his delicate charge. Unfortunately he seems to have taken a severe view of his duties as amateur father ; and on one occasion, many years later, when he handed to a prize-winner a copy of *Lorna Doone*, he mentioned, with a humorous twinkle, that he had often chastised the author by striking him on the head with a brass-headed hammer. We have it on

49   G

the authority of Mr Stuart J. Reid that Blackmore
neither then nor subsequently felt the least gratitude for these attentions, and was wont to refer
to his distinguished contemporary in language
the reverse of flattering.   And what he felt about
his schoolfellow, he felt—or Mr Reid is mistaken—
about his school, the retrospect of the misery and
privations of his boyhood affecting him to his
latest hour with a lively sense of horror and
reprobation.

One would not have thought it.   The opening
chapters of *Lorna Doone*, though candid, seem
written with relish of the little barbarians at play,
just as if Blackmore had settled with himself that
the trials of child's estate were goodly exercises
for the larger palæstras of life and literature.
The filial note is never wanting, and those classic
pages, so redolent of the place, and so descriptive
of its customs, even to the verge of exaggeration,
appeal to the younger generation of "Blundellites"
as a splendid and enduring achievement, to which
Mr Kipling's *Stalky and Co.*, and Mr Eden
Phillpott's *Human Boy*, and even *Tom Brown's
Schooldays*, must humbly vail.

It would be a considerable satisfaction to
report that the scenes which Blackmore pictured
are still in all respects as he painted them; but
to do so would be to tamper with truth, and lead
to unnecessary disappointment.   In the first
place, the school, as a society of men and boys,
was removed in 1882 to a new and more convenient abiding-place about a mile distant, where
it has renewed its youth, and flourishes with such
a plentitude of numbers as was never known on
the traditional site by the bank of the Lowman.

The venerable buildings—it moves a nausea to tell—have been remodelled into villas. Apparently there was no remedy, for, although there was talk at the time of acquiring them as a local museum and library, like the Castle at Taunton, nothing came of it all, Tiverton being a small town, and philanthropists few and far between. To be sure, some stipulation was required that the elevation should be preserved *in statu quo;* but this has been only partially observed. The new residents could not be expected to live in dungeons, and so, for the admission of air and sunshine, the Jacobean windows have been extended and deprived of their pristine proportions. Within, the carved oak ceilings and panels have fled before an invasion of varnished deal, and the whole of the beautiful interior has become a memory.

Would that I could stop here, but stern Clio bids me go on and declare that, a quarter of a century ago, might have been seen over the outer gateway an original brass plate with a curiously inaccurate inscription, recording the circumstances of the foundation in 1604, with a pair of ambitious elegiacs, which not even the most lenient Latinist could with safety to his soul pronounce elegant. This brass is now at Horsdon, in charge of the new school, which has also the mystic white "P.B." pebbles that adorned the pathway outside the boundary wall. The pathway is another ghost. Not only have the pebbles, both white and black, been uprooted, but sacrilegious hands have been laid on a most sensible and delightful old barricade, formed of heavy posts and heavy angular beams, which ran the whole length of the wall, and was closed at each end with a gate. How Dr Johnson would have loved it !

But the zeal for improvement, which set in during the seventies, is not accountable for all the changes that have marked the spot since Blackmore's time ; and without more explanation, many of the allusions in *Lorna Doone* must appear mysterious and unintelligible. When Blackmore was at the school, the converging lines of railway, with their passengers and goods stations, and multiplex ramifications, and the adjacent coal-yards and slaughterhouse, were still in the future, and the sites they now occupy were pleasant meadows. At the north-west corner, the point nearest the school, was a "kissing"-gate, whence a footpath, traversing the first meadow, led to another gate of the same amorous description. The main path then struck across to the right and joined the coach route, afterwards called the "old" London road, opposite Zephyr Lodge. Another track pursued an easterly direction to a pretty white timber bridge, which spanned the Lowman with a shallow arch, and near which was the celebrated Taunton Pool. This bridge afforded access to Ham Mills, remembered as a couple of low, white thatched cottages, very picturesque, whither it was the custom of the inhabitants to repair for Sunday junketings.

From the entrance-gate near the school to the corner of the London road ran a quickset hedge, which extended to a point over against a comparatively modern building, which still exists and formerly served as a turnpike, the old London road having been moved further up the hill to make room for the Exe Valley railway bridge. In a similar fashion, the construction of the branch line to the Junction, or "Park" station, as the old people call it, necessitated a great diversion of the Lowman, which previously described a zigzag erratic course, and shot much nearer to the Lodge and London road, so that the little torrent, known to the natives as the Ailsa, and to Blackmore and his boarders as the Taunton brook, joined it almost at right angles.

Blackmore, of course, described the locality as he knew it in his own schooltime. He does not appear to have urged his researches so far back as the assigned age of John Ridd, or he would have eschewed certain anachronisms which, in default of this precaution, have crept into his narrative. They are of no particular consequence, but may be mentioned, as it were, by the way.

To begin with, there were no iron-barred gates for the boys to lean against in 1673, nor for twenty years afterwards. Until 1695, there were only wooden gates, with a small door for entrance, and it may be noticed incidentally, that at the time of their removal they were much decayed. Nor again, in 1673, were there any porter's lodges. These accessories were first built at the close of the seventeenth century. There being no lodges, the porter was evidently the invention of a later date—1699, apparently. The "old Cop" of the romance, with his sympathetic boots and nose, was the identical functionary of Blackmore's youth. His name was George Folland, and he succeeded Hezekiah Warren in 1818.

Another chronological error has to do with

the Homeric fight between John Ridd and Robin Snell, which the author paraphrases as an "item of importance." As such I will treat it—to the extent of proving that it can never have taken place. The fleshly existence of the victor has been warrantably challenged, but no such question can arise as to his antagonist. Not that he was called Robin, but the voluntary statement that he became thrice Mayor of Exeter is a plain indication of the person implicated. Now, a visit to the north aisle of the choir of Exeter Cathedral will reveal the presence of three gravestones placed there to the memory of his father, his mother, and himself, with their arms. The inscription which mostly concerns us here is the following :—

"Here, at the Feet of his Father, lyeth the Body of John Snell, Esq., who served this City three times as Mayor, and several times as one of her Representatives in Parliament, served her faithfully and diligently, fearing God and honouring the King. He died ye 26 of Aug. A.D. 1717, ætat suæ 78. Here also lyeth Hannah, his virtuous and religious wife."

The Rev. John Snell, the mayor's father, was a notable man. Son of the Rev. Arthur Snell, M.A., and born at Lezant, Cornwall, in or about 1610, he was educated at Blundell's School, Tiverton, and Caius and Gonville College, Cambridge, where he graduated M.A. In February 1634-5, he was instituted to the rectory of Thurlestone, South Devon, from which he was ejected in or about 1646. Reinstated in his living at the Restoration, he was, in 1662, elected Canon Residentiary of Exeter Cathedral. This honourable post he resigned January 4, 1678-9, and died the following April. It may be added, as an almost, if not quite unprecedented circumstance, that he was succeeded in his canonry by two of his sons, Thomas and George ; and, as a Rev. John Snell, Vicar of Heavitree, died Canon of Exeter, September 4, 1727, I am by no means certain that a fourth member of the family —probably a grandson of the original John Snell —did not rise to the same office and dignity.

It is natural to inquire whether there can be found any explanation of this prosperity. The answer is partially, yes. As chaplain to the Royalist garrison, the rector of Thurlestone went through the siege of Fort Charles, Salcombe, and in Walker's *Sufferings of the Clergy* may be read the story of his persecution by the lying Roundheads, when his first-born son was a boy in jackets.

Many more particulars might be adduced— especially the tradition that "Robin" Snell was killed in a riot—but enough! There remains the question, how came the novelist to know or care aught about this personage. On this point there can be no mistake, as I had it from Mr Blackmore himself that he remembered a schoolfellow named Snell, who must have been either my father or my uncle, the late Mr W. H. Snell, who entered the school on the same day (August 16, 1837) as Blackmore. The latter was uncommonly well posted up in the history of his family, and from him probably the information was derived. There are many Snells in Devonshire. The principal families of that name were long settled in the neighbouring parishes of

Chawleigh and Lapford, where they were small landowners, and intermarried with the Kellands and Melhuishes. Curiously, as one may think, in John Ridd's time Grace Snell, of Lapford, wedded Dr Thomas Bartow, son of Peter Bartow, of Tiverton, and thus became sister-in-law to Philip Blundell, of Collipriest, who was of the kindred of the famous Peter, and a feoffee of the school.

While it is natural to regret, and needful to state the alterations that have taken place in the time-honoured premises and their immediate surroundings, it must not be supposed for a moment that modern vandalism has wiped out every feature of interest. The "Ironing Box," or triangle of turf, whereon John Ridd fought his great fight with Robin Snell, is still there. So also are the paved causeways and rows of mighty limes (save for sad gaps caused by a recent storm), and the porches and the lodges,—all vestiges of former days of which the present generation of Blundellites are not unmindful. Every seven years do they meet—old boys and new—in the historic Green, thence to perform a pilgrimage on St Peter's Day to St Peter's Church, after the example of their ancestors, which pleasant and pious custom neither time nor circumstance will, it is to be hoped, cause to fall into desuetude.

"Blundellites" is à la Blackmore; the more usual, the official, appellation is "Blundellians." The school magazine is called *The Blundellian*, and I am indebted to an anonymous letter which appeared in its columns (April 1887), and was indited, no doubt, by my late friend, the Rev. D. M. Owen, for quotations from a private communi-

cation, unquestionably the production of R.
D. Blackmore himself.   The extracts are as
follows :—

"I am much obliged for a copy of the
Blundellite, which certainly was the ancient and
therefore more classical form of the word.   My
father always called himself a 'Blundellite,' and
so did my uncles, and I believe my grandfather.
All went from Peter to Ex. Coll. (Oxford);
however, the juniors have fixed it otherwise and
so it must abide. . . . 'Blundellian,' if anything,
is the adjectival form, at least according to
my theories, though even then 'Blundelline'
would seem more elegant.   'Scholæ Blundellinæ
Alumnus' is in most of my father's school-books
(in 1810).   And I think we find the distinction
between the 'ite' and the 'ian' in good writers,
e.g., a 'Cromwellite,' but the 'Cromwellian' army,
a 'Jacobite,' a 'Carmelite,' etc. . . . All, I maintain, is that, in my days, we never heard of a
'Blundellian,' *i.e.*, in school talk, or from the
masters."

Blackmore's mention of his grandfather, by
which he evidently intends his paternal grandfather, having been at Blundell's school, is worthy
of note.   Many years ago the novelist himself
acquainted me with the fact, but the curious
thing is that the name of John Blackmore, the
elder, apparently does not occur in the school
register.   This has recently been edited by Mr
Arthur Fisher, who shows that during certain
periods it was ill kept, and there seem to have
been frequent omissions.   One of the uncles
must have been a brother of his mother, and,
strange to say, his name also is wanting.   The

H

entries referring to other members of the family
are :—

1162. JOHN BLACKMORE, 15, son of John Blackmore, clerk,
Charles, South Molton, Aug. 13, 1809—June 29, 1812.
1498. RICHARD BLACKMORE, 15, son of John Blackmore,
clerk, Charles, South Molton, Feb. 19, 1816—Dec. 18,
1817.
1258. RICHARD DODDRIDGE BLACKMORE, 12¼, son of Rev.
John Blackmore, Culmstock, Wellington, Aug. 16,
1837—Dec. 16, 1843 ; elected to an exhibition on ——
1843 ; Giffard Scholar at Exeter Coll., Oxford.

Blackmore's schooldays are now so remote,
the survivors so few, that it is hard to recover
many details.   I have been favoured, however,
with communications from two of his contem-
poraries—Colonel H. Cranstoun Adams and the
Rev. E. Pickard-Cambridge ; and at this distance
of time it is not likely that much more can be
gleaned.   Colonel Adams writes :—
  " He was a very quiet little fellow, and was
looked upon as being very clever.   He was
always ready to help any juniors in their work,
and often assisted me.   There was really nothing
very particular about him, except that he was
quieter than the average run of boys.   He joined
in all the games, and I recollect his having one
fight in which he got very much knocked about ;
but he was extremely plucky about it, and his
opponent got a caning for daring to fight a
monitor, which Blackmore was at the time. . . .
He was a popular boy, and kind-hearted ; but,
although he was looked upon as clever, I don't
think any of us thought he would become the
author of such a work as *Lorna Doone.*"
  Mr Pickard-Cambridge sends the following :—
  " R. D. Blackmore was a day-boy, and I

believe remained so; but it is so long since my schooldays that my memory fails me. He was a clever boy at schoolwork. I used to go and stay with him at his father's vicarage, Culmstock, at the Easter holidays, and when there became acquainted with Temple and his relations. After we left school, I never saw him, but learned his mode of life from public reports.

"He was a small, unhealthy-looking boy, and I could never have dreamt that he would turn out such as I see him in his photograph by Mr Jenkins.

"Now it may be interesting if I tell you what happened one afternoon as I and Blackmore were walking up the Lowman. We came to a gate at the end of a field, and just before we got over it, I saw something sitting on the gate at the opposite end of the field. It was a figure dressed in white clothing, no head appearing, and while I was wondering what it was, it suddenly disappeared to the right of a gate thro' a hedge.

"I said to Blackmore, 'Did you see that white figure sitting on the gate?'

"'Yes,' he said, 'I could not make out what it was.'

"When we got to the gate, we hunted the hedge and all about by the stream, but could not find or see anything; so we came to the conclusion that it must have been a ghost. When we got back to the school, I believe we told what we had seen; anyhow, we thought no more about it. But about three days afterwards, some people coming by the coach from Halberton saw the same apparition about the same spot, and told of it in the town, and it came to our ears, and then we immediately related what we had seen.

"This was a great confirmation of our story, and there it must end.   But I can state that all that I have said was true.   I am no great believer in ghosts, but have related the above whenever in conversation ghosts have come to the front."

CHAPTER V

THE TOWN OF THE TWO FORDS

An imaginative mind, anxious for exercise, might easily find a worse pretext than the probable appearance of Tiverton at different epochs in its history. Three monstrous fires—in 1598, 1612, and 1731—have reduced the town to ashes, so that, despite its antiquity, it presents, on the whole, an extremely modern aspect, which, as time goes on, tends to become accentuated. Still certain buildings remain—not many, I fear—from which, like Richard Owen in another sphere of palæontology, the lover of the past may gather ideas for his reconstructive task. *Ex pede Herculem.*

Every stranger, on arriving at Tiverton, is at once struck by the Greenway almhouses, with their quaint little chapel. These were miraculously preserved in the earlier devastations, when, according to contemporary notices, the fire "invironed those sillie cottages on every side, burning other houses to the grounde which stood about them, and yet had they no hurt at all." In the third welter of flame the almhouses were less fortunate, and it is a singular fact that the

¹ *Lorna Doone*, chapter iii.

only life lost on this occasion—on the two previous
there had been many victims—was that of an
inmate who obstinately refused to quit the
building, saying, "Who ever heard of an
almshouse being burnt?"   When, at last, he
was convinced of the peril of optimism, and he
would fain have made good his escape, it was too
late—all egress was barred.   Even in this,
however, there was something miraculous, for,
though the almshouses were burnt and transformed into fiery catacombs, the chapel was
inexplicably preserved, and remains to this day,
with all its rich ornaments and emblematical
figures untouched.   The inscriptions, however,
or, as Blackmore playfully expresses it, "the souls
of John and Joan Greenway" are not "set up in
gold letters."   Had the name "Gold Street"
anything to do with this idea?

The founder of the almshouses was John
Greenway, born about 1460, of whom little is
known that is authentic.   Apparently of lowly
origin, "by ability and industry he acquired an
ample income" as a merchant.   So says Harding,
but it is seldom that ample incomes are acquired
by brains and diligence alone.   The stroke of
luck may almost always be charged as a con-
tributory factor.   If legend may be believed,
Greenway was positively inspired to wealth-
making.   A simple weaver, young and without
prospects, he dreamed a dream which was thrice
repeated.   Each time a mysterious voice admonished him to proceed to London town, and there,
on London Bridge, to await a cavalier on a white
nag, who would have a message for him.   The
sanguine youth obeyed these supernatural instruc-

tions ; and, taking his stand on the appointed spot, was accosted by an unknown horseman, by whom he was told to return forthwith to Tiverton and dig in a certain quarter. Again Greenway obeyed, and was rewarded by the discovery of a crock or pot of gold, which, as his initial capital, enabled him to launch out into business, and ultimately to found these almshouses in 1517. There is a notion that amidst the exterior carvings of St Peter's Church, where Greenway built him a lovely chantry with wagon roof and Renaissance door, is sculptured the crock of plenty, but hitherto—owing perhaps to *embarras de richesse*—it has escaped detection.

Now the embellishments of Greenway's two chapels deserve close attention, not only on account of their beauty, but for other reasons that will immediately appear. Greenway is represented by his arms (*a chevron between 3 covered cups, on a chief 3 sheep's heads erased*), his staple-mark, and his cipher, which are figured on shields inserted in the quatrefoil of the cornices of the chapel in Gold Street and its porch ; and by the following rhyme inscribed in bold letters under the main cornice :—

> " Have grace, ye men, and ever pray
> For the sowl of John and Jone Grenway."

These marks of parentage are merely what one would expect, but the walls have other symbolism, some of which demands comment. In two compartments of the upper cornice are to be found the arms of Courtenay and an eagle rising from a bundle of sticks. These devices are repeated on a larger scale over the archway, with the addition of the arms of England.   The eagle montant, to borrow a term from falconry, is understood to typify the mythical phœnix, and may be regarded as alluding to the vicissitudes of that illustrious and ever-resurgent family.

The arms of England present no difficulty. They are to be explained by the marriage of William Courtenay, 10th Earl of Devon, with Katherine, youngest daughter of Edward IV., her elder sister Elizabeth being the consort of Henry VII.   Miss Strickland, by the way, records a quaint incident in connection with a tournament held at the wedding of Prince Arthur, when " Lord William Courtenay (brother-in-law of the Queen) made his appearance riding on a red dragon led by a giant with a large tree in his hand."   What time the almshouses were building Katherine de Courtenay was actually resident at Tiverton Castle, and she was buried, in 1527, with immense pomp in the Earl of Devonshire's chapel, which was destroyed by the Puritans, and is believed to have stood on the north side of the chancel in St Peter's Church.   In her honour was erected that large achievement in the centre of the porch, consisting of Courtenay and Rivers quarterly, impaling quarterly, 1st France and England quarterly, 2nd and 3rd Burgh, 4th Mortimer.   It is surmounted with the Courtenay badge before-mentioned, and the supporters are St George and a woman.

It would be incompatible with the limits of this work to enter upon a minute description of all the charming imagery of this beauteous chantry. Much of it speaks for itself, but it may be as well to put the reader on his guard against a false blazoning of one of the coats of arms, which displays what looks suspiciously like a tiara. It may possibly be permissible to use the term, but subject to the understanding that we have here nothing to do with any papal insignia. *The three clouds radiated in base, each surmounted with a triple crown*, are for the Drapers' Company ; just as the *Barry nebulée ; a chief quarterly, on the 1st and 4th a lion passant guardant, on the 2nd and 3rd two roses*, are for the Merchant Venturers of London. Attention may also be drawn to a series of sermons in stones, or small sculptures illustrating the chief events in the life of our Lord ; on account of the height at which they are ranged, they might easily be passed unnoticed.

Viewing the decorations generally, we cannot but observe that the place of honour is assigned to the Courtenays ; and, probably on the strength of this fact, Harding speaks of the Marquis of Exeter as Greenway's great patron. In this he may be mistaken, since, on the death of her husband, the Lady Katherine succeeded to the manor of Tiverton, and doubtless exerted much influence in the town and county during the sixteen years of her widowhood. This brings us to the stately home in which, more than anywhere else, those sorrowful years were spent.

Due north of St Peter's churchyard, from which only a wall parts them, are the precincts of Tiverton Castle whereof there exist somewhat extensive remains in varying degrees of preservation. This was for several centuries one of the chief residences of the Courtenays, and in the Middle Ages was a strong place of arms. On the west is a precipice, which runs down sixty feet

I

sheer to the River Exe and secured the castle on that side; in other directions it had towers and turrets, and ramparts and moats, and all that military science then knew in the way of elaborate fortification. Two of the towers yet stand—a square and a round, while the ivy-covered ruin, which is detached from the rest of the buildings, at the south-west angle of the castle grounds, is supposed to represent the oratory or chapel. From its position it was evidently distinct from the Earl of Devonshire's Chapel, mentioned above, and must have been a private sanctuary reserved to the household.

The castle is stated to have been built by Richard de Redvers or Rivers, who was an Earl of Devon in his time—about 1106; it came into the possession of the Courtenays on the extinction of the Redvers family in 1274, when Hugh de Courtenay, great-grandson of Mary de Redvers, succeeded to all their estates. His immediate predecessor was Isabella de Fortibus, born Redvers, who is credited with the gift of an ample stream of water known as the Town Lake, a section of which, enclosed between paved banks, may be observed in Castle Street. She, of course, was *not* a Courtenay; and it is with these rather than with other possessors of the castle that we are mainly concerned. As, with brief intervals, they were the ruling element in the town for a period of three centuries, it is natural to inquire what manner of men were those great lords, and how it went with the neighbourhood when they were uppermost.

With their emblems around us, and with the odour of sanctity investing the places where those emblems appear, there is a palpable danger of attributing to the Courtenays a larger measure of piety than is at all their due. Of him who is called sometimes the Good, sometimes the Blind Earl, no word of censure may be spoken; and as for the husband and descendants of Katherine—William, Henry, Edward—their tragic fates evoke that infinite compassion for which the blood of the innocent cries always, and never in vain. Even the guilty Courtenays were not devoid of redeeming qualities; they were stout warriors, and loyal to their king. Yet two of the race, father and son, both of them named Thomas, were the authors of a felon deed—a deed as black as any that soils the pages of history, or swells the calendar of crime. To all appearance the plot was hatched in Tiverton, and Tiverton yeomen were the willing, or unwilling, instruments of the scandalous theft, the inhuman murder. The whole may not be told here; let what follows suffice.

On Thursday, October 23, 1455, Nicholas Radford, sometime "steward" of the Earl of Devon, now an old man and a justice, was dwelling in God's peace and the king's in his own place at Upcott, in the parish of Cheriton Fitzpaine. The same day and year came Sir Thomas Courtenay, eldest son of the earl, with a body of retainers to the number of ninety-four, armed with jacks, sallets, bows, arrows, swords, bucklers, etc., who beset the house at midnight, and with a great shout fired the gates. Naturally at that hour Radford, his wife, and his servants, were in bed, but awakened by the sudden commotion, the good old man opened his window, and demanded whether there were among them any gentlemen.

"Here is Sir Thomas Courtenay," answered one of the yeoman; and almost at the same moment the knight called out to him, "Come down and speak with me."

The old man, however, would not comply, until Courtenay swore as a true knight and gentleman, that neither his person nor his property should be molested. Relying on this promise Radford descended with a lighted torch and ordered the gates to be thrown open, whereupon, much to his alarm, the rabble of followers began to stream in. The knight reassured him, and standing by his cupboard, condescended to drink of his wine. Whilst Courtenay held the master of the house with tales, his men plundered the mansion of its treasures. Money and bedding, and furs, and books, the ornaments of his chapel and the like—they carried them all away on Radford's own horse, and did not spare even his sick wife, but rolling her out of bed, took away the sheets she was lying in.

Sir Thomas now said to the justice, "Have done, Radford, for thou must need go with me to my lord my father." The old man expressed his readiness, and bade his servant saddle a horse, only to receive the reply that his horse had been removed and laden with his own goods. Hearing this, Radford said to his visitor,

"Sir, I am aged, and may not well go upon my feet, and therefore I pray you that I may ride."

"No force (odds), Radford," was the answer, "thou shalt ride enough anon, and therefore come on with me"

Accordingly they went on together about a stone's throw, when Sir Thomas, having secretly conferred with three of his men—two of them Tiverton yeomen—set spurs to his horse and rode on his way, exclaiming, " Farewell Radford ! "

In a trice Nicholas Philip slashed the old justice across the face with his sword, and as he lay on the ground, dealt him another stroke, which caused the brain to drop out from the back of his head. His brother, Thomas Philip, cut the victim's throat with a knife, while the third man, with surely supererogatory caution, pierced him through the back with a long dagger. Thus was Nicholas Radford feloniously and horribly slain and murdered.

As an aggravation of the crime, on the following Tuesday the old man's godson, Henry Courtenay, with certain of the ruffians, arrived at Upcott, where the body of Radford lay in his chapel, and opened a mock inquest. One of them, Richard Bertelot, sat as coroner, and the murderers were summoned by strange names. They answered, "scornfully appearing," made what presentment they chose, and gave out that they should accuse Radford of his own death. They then compelled his servants to carry the body to the church of Cheriton Fitzpaine, John Brymoor, *alias* Robyns, a singer, leading the way with derisive songs and catches, as it was borne along.

Gaining the churchyard, they took the murdered man out of his coffin, rolled him out of his winding-sheet, and cast him all naked into the grave, where they threw upon his head and body sundry stones that Radford had provided for the making of his tomb, crushing them. They had no more pity or compassion for him than for a Jew or a Saracen.

It seems that in January of this year the justice had sold a good deal of land, including the manors of Calverleigh, Poughill, and Ford, for £400, and this large sum in cash is believed to have been the incentive of the murder. The Earl of Devon, who was no doubt accessory before the fact, speedily prepared an expedition to Exeter in order to obtain possession of such goods and chattels as Radford had lodged with the Dean and Chapter; and in November, he and his son Thomas assembled an armed retinue of a thousand or more at Tiverton, and marched to the city. We need not follow their proceedings there—they were outrageous—and, as signalising the barbarous character of the age, be content to note that neither the Earl nor his son received the penalty they deserved. Providence, however, suffered neither of them to escape. The Earl was poisoned at Abingdon, and his son and successor beheaded at York, after being taken prisoner at the battle of Wakefield, 1461.

The subsequent history of the castle must be traced briefly. After passing through various hands, it was purchased by Roger Giffard, fifth son of Sir Roger Giffard, of Brightleigh, in the parish of Chittlehampton, who pulled down the greater part of the buildings, and named it " Giffard's Court." Nevertheless, it was in a condition to repel an attack by the Parliamentarian forces under Massey in October 1645, though two days later it was stormed by Sir

Thomas Fairfax at the head of an army out-numbering the somewhat disaffected garrison by thirty to one. The owner of the castle was then Roger Giffard, grandson of the first-named Roger, and despite the fact that the defence of the place was entrusted to Sir Gilbert Talbot, as military governor, there is no reason to suppose that Giffard was an absentee. Like his more famous kinsman, Colonel John Giffard, of Bright-leigh, Roger was a devoted Royalist, and is mentioned among those persons who were fined for their loyalty. Blackmore's reference to bales of wool used in the defence is strictly historical (see *Lorna Doone*, chapter xi.).

The modern house was built in 1700 for Peter West, who came of an old Tiverton mercantile stock connected with the Blundells. In 1594 John West had married Edy, daughter of James Blundell, and niece of Peter Blundell and his sister Elinor, wife of John Chilcott, of Fairby, and mother of Robert Chilcott, the founder of Chilcott's School, which stands at the lower end of St Peter Street, and, with its mullioned and transomed windows, its handsome archway, and solid, iron-studded, black oak door, forms an interesting specimen of Jacobean architecture. Peter West's daughter Dorothy took for her bridegroom Sir Thomas Carew, of Haccombe, and thus manor and castle passed into the possession of the distinguished family which still owns them.

We have enjoyed many opportunities of estimating the wealth and importance of the "woollen" merchants of Tiverton; but, if any-thing yet lack, the reader may station himself before the great House of St George, nearly opposite Chilcott's School, and consider it at his leisure. This seemly residence, with its garden close, was built apparently by George Skinner, merchant, whose initials were formerly to be seen on the northern termination of the hood-mould. On the southern termination is the date 1612— the date of the second great fire. As the house is thoroughly Jacobean in style, it is natural to conclude that it is in all essentials the identical structure erected in that memorable year, but the confused account in Harding's *History of Tiverton* contains documentary evidence showing that it was "demolished and consumed by reason of the late unhappy wars" (*i.e.*, the Civil War), and suggests that the "messuage" was rebuilt at various periods, from 1541 onwards. I shall not attempt to unravel the mystery, but content myself with observing that, beyond any question, the building has been altered, and that within living memory. Once, and for long, it rejoiced in another storey, but modern wisdom having determined that the edifice was "top-heavy," the upper portion was removed.

About the year 1740 the manufacture of serges, druggets, drapeens, and the like began to decline, and, later, the effects of the American Revolution were severely felt in the town. In 1790, however, there were still a thousand looms and two hundred woolcombers in the neighbourhood. Then came the great war with France, which almost paralysed the local firms ; and on its cessation the Tiverton manufacturers vainly endeavoured to restore old connections with the Continent. It was plain that the ancient trade

CHAPEL, GREENWAY'S ALMSHOUSES, TIVERTON (page 61).

in wool, on which so many depended, was in its last throes. The end was sudden and dramatic. One morning, when the workpeople were at breakfast, the inhabitants of Westexe were startled by the loud report of a gun, and the news soon spread that Mr Armitage, the manager of a large mill, which had been built in 1790, and in which, as in a last refuge, the remains of the staple industry were concentrated, had shot himself in the counting-house.

The ruin of the place now seemed certain. Happily, however, the following year (1815), Messrs Heathcoat, Boden, and Oliver purchased the mill, and by extensive additions, converted it into an immense lace factory. In 1809 they had obtained a fourteen years' patent for a greatly improved bobbin-net machine, of which Mr Heathcoat was the inventor, and erected a factory at Loughborough. The firm removed to Tiverton in consequence of the injury done to the machines by the Luddites, and thither a number of their men accompanied them. Some of the Leicestershire "hands," about the year 1820, had a dispute with Mr Heathcoat, who had become sole proprietor of the factory, and, this having ended in their discharge or voluntary retirement from his service, they determined to set up an opposition concern. It is believed that the artisans had machines of their own brought down along with those of Mr Heathcoat and installed in the mill under some arrangement with him. Anyhow, they resolved to start lace-making on their own account.

Money, of course, had to be provided, and this to a limited amount—very limited for such

K

a venture—was found them by a physician of the
town named Houston, whilst premises were
secured behind, or near what is now the Golden
Lion Inn, Westexe. Here the quixotic scheme
was launched, and here it came to an inglorious
end, after a futile imitation of the frog in the
fable. The credulous doctor, who lived in a
house, now a saddler's shop, next the "White
Ball," and whose backyard abutted on the
infant factory, lost what he had lent, and no
doubt learnt a lesson.

Hardly more felicitous was Mr George
Cosway's attempt to resuscitate the woollen
industry. Mr Cosway "took up arms against
a sea of troubles"; his capital was none too
large, and in the face of powerful competition in
other parts of the country, his factory in Broad-
lane was never a conspicuous success. On his
death it was closed, and that finally. Mr Cosway
belonged to the same family as the famous
miniaturist, one of whose larger paintings,
designed for an altar-piece, hangs on the north
wall of St Peter's Church. The subject is "St
Peter delivered by an Angel," and the picture
was Richard Cosway's gift to the town of which
he was a native. The larger painting on the
other side of the vestry door, the subject of which
is "The Adoration of the Magi," is a very fine
work by Gaspar de Crayer, and an almost exact
reproduction of a picture by Rubens in the
Antwerp gallery.

It would be improper, I suppose, to refer to
Tiverton without mentioning Lord Palmerston,
whose Parliamentary connection with the borough
extended from 1835 to 1865—just thirty years.

As an Irishman, the popular statesman must have been perfectly at home in the town, which is always lively at election times, and during his early acquaintance with it, had an unenviable reputation as a rival to Donnybrook Fair. Most of the inhabitants had their chosen inn, the tradesmen being accommodated in the parlour, the artisans in the bar, and the labourers in the kitchen; and the consumption of beer and spirits almost exceeds belief. One would make ten glasses of grog his nightly quantum, another was not content with fewer than eighteen, while a third drank gin and water by the bucketful. Every now and then women would have a fight in the streets. A ring would be formed, whereupon the trulls grappled with each other, and with their long hair streaming down their backs, and blood down their faces, presented a pitiful and degrading spectacle. Things are better now.

Speaking of the Tiverton inns reminds me that John Ridd and Fry lodged, on the eve of their departure, at the "White Horse," in Gold Street. This tavern is still in existence, and as it is not specially picturesque, the reader may be at a loss to conceive why Blackmore should have selected this particular house of entertainment. The novelist, however, knew what he was about. In the seventeenth century it may have been the most important inn in the town. On the entry of the Royalists into the town in the month of August, 1643, they were stoned by the mob, many of whom were killed or wounded by the fire of the soldiers; "and," says Harding, in recounting the circumstance, "the effect produced was a dispersion of the remainder, when one, John Lock, a miller, was taken and executed at the sign of the White Horse, on the north side of Gold Street" (*History of Tiverton*, vol. i., p. 58).

CHAPTER VI

THE WONDERS OF BAMPTON

THE country between Tiverton and Bampton
reminds us how comparatively new are many of
our main roads. Beginning with the town,
although Bampton Street is one of the principal
thoroughfares, this is not the case with Higher
Bampton Street; and of both it may be stated
with absolute assurance that they do not owe
their names to accident or caprice. They were
christened thus because they were a direct con-
tinuation of the old road from Bampton, the
whole of the present route through the picturesque Exe valley not having been constructed
until long after the days of John Ridd and the
less mythical Bampfylde Moore Carew. For
this reason "Jan," on his way home, would have
proceeded first to Red Hill, with the inn at its
foot;[1] and hereafter we shall cease to wonder
that Carew and his companions fell in with the

---

[1] This is, of course, assuming that they did not take the
turning to Bolham. By an apparent anachronism, Blackmore talks of "the village of Bolham on the Bampton Road"
(*Lorna Doone*, chapter lx.) as the place where the ladies'
coach was stopped by Faggus. There was no *coach*-road
passing through Bolham at that date.

convivial gipsies at the same " Brick House,"
since it adjoined the king's highway.   Hence, he
climbed the steep ascent of Knightshayes, from
whose summit he might have cast a last lingering
look at the town.   Afterwards he would, for some
time, have seen nothing but the hedgerows and a
stretch of desolate road.

Even to Ridd, however, the glory of the Exe
was not utterly forbidden, inasmuch as from
Bolham onwards there was some kind of road.
Moreover, on the opposite side of the river was
an accommodating lane, from which lesser lanes
scamper off to the "weeches" of Washfield and
Stoodleigh Church, and which, steadily pursued
in its northward trend, has coigns of vantage
imparting grateful visions of Rock, with its
sweet old cottages, and the romantic Fairby
Gorge, and the woody amphitheatre of Cove
Cliff, together with such pretty accessories as a
wayside spring, trim dairies, rich orchards, a
modern suspension bridge, an old-world bridge,
and beside it a quaint little lodge, with its porch
and its bonnets of thatch—a miracle of rustic
beauty!   But it really matters not from which
side the landscape is viewed, the prospects are
equally charming ; and the only cause for regret,
from an æsthetic standpoint, is the railway, whose
rigid track, bisecting the valley as far as the
Exeter Inn, brusquely intrudes on its soft
contrasts of forest, stream, and lea.

From the inn, one branch of the new road
still follows the river through a sylvan paradise,
while another, nearly parallel with an older lane,
yclept Windwhistle, leads on to Bampton along
the tributary Batherum.   On quitting that high-

way of loveliness, the Exe, one is conscious of a difference—the outlook is more tame. However, as one approaches the town, the scenery improves, and of the town itself it must be conceded that it is beautifully situated among the hills.

For me, Bampton is a place with sacred memories; but I am well aware that, to sound its depths of sentiment, an initiation is necessary. A stranger strolling listlessly through the church-yard, or seated with callous heart against a walled-up yew—to him it is all a void. What can he know of all the unrecorded history which, for certain souls, has transfigured the spot into a shrine? Moreover, although a fair resident informed me recently that Bampton "stands still," I have an uncomfortable conviction, forced upon me in a brief visit, that this is not quite the case, that it has exchanged some of its old Sabbatic calm for an irreverent spirit of enterprise and strivings to be "up-to-date." Thanks to a disciple and friend of the late Mr Cecil Rhodes, the quarries have been galvanised into stupendous energy, and, aided by the contrivances of modern science, are now working at high pressure, and all Bampton is cock-a-whoop over the same. Well, well, one must have patience. Only suffer me to write of *my* Bampton, which was also Blackmore's Bampton, not the Bampton that now is.

In those far-off days of 1891-3, the quarries were not wholly quiescent; even then they were shedding their riches, but in a decent, leisurely way, leaving many a grass-grown plot and fern-clad lovers' walk, and tokens of vanished industry in what we termed " the rubble-heaps." The

distinctive feature of Bampton stone is that it
contains a large proportion of "chert" or flint,
which makes it good for roads. The principal
structures in the neighbourhood—including the
county and other bridges—are built of it, and,
judging from the age of the church tower, these
black limestone beds have been worked for at
least six hundred years.

The topography asks some explaining. A
noter hies here, noting. Somebody has told him
of Bampton Castle, and forthwith the heady ass
swoops on a circular shed on the quarry plane as
a relic. To be sure, at the south-east entrance of
the town there are plentiful suggestions of military
operations. The wind-swept knoll, whence you
catch the first glimpse of Bampton, would be a
fine station for a park of French artillery, to
which the exposed railway station, with its less
warlike engines, could offer but a faint resistance.
A few paces further on, and you come to what is
uncommonly like a bastion, crowned by the
pseudo-Bampton Castle. Of the real Bampton
Castle, at the opposite end of the town, nothing
remains but the site and some rather doubtful
fortifications in what is now an orchard.

But there *was* a castle, for in 1336 Richard
Cogan had a licence from the Crown to castellate
his mansion-house at Bampton, and to enclose his
wood at Uffculme, and three hundred acres for a
park. The exact site of the castle is believed to
have been on a lower level, but closely adjacent
to the exis.ing Mote. The origin and purpose of
this great mound, which is artificial, is not
perhaps free from obscurity, but a former resident
favours the following elucidation: The name of

COMBE, DULVERTON [page 91].

the place is derived from the Saxon word *mot* or *gemot* (a "meeting"), and it was probably the seat of the Hundred-mote, or court of judicature, Bampton being the head manor of the hundred.[1] It was also a burgh, or fortified place, and by the laws of King Edgar the Burghmote, or Court of the Borough, was held thrice a year. The parish, it may be observed, is still divided into Borough, East, West, and Petton quarters, and the ancient office of portreeve is yet retained. Some time before Domesday and the Geldroll, the king gave Bampton to Walter de Douay. From Walter's son, Robert de Baunton, the lordship passed through the Paynells to the Cogans, and from the Cogans to the Bourchiers, Earls of Bath, who, so far as is known, were the last owners of the barony to reside at the castle. The Bourchier knot is to be seen in the church—on the screen and the roof-bosses.

Apart from such rather dry particulars, it is not much that I can tell you of the public annals of Bampton, but one morsel relating to the Bourchier reign you must swallow, if only for its rarity. In May 1607, Walter Yonge, of Colyton, thus wrote in his diary : " There were earthquakes felt in divers parts of this realm, and, namely, at Barnstaple, Tiverton, and Devonshire ; also I heard it by one of Bampton credibly reported that there it was felt also. And at Bampton, being

[1] Perhaps a more likely explanation is that it was a Norman motte, specimens of which are to be found not only in England, but in France, and which is depicted in several scenes of the Bayeux. These earthworks are usually planted not on hill-tops, but on low sites in or near villages, and not far from a church.

L

four"—Tush, Squire Yonge, it is full seven—
"miles from Tiverton, there was a little lake
which ran by the space of certain hours, the
water whereof was as blue as azure, yet notwithstanding as clear as possible might be.
It was seen and testified by many who were
eye-witnesses, and reported to me by Mr Twistred,
who dwelleth in the same parish, and felt the
earthquake."

Can it be that this "little lake"—good
Devonshire for running water—was the shut-up
and buried, but by no means dared or dead,
Shuttern stream? Perchance it was. Flowing
under broad Brook Street, in times of flood he
emerges and revenges himself for his confinement,
spreading across the roadway, and swamping the
sunken cottages, and waxing a lake indeed, in
the Biblical acceptation of the term. But the
Shuttern was not shut up or buried for many a
year after the miracle. He flowed muddily along
in open channel, though straitly enclosed by
banks and spanned at intervals by bridges—a
poor copy of a Venetian canal and a rare play-
ground for the oppidan ducks. Now they have
to waddle their way, and a long way it is for
some of them, to the Batherum, a few, it may be,
tumbling down the hill from Briton Street. And
let not Master Printer, in his wisdom, correct to
"Britain Street," as he hath aforetime been moved
to do. For "Briton" is the recognised and
official spelling, and who is he that he should
alter and amend what has been approved by
lawful authority?

The Conscript Fathers of the town are
greatly exercised at such odious disguisings of

the true and proper form, which they rightly decline to sanction or accept. I am with them, heart and soul. Here in Beamdune, in this very street, the ancient Britons—'twas in 614—fought a great fight for freedom against the West Saxons, and there were slain of them forty and two thousand. The present inhabitants are descended from the vanquished, the Britons. You doubt it? Then little you know of their intermarriages. An outsider has no chance. Why even the pedlars and pedlaresses complain of Bampton's closeness. "They're no use," they exclaim, "they deal only with their own people." You still doubt? Then I renounce you as a heathen man and a publican.[1]

Bampton's chief boast is its fair, which is held on the last Thursday in October, and attracts thousands of visitors, many of them coming from considerable distances. It is not easy to say precisely why, since there are other places nearer the moor, but for a long succession of years the town has served as the principal mart for the wild Exmoor ponies, deprived of which the fair would no doubt rapidly dwindle. These shaggy little horses—a good number of them mere "suckers"—are sold by auction, and the incidents connected with their coming and going, and their manners in the sale-ring, constitute the "fun of the fair."

[1] This story, repeated in directories and guide-books for generations, receives short shrift from Mr R. N. Worth. "It has been claimed as the Beamdune where Kynegils defeated the Britons in 614, but that was Bampton in Oxfordshire" (*History of Devonshire*, p. 98). *Sic transit gloria mundi.*

On the last occasion when I travelled to
Bampton Fair, my compartment was entered by
a gipsy belle with abundance of raven hair in
traces, the dark complexion of her race, the
regulation earrings and trinkets, and much con-
versational fluency.   She had come up from
Exeter on the chance of meeting with some of
her people whom she had not seen for several
years.   That brought to my recollection a
prevalent belief that the Romany folk have a
septennial reunion, no doubt intended to be
cordial and friendly in the extreme.   Nevertheless,
I can answer for it that the intention is not
always fulfilled, for on one fair day two rival
tribes fought a pitched battle with blackthorns,
etc., in the orchard of the Tiverton Hotel.   And
the women will fight like the men, and with the
men.   They are artful beggars.   A gipsy matron
guided round a youngster of three or four years,
with his small legs already encased in trousers,
to claim a penny, because on one hand he had
little excrescent thumbs.   The boy could hold
a penny between these thumbs, and, on being
given a coin, was told to say " Thank you," his
mother expressing her gratitude with the wish,
" May you enjoy the lady you loves ! "
It is a safe assumption that no one visits a
place of the size of Bampton—at all events, at
ordinary times—without having a look at the
church.   Ten years ago you would have been
rewarded with the spectacle of high pews, over
the backs of which I can remember feminine
eyes taking stock of the congregation.   Nose
and mouth were not visible, and consequently
the fair damsels had somewhat the appearance

of hooded Turkish ladies. Now that Bampton
Church has been swept and garnished and
the arcade straightened—it fell over quite two
feet and crushed the timbers in the aisle—the
building hardly seems the same, but the most
valuable features, to an antiquary, remain untouched.

Entering the chancel from the churchyard,
you will find against the north wall fragments
of bold and graceful sculpture, with tabernacle
work, tracery, shields, the symbol I.H.S., and
the Bourchier knot and water bouget, or budget,
as it is sometimes written. Perhaps "bucket"
may be permissible as a variant, since the bearing,
which is in the form of a yoke with two pouches
of leather appended to it, was originally intended
to represent bags slung on a pole which was
carried across the shoulders—an arrangement
adopted by the Crusaders for conveying water
over the desert. To return to the fragments,
they were part of two ancient monuments which,
according to the Rev. Bartholomew Davy, formerly
stood in the chancel ; on their removal, about a
hundred years ago, the sides were used to line
the wall.

That the monuments covered the remains of
Sir John Bourchier, knight, Lord Fitzwarner,
created Earl of Bath July 9, 1536, and those
of his father, is certain. The will of the former,
bearing date October 20, 1535, and proved
June 11, 1541, expressly directs that his body
shall be buried in the parish church of Bampton,
Devon, in the place there where his father lies
buried, and that a tomb or stone of marble be
made and set over the grave where his body

shall be buried, with his picture, arms, and recognisances, and the day and the year engraven and fixed on the same tomb within a year after his decease. During the restoration the workmen discovered under the place where the organ now stands, a vault containing several ridged coffins, believed to be those of members of the Bourchier family, but, as the dates were not taken, this is merely a matter of speculation.

Behind the organ is a triptych of black marble, one compartment of which perpetuates the memory of a lady. The two others contain the following inscriptions :—

"Vnder lyeth the body of Arthur the sone of John Bowbeare of this Town, Yeoman, who departed this life the 17 day of December Anno Dom 1675."

" Here vnder lyeth ye body of John the sone of John Bowbeare of this Town, Yeoman, who departed this life the 12 day of May Anno Domi 1676."

According to local tradition, Arthur and John Bowbeare were giants, like John Ridd ; and it will be noted as a further coincidence that they were of the yeoman class. The name is still pre-served in Bowbear Hill, to the south-east of the town, and in Higher and Lower Bowbear Farms. Another interesting point is that John Ridd may have entered the town of his fellow-giants, who were still alive, though soon to die, not by the old Tiverton road, but by an ancient track which ran down Bowbear Hill. This track, now dis-used, was an old Roman road, and, having been paved, is still known as Stony Lane.

Giants are said to be usually short-lived—a charge which cannot be laid against the Vicars of Bampton. On consulting the list I find that from 1645 to 1711 the living was held by the Rev. James Style, from 1730 to 1785 by the Rev. Thomas Wood, and from 1785 to 1845 by the Rev. Bartholomew Davy. In the case of the last-mentioned divine—familiarly known as "old Bart Davy"—the patience of some member of his flock was evidently exhausted, for one fine morning there was found, nailed to the church door, the following lamentation :—

> "The Parson is a-wored out,
>   The Clerk is most ado ;
>   The Saxton's gude vor nort—
>   'Tis time to have all new."

According to the son of the last parish clerk of Bampton, there was a servant of Mr Trickey, of the Swan Inn, named Joe Ridd, or Rudd, who amused the townspeople of a generation or two ago with stories of the "girt Jan Ridd," of Exmoor, ostensibly an ancestor. One of these stories was that the huge yeoman, "out over," broke off the branch of a tree and used it as a weapon. This circumstance gives special point to the statement in chapter liii. of *Lorna Doone*, that "much had been said at Bampton about some great freebooters, to whom all Exmoor owed suit and service, and paid them very punctually." Moreover, in Mr Snow's grounds at Oare is a mighty ash, whose limbs incline downwards, they (it is said) having been bent out of their natural set by the constraining power of the matchless Ridd.

Blackmore not only conducts his hero and heroine through Bampton as a place on their line of route, but alludes to it respectfully (see chapter xiii.) as one of the important towns on the southern side of the moor, though he dare not for conscience' sake compare it with metropolitan Taunton.

A BIT OF OLD DULVERTON.

CHAPTER VII

WHERE MASTER HUCKABACK THROVE[1]

THE stage from Bampton to Dulverton was not easy for John Ridd and his serving-man, nor is it easy for us. From the very heart of the town is a toilsome ascent to High Cross, fitly so named, and reputed to be haunted. Chains have been heard to rattle there, and the enemy of mankind is alleged to have a predilection for the spot. On this subject an old Bamptonian once told me an amusing story. In the days when the "boneshaker" wooden bicycle was a novelty, and the Barretts (relations of Mrs Barrett Browning) resided at Combehead, someone belonging to the house was riding down the hill in the twilight on his machine, which was rattling and creaking to a merry tune. Half-way down he encountered a labourer, who, never having seen or heard of anything of the kind, and totally at a loss to account for the phenomenon in the

---

[1] "And truly, the Dulverton people said that he was the richest man in their town, and could buy up half of the county armigers" (*LornaDoone*, chapter xiii.). Some of the local "armigers" figure in the following pages.

M

"dimpse," as he would have called it, inconti-
nently jumped to the conclusion that the strange
shape advancing towards him was that of
Apollyon, and, in abject terror, turned and
fled.

Whatever the explanation may be—whether
it is the beetling trees or the unfrequentedness—
there is no doubt, as is proved by the universal
testimony of those who have used the road,
especially by night, that it differs from most roads
in being distinctly uncanny.

Combehead is the property of the lord of the
manor (Mr W. H. White), and the manor is,
roughly speaking, the parish.   But just as there
are wheels within wheels, so there may be
manors within manors, and it happens that
Mr Wensley, an excellent yeoman who lately
purchased the farm which he had previously
occupied as a tenant—Birchdown, at the right
base of the hill—is also a lord, though he
modestly disclaims any intention of proceeding
to the Upper House of Parliament.   Locally,
however, he has his rights, and I believe the
other lord has to pay his lesser brother "quit-
rent" for certain land "within the ambit" of the
manor of Bampton.

From the summit of Grant's Hill one gains
the first sight of Somerset, and very prepossessing
one finds it, with the twin valleys of the Exe and
Barle cleaving the high ground, and Pixton
enthroned between.   By their junction the two
rivers form a wide basin in which lies the town-
ship of Exebridge.   This, as will be shown, was
the scene of one of the exploits of the famous
Faggus.   There is nothing uncanny about

Exebridge ; indeed, it may be called an open, sunny hamlet. Nevertheless, the river here has its black pool, to which was "banished"—when or for what reason I cannot say—Madam Thorold, of Burston, an old house in the neighbour-hood. In like manner, but rather less cruelly, Madam Gaddy, of Great House, Bampton, was "banished" to Barton, with leave to return at a cock's-stride a year. When she gets back, she will be horrified to find her grand old mansion gone and a modern public-house usurping its name and place. Similarly, the late Captain Musgrove, of Stone Farm, Exford, is reputed to have been conjured away by so many parsons to Pinkery Pond, whence he is on his way back at the conventional cock's-stride.

As chance wills, without going out of my way, I have it in my power to supplement these brief, but poignant, accounts of the supernatural with other and more detailed ghost-stories derived from the history or traditions of the Sydenham family. Close to Dulverton Station are two roads branching off to the left; either of these will conduct you to the village of Brushford, and from there to the entrance to Combe, a beautiful Elizabethan manor-house built in the usual shape of an E. The Sydenhams were a distinguished Somerset-shire family, and, although some of its branches are extinct, and others fallen from their high estate, there are left ample proofs of its former greatness, and, if I may be permitted to say so much of those whom I have been privileged to know as friends, "still in their ashes glow their wonted fires."

It was in 1568 that John Sydenham bought

the manor of Dulverton from Francis Babington, a gentleman of the Privy Chamber, but the connection of the family with Dulverton is of much longer standing ; and as a John de Sydenham is mentioned as marrying Mary, daughter and heir of Joan Pixton, of Pixton, in the fourteenth century, this may perhaps be taken as the period of their first settlement in the neighbourhood.   They had other homes in Somerset—notably at Brympton d'Evercy, near Yeovil, now the property of Sir Spencer Ponsonby Fane ; and the canopied monument, erected in the little church hard by, to a Sydenham by a Sydenham, is worth going a day's journey to see.

So far as the house and estate of Combe are concerned, they first came into the possession of the Sydenhams through the marriage of Edward, son of John Sydenham, of Badialton (Bathealton), with Joan, daughter and heir of Walter Combe, of Combe, in 1482.   Part of the original mansion still remains, and is used as servants' quarters ; the house, however, was rebuilt during the reign of Elizabeth, and probably towards its close, as two medals, struck to commemorate the defeat of the Armada, were found, some few years ago, beneath the floor of the entrance porch.   The main entrance of the older building appears to have been in the east wing, where cross-beams, over what were once two very wide doorways, are still to be seen.   The second doorway opened into the inner court or quadrangle.   The stone, a species of shillett, was quarried near the house, and, instead of mortar, clay was largely used. A better sort of stone was employed in the later building, with plenty of lime and sand. The oak work is magnificent.

There was a close connection between the Sydenhams of Combe and those of Brympton. Humphry, well-known as the "silver-tongued," Sydenham, was a scion of the latter branch. He entered at Exeter College, Oxford, became Fellow of Wadham in the same university, and then chaplain to Lord Howard, of Escrigg, and Archbishop Laud successively. Appointed rector of Pockington and Odcombe, he resided in the latter place (Tom Coryate's native village); and his preferments included a prebendal stall at Wells. On the establishment of the Commonwealth, he was deprived of his living by the Commissioners, and retired to Combe, where he performed the church service for tenants and others who chose to attend in the chapel-room over the hall. This eloquent divine was buried at Dulverton.

Major Sir George Sydenham, another brother of Sir John Sydenham, of Brympton d'Evercy, and a knight-marshal in the army of Charles I., had married his cousin Susan, daughter of George Sydenham, of Combe; and, whilst staying with his wife at her father's house, received an urgent summons to accompany his brother on some public occasion. Nothing more was heard of him until one night, as his wife was sleeping peacefully, he appeared to her in his military dress, but deathly pale. Starting up in affright, she exclaimed that her husband was dead, and announced her intention of joining him. Accordingly, the next morning she set out, and on the way was met by a messenger who unluckily confirmed her presentiment, saying that her lord had died suddenly.[1]

Ever since then the spirit of the major has had an uncomfortable trick of turning up at unexpected hours in the mansion in which he made his first apparition. One day Mrs Jakes, a tenant of the family, was ascending the stairs, when she met a strange figure coming out of one of the rooms, and, according to her account, motioned as if he would snuff the candle for her. She was not alarmed, because Sir George looked kindly on her, and it was only later that she remembered the story of the ghost.

More extraordinary still were the circumstances of another visit. When the late rector of Brushford was a young man, he invited a college-

---

[1] It may be worth mentioning that an incident similar to that which marred the happiness of Susan Sydenham occurred in the life of the celebrated John Donne. In 1610, on the third day after his arrival at Paris, he was left alone in a room where he had been dining with Sir Robert Drury and others. Half an hour later the knight returned, and was surprised to find him in a curious sort of ecstasy. At first he was unable to speak, but after a time he declared—

"I have seen a dreadful vision since I saw you. I have seen my dear wife pass twice by me through this room, with her hair hanging about her shoulders, and a dead child in her arms."

Sir Robert suggested that it was nothing but a dream, which he advised him to forget, but Donne replied, "I cannot be surer that I am now living than that I have not slept since I saw you, and I am so sure that at her second appearance she stopped, looked me in the face and vanished."

As he seemed so certain, a messenger was sent to Drury House, who brought back the news that he had found Mrs Donne ill in bed, after the birth of a dead infant—an event which had happened on the very day and hour that her husband had seen the vision.

friend to stay with him. The evening of his
arrival was spent in the usual way, with plenty of
fun and pleasantry, after which the party broke
up for the night. The following morning the
guest came down in the same good spirits, but
he had a tale to tell.

"You fellows thought you were going to
frighten me last night," he observed. Everybody
disclaimed such an intention, and begged to
know what he meant. There were signs of
incredulity on the part of the collegian, and then
he was induced to explain that an old cavalier
arrayed in a wide cloak and Spanish hat had
presented himself at his bedside. The spectacle,
however, had given him no concern, as he had
taken it for a practical joke.

Major Sydenham's portrait was painted at
Combe, and is still in the possession of the
family. It is that of a man with the pointed
beard and moustache of the period, wearing a
cavalier's hat and feather; and within living
memory was concealed behind curtains. In view
of what was said about the subject, this was not
unnatural, but the picture itself had a peculiar
quality. A boy, it is remembered, refused to
look at it, and hid under the table, because the
eyes followed him.

I have not yet done with the Sydenham
phantom. As may easily be supposed, the
country-side has its legends of these great people,
who, it is averred, drove a carriage with six or
eight horses shod with silver. Amongst the
legends is one that narrates the laying of Major
Sydenham's ghost, whose visits became so
frequent and inopportune that the family at

Combe resolved on serious measures to prevent
their recurrence.   They communicated with the
Vicar of Dulverton, desiring him to perform the
rite of exorcism, and accordingly that divine,
attended by his curate, proceeded to the large
upper room still known as "the chapel," where,
as we have seen, the "silver-tongued" Sydenham
had so often read prayers under the Commonwealth.   At the conclusion of the service the
man-servant was ordered to lead a handsome
watch-dog to Aller's Wood, on the border
of the present highway to Dulverton, and there
release him.   Particular instructions were given
him on no account to hurt or ill-use the animal,
but these he seems to have disobeyed.   The
result was a sudden flash of lightning, followed
immediately by a loud clap of thunder, in the
midst of which the dog disappeared.   On
returning to the house the terrified emissary
reported the occurrence, but the opinion was
expressed that the spirit had been effectually
laid.

The country-side, however, was unwilling to
resign its ghost, and, amongst other "yarns,"
the following has been told.   There is a stone
staircase at Combe, and one step was always
coming out.   If it was put back one day, it was
found dislodged the next ; and this was believed
to be Major Sydenham's work.   At length the
two Blackmores, father and son, were sent for.
They were masons of Exebridge, and skilled men
at their trade, of which they were proud.   They
thought they had secured the step in its place
firmly.

"Damme, Major Sydenham, push it out if

TORR STEPS, HAWKRIDGE (page 109).

you can," exclaimed one of them. No sooner said than done.

I now come to what may be either the basis or a variant of the main tradition, unless, as may well be the case, it is an entirely independent narrative — namely, a circumstantial relation quoted in the *Treatise of the Soul of Man,* which edifying composition was published in 1685. It is, word for word, as follows :—

" Much to the same purpose is that so famous and well-attested story of the apparition of Major George Sydenham to Captain William Dyke, both of Somersetshire, attested by the worthy and learned Dr Thomas Dyke, a near kinsman of the captain's, and by Mr Douch, to whom both the major and captain were intimately known. The sum is this :—The major and captain had many disputes about the Being of a God and the immortailty of the Soul, on which points they could never be resolved, though they much sought and desired it, and therefore it was at last fully agreed betwixt them, that he who died first should on the third night after his funeral, come betwixt the hours of twelve and one, to the little house at Dulverton in Somersetshire ; and the captain happened to lie that very night which was appointed in the same chamber and bed with Dr Dyke. He acquainted the doctor with the appointment, and his resolution to attend the place and hour that night, for which purpose he got the key of the garden. The doctor could by no means divert his purpose, but when the hour came he was upon the place, where he waited two hours and a half, neither seeing nor hearing anything more than usual.

N

"About six weeks after, the doctor and captain went to Eaton, and lay again at the same inn, but not the same chamber as before. The morning before they went thence the captain stayed longer than was usual in his chamber, and at length came into the doctor's chamber, but in a visage and form much differing from himself, with his hair and eyes staring and his whole body shaking and trembling. Whereat the doctor, wondering, demanded, 'What is the matter, cousin captain?' The captain replies, 'I have seen my major.' At which the doctor seeming to smile, the captain said, 'If ever I saw him in my life, I saw him but now,' adding as followeth. 'This morning (said he) after it was light, someone came to my bedside, and suddenly drawing back the curtains, calls, 'Cap, cap,' (which was the term of familiarity that the major used to call the captain by), to whom I replied, 'What, my major.' To which he returns, 'I could not come at the time appointed, but I am come now to tell you that there is a God, and a very just and terrible one, and if you do not turn over a new leaf, you will find it so.' This stuck close to him. Little meat would go down with him at dinner, though a handsome treat was provided. These words were sounding in his ears frequently during the remainder of his life, he was never shy or scrupulous to relate it to any that asked him concerning it, nor ever mentioned it but with horror and trepidation. They were both men of a brisk humour and jolly conversation, of very quick and keen parts, having been both University and Inns of Court gentlemen."

The intimacy to which this narrative bears witness, though easily accounted for in officers of the same regiment, is further explained by the fact they were near neighbours at home. The Sydenhams, as has been shown, dwelt at Combe, and the Dykes, I may now add, at Pixton, the former residence of the Sydenhams, whilst the salutation "Cap, cap" indicates much friendliness. The Dyke dynasty came to an end when Sir Thomas Acland (seventh baronet) married Elizabeth Dyke, and joined her estates at Dulverton and elsewhere to his own vast patrimony. With them I am not concerned, more than to state that they were the grand-parents of John Dyke Acland, who wedded in 1771 the Lady Christian Harriet Caroline Fox-Strangways, sister of Stephen, first Earl of Ilchester.

In the commonplace book of Thomas Sayer, parish clerk and schoolmaster of Dulverton, I find the following entries relating to the family :—

"Jn⁰ Dyke Acland, Esq., married Jany 7, 1771. The above Jn⁰ Dyke Acland born Feb. 18, 1746, and died Nov. 15, 1778. The old Sir Thos. Dyke Acland, Father of above Jn⁰ Dyke Acland, born Aug. 12, 1722, and died Feby 20, 1785."

The same manuscript includes particulars regarding Pixton House, which prove the existing structure, the "frozen music" of which is superbly classical, to be differently laid out from its predecessor, which we may conjecture to have been of some type of English domestic architecture, and, according to Sayer's measurements, contained some fine rooms. The old house was pulled down in February 1803, and the new, built by Hassell, of Exeter, was finished in November 1805. This work was carried out on the initiative of Lady Harriet Acland, after whom the private road through the serried woods of the sequestered Haddeo valley is named "Lady Harriet's Drive"—doubtless, because she ordered its construction.

Two or three years ago Mr Broomfield, of Dulverton, showed me an old picture, dim, dirty, and discoloured, yet significant. Through the crust of time one could discern a man, a woman, and a boat; and the attitudes and certain of the details convinced me that the faded, and not very valuable, heirloom represented a scene in the life of the great lady of Pixton, to which *she* must have looked back with horror, and her posterity will ever refer with pride. I will try to interpret that picture, and conjure up the scene it so feebly portrays.

It was the year 1777, and Major Acland's grenadiers, forming the advanced guard of General Fraser's brigade, were advancing against the American insurgents. Lady Harriet had already endured cruel privations, and in the course of the previous year had nursed her husband through a dangerous bout of sickness, contracted in the campaign. Now it had begun again. Only a short time before, the tent they were sleeping in had caught fire, and most of their clothing had been burnt. It was winter, and bitter cold.

Now, however brave a woman may be, unless she is a professed Amazon, she is not expected to fight, and, as an action was about to take place,

Acland requested his wife to remain with the baggage. In a small log-hut with three other ladies—the Baroness Ruysdael, Mrs Ramage, and Mrs Reynell—Lady Harriet spent hours of agonising suspense, the high notes of the incessant musketry fire mingling with the diapason of the artillery, to be varied erelong by the groans of the wounded borne into their place of shelter, and littering the ground around.

After a while the news reached Mrs Ramage that her husband had been killed. Then came another message that Lieutenant Reynell had been dangerously wounded; and finally, at the close of the day, Lady Harriet received the information that Major Acland, seriously hurt, was in the hands of the enemy.

With equal courage and affection, the devoted woman resolved to go in search of him, and that without delay. Accordingly, with Dr Brudenell, chaplain of the regiment, she entered a small boat and proceeded down the river to the enemy's outposts. Here they were challenged by the sentry, and Brudenell, hoisting a white handkerchief on a stick, attempted to explain their errand. The sentinel, however, proved obdurate, not only refusing to carry any message to the officer in command, but warning them not to move, or he would fire on the boat. So all through that inclement night, insufficiently clad, without a particle of food, and in imminent danger of becoming a target for the foe, they sat and waited.

With the morning their situation improved. The general, on being made cognisant of the facts, received the lady with soldierly sympathy, and accorded her full permission to attend on her husband until his recovery.

Soon after they returned to England, and to Pixton, but Colonel Acland was born to ill-luck. He fought a duel on Bampton Down, November 11, 1778, with Captain Lloyd, an officer of his own regiment, whom he had offended by praising the humanity of the American people, and caught a chill. Four days later he was dead.

Lady Harriet had two children—Elizabeth Kitty and John Dyke. The latter, after succeeding to the baronetcy, died at the age of seventeen, whilst his sister married, in 1796, Lord Porchester (afterwards second Earl of Carnarvon), and died in 1816. Lady Harriet outlived both husband and children, dying in 1818.

The present possessor of Pixton is the Dowager Countess of Carnarvon ; and her sons are the lineal descendants of the intrepid woman whose adventures I have described.

Pixton Park, with its beeches and herd of fallow deer, and Lady Harriet's Drive, flanked on each side by gorgeous oak woods or oak coppice, vocal with streams, and centred by brown Haddon, are among the features which enable Dulverton to maintain its proud claim to extraordinary beauty of scenery. In this respect it has no superior in the West Country, and Tennyson, who visited the neighbourhood not long before his death, went away delighted with it. An account of this visit appears in the life of the poet by his son, the present Lord Tennyson ; and, although rather inaccurate in some of the details, yet, as a piece of impressionism, deserves to be reproduced.

"In June, Colonel Crozier lent us his yacht, the *Assegai*, and we went to Exmouth, and thence by rail to Dulverton—a land of bubbling streams, my father called it.

"Lord Carnarvon had told him years ago that the streams here were the most delicious he knew.

"We drove up the Haddon valley, and to Barlynch Abbey on the Exe. The ragged robin and wild garlic were profuse. We returned by Pixton Park.

"The Exe is 'arrowy' just before its confluence with the Barle, running, as my father remarked, 'too vehemently to break upon the jutting rocks.' We sat next on a wooden bridge over the Exe, and he said to me, 'That is an old simile, but a good one: Time is like a river, ever past and ever future.'

"In the afternoon, we drove through the Barle valley to Hawkridge, then to the Torr Steps, high up among the hills, with an ancient bridge across the river, flat stones laid on piers. Some tawny cows were cooling themselves in mid-stream; a green meadow on one side, on the other a wooded slope. 'If it were only to see this,' he said, 'the journey is worth while.'

"We climbed Haddon Down [Draydon Knap?], and then to Higher Combe—a valley down which there was a most luxuriant view, the Dartmoor range as background, almost Italian in colouring."

Lord Tennyson adds, that, at Dulverton, his

father began the Hymn to the Sun in a new metre, for his "Akbar."

A most exquisite view is to be obtained from Baron's Down, situated on the lofty height of Bury Hill. Formerly the seat of the Stucley Lucases (who were as great in stag-hunting, or nearly so, as Tennyson was in poetry), it afterwards served as the country-house of Dr Warre, Headmaster of Eton, who resigned his tenancy, much to the regret of his neighbours and friends, as recently as last year.

Of Dulverton town, as distinct from its environs, it is impossible to say much. It is, however, one of the chief centres of Exmoor stag-hunting and fishing, and the hotels, which thrive on these attractions, provide adequate accommodation. Owing to the constant stream of fashionable visitors from all parts of the world, Dulverton, though in point of size a mere village, wears, during the season, a quite cosmopolitan aspect ; and, as if to emphasise its superiority to other rustic communities, the enterprising inhabitants have lately caused to be installed a system of electric lighting by means of high poles with wire attachments.

Here, it will be remembered, dwelt Master Reuben Huckaback, John Ridd's maternal uncle, who, when bound on the back of the frightened mountain pony, described himself as "an honest hosier and draper, serge and long-cloth warehouseman, at the sign of the Gartered Kitten, in the loyal town of Dulverton." Huckaback, I am disposed to think, was Blackmore's creation, the name in itself being suspicious. What is Huckaback ? Nuttall defines it as "a kind of linen with raised figures on it, used for tablecloths and towels "—the sort of thing that a shopkeeper in Uncle Ben's line would be likely to sell. Blackmore, no doubt, somewhat exaggerates the commercial advantages of Dulverton, but in the good old days, tradesmen managed to subsist very comfortably, and even to retire on a competence. The premises now occupied by Mr Bayley were probably those Mr Blackmore had in his eye, though their spick-and-span appearance does not suggest anything venerable. The proprietor, however, has good warrant for ascribing a decent antiquity to the house, whose traditional sign is the Vine, not the Gartered Kitten. That it may have been partially remodelled or reconstructed since the seventeenth century, is readily granted, as being in the nature of things, but, having been the head shop at Dulverton time out of mind, it is, at all events, in the apostolic succession.

Some Dulverton streets bear interesting names. Thus we have Rosemary Lane and Lady Street. The latter was formerly much narrower at its entrance into Fore Street, and an old inhabitant once told me that he believed that anciently it had been built over, and that the front of the superincumbent structure was adorned with an image of the Virgin Mary.

The widening process involved the demolition of two ancient cottages, which had formed the Nightingale Inn ; and amongst the débris was discovered an old coin, on seeing which a local connoisseur forthwith pronounced it Spanish, adding that it had been probably left by the Dons when they invaded England in 1600. A

o

companion denied that England was ever invaded
by the Spaniards, but the other would not be
contradicted. "He knowed they did, and it
weren't likely they could pass Dulverton without
stopping for a drink." In point of fact, the coin
was a poor specimen of a sixpenny bit, struck
in 1566.

CHAPTER VIII

BROTHERS BARLE AND EXE[1]

IT is now time to quit Dulverton, and one has to face the somewhat complex question in which direction one's steps should next be turned. There are three main routes—by the railway to Barnstaple; by the "turnpike" to Dunster and Minehead; and by one of several roads to Simonsbath, the heart of the moor. All these ways lead to interesting places—places much too interesting to be passed by; and it is at one's choice which to seek out first. That is assuming that one intends to establish Dulverton as one's base, making longer or shorter excursions to the spots hereafter to be named. To recommend such a course, however, would be obviously impolite to other towns equally avid of patronage. They must all be visited in turn—so much is certain.

As a start must be made, and a selection may not be avoided, I will fall back on the line I always followed as a boy, and once more breast Mount Sydenham, with its chaplet of firs. When

---

[1] In chapter iii. of *Lorna Doone*, Blackmore speaks of Dulverton as a town near which "the Exe and his big brother Barle have union."

the panting and perspiring traveller reaches a turn of the road he may hap to espy a hollow in a field on the left. That is Granny's Pit, where an old woman with dishevelled tresses has been viewed, bewailing her daughter. A few more paces bring us to the grove of firs, whence the sinuous Barle may be surveyed far below in all his sylvan glory. This may be Blackmore's "corner of trees," if Ridd followed this route, and not Hollam Lane, which runs parallel with it. Stepping back into the lane, one soon finds oneself on Court Down, which, though not of any great extent, is a genuine bit of moorland "debated" by green fern, and purple heather, and golden gorse, embosomed in which there may stand at gaze fleecy, white-faced sheep of the horned variety peculiar to Exmoor.

Nature's "much-admired confusion," however, is exhibited on a much grander scale in the undulating sweep of Winsford Hill, which, from Mountsey Hill Gate to Comer's Gate, boasts four miles of continuous brake. This free and joyous expanse is the native heath of Sir Thomas Acland's wild Exmoor ponies, which, in their shaggy deshabille may at times be seen grazing on the rough sward, or scampering playfully over moss and ling. They suffer none to approach.

At Spire Cross is a confluence of roads, that to the left being one way to Torr Steps, an old Keltic bridge formed of large, loose slabs laid athwart low piers, which bears a family likeness to Post Bridge on Dartmoor, but the latter is grooved for chariots. It is well to point out that this charming vestige of prehistoric civilisation—

a gem in a lovely setting — is by no means isolated. The remains of several British castles are to be found in the neighbourhood, Mountsey Castle being quite near ; and up on the hill, not far from Spire Cross, but in the opposite direction, is a menhir. The stone carries an inscription, which, though extremely rude and partially obliterated, is yet distinctly legible; and the monument is supposed to mark the burial-place of a Romanised British chieftain—the "grandson of Caractacus," which is the English rendering of "Carataci Nepos." Dr Murray recently took a "squeeze" of the face of the stone, from which a cast was made, now at Oxford ; and both he and Professor Rhys, who accompanied him, were convinced of the genuineness of the scrawl. The actual lettering appears to be : CVRAACI EPVC. Moreover, beside the road to Comer's Gate are three immense cairns, known as the Wambarrows. This is the highest point of Winsford Hill—1405 feet above the level of the sea.

Around all these spots cluster superstitions weird or bizarre. The menhir is an index of buried treasure. The Wambarrows are the haunt of a mysterious black dog. Round Mountsey Castle a spectral chariot races at midnight, to disappear into a cairn in a field at the foot of the hill. As for Torr Steps, the legend is that they were placed there by the devil, who menaced with dire penalties the first mortal that should presume to use them. The sable monarch took his seat on one bank of the stream, while the other was occupied by a parson, eager to try conclusions with him. The holy man was astute, and, as a preliminary measure, dispatched a cat across the bridge. On touching the opposite side she was ruthlessly rent in pieces, whereupon, the charm having been shattered, the parson boldly strode over the causeway and engaged the devil in a conflict of words, each abusing the other in good set terms. In the end the enemy of mankind retired vanquished, resigning the bridge to all and sundry. Close above these steps was one of the two homes of Mother Melldrum (see *Lorna Doone*, chapter xvii., where Blackmore alludes to the legend of their origin).

It appears that the Oxford *cognoscenti* went down into the stream in a vain search for more inscribed stones. This reminds me of a curious story of the Barle, the willows on whose banks, by the way, overhang its amber bed so as to form almost an arch. On a hill to the right, looking downstream, stands Hawkridge Church, and what is termed, in contradistinction to the parish, Hawkridge town. Well, once upon a time a villager was asked to take the place of the bass-singer in the choir for one Sunday only, and consented. A day or two later he was discovered by the incumbent, a well-known hunting parson, wading up and down the little river apparently without aim or object. The cleric drew rein, and, much amazed, inquired the meaning of this extraordinary procedure. "Plaze your honour," was the reply, " I be trying to get a bit of a hooze on me."

In other words, he was attempting to catch a cold, so that he might become hoarse, this being, as he thought, the best means of qualify-

ing himself for the successful discharge of his
duty.

" Where the swift Exe, by Somerset's fair hills,
  In curving eddies, borders pastures deep,
  Near fern-fringed slope of lawn, where babbling rills
  Sing sweetest music, mid thick foliage peep
  Five bridges, and thatched roofs. The grey Church Tower
  O'er all looks down on groves of oak and pine :
  Red deer, red Devons, ponies of the moor,
  Delight the traveller in this home of mine."

This acrostic, in praise of a charming village,
is the composition of the Rev. Prebendary W. P.
Anderson, vicar of Winsford, who has resided
there ever since 1857, and the lines show that
his experience of the place has been like the
place itself—happy.   Far otherwise was it with
one of his predecessors.   In the church porch
may be seen a list of the parish clergymen, not
so dry as such lists are wont to be, from which
it appears that early in the fourteenth century
Winsford had a blind vicar—one Willelmus.
Being unable to perform all the duties of his
office, he was allowed two coadjutors, of whom
it is recorded, to their eternal infamy, that they
were deprived "for starving the Blind Vicar."
This conduct, inhuman at the best, was the more
scandalous in that the Priory of Barlynch, to
which the advowson belonged, had, in 1280,
endowed the vicarage with the whole tithe of
wool, lambs, chicken, calves, pigs, sucklings,
cheese, butter, flax, honey, and all other small
tithes and oblations and dues pertaining to the
altar offerings.   And yet he starved—the Blind
Vicar !

Barlynch Priory, a community of Austin

Friars stood, where its remains yet stand, some two or three miles down the Exe. Shaded by what the old charter calls "the mountain of the high wood of Berlic," its situation was in the highest degree romantic; and if the prior had a lust for venery, his taste might easily be gratified, for in the adjacent woods or "copes," the deer would have found abundant shelter, and thither they doubtless resorted to pass the long summer day under the dense foliage.

Returning to Winsford, Mr Anderson's lines omit one trait which to many will seem the chief glory of the village—namely, the old inn. The "Royal Oak" is a hostelry such as one does not see every day. Its thatched roofs, and low ceilings, and projecting windows, and general crinkle-crankle are eloquent of the olden time, and the sign, as was the case with all ancient signs, hangs from its own post—a reminder of Boscobel. Hence, by a beautiful rustic lane the traveller wends his way to Exford, and on the outskirts of the village encounters the church.

On a pedestal in the churchyard stands the mutilated shaft of a venerable preaching cross, and hard by the gate one observes an "upping-stock," or "upstock," for the convenience of women in mounting their horses after divine service.

Before Exmoor was disafforested and, yet later, made a parish of itself, it is probable that Exford was the ecclesiastical capital of the district —at any rate, of the southern portion of the moor. The parish stands on the very verge of the old forest, and during the reign of King John was actually brought within its limits. Lanes in the neighbourhood were, in more scrupulous times, the forest-bounds, and along these tracks, still passable, were certain marks mentioned in the Perambulations, almost all of which can be identified. One such track, partly diverted from its old course—which, however, may be easily traced—led from what is now a cottage, but was once a small farmhouse, straight to the church. This cottage bears the name of Prescott, and still contains a round-headed stone doorway, and a little square window let into the side of the big fireplace. The late vicar, the Rev. E. G. Peirson, suggests that this may have been the original priest's cot or parsonage house. "I like to think," he says, "that my predecessors, before they came into permanent residence here, used to stop at that house when they came over the moor, and clean themselves before going into the church." He adds, however, that in that case the cottage or its name must date a long way back, as there would seem to have been clergy resident at Exford early in the twelfth century.

Mr Peirson's theory is pretty, but a simpler explanation is that the cottage belonged to the glebe. It is curious that just at the point where the old lane used to strike the churchyard, a few projecting stones still form a rough stile over the wall.

Probably it will affect most people with a feeling of surprise that there should be any connection between a place so far inland as Exford and smuggling, yet the same is true. In an orchard above West Mill was formerly an old malt-house, where malt was made and whisky distilled. But the most interesting spot to excise

P

men lay rather to the north, at Pitsworthy
Cottage.   Here was an old stone building used
as a turf-house ; but the room where the turf was
stowed had a party-wall concealing another
chamber, to which access could be obtained only
by a secret entrance under the office of the thatch.
Ordinarily this was blocked by a large stone
fitted with a swivel.   Long after, pieces of hoops
and decayed staves were discovered in this hiding-
place.   Wooden hoops are seen even now round
brandy casks, but these were smaller and adapted
to the kegs which the smugglers, landing under
Culbone, transported to Hawkcombe Head, and
Black Mire, and White Cross, and right down to
Pitsworthy.   There was no road across the moors
in those days—I am thinking of the "forties"—
and a man called Hookway is remembered as
travelling from Culbone with pack-horses.

More of smuggling anon.   Meanwhile, I am
disposed to record, for the first time, the nefarious
doings of Jan Glass and Betty, his wife.   Sheep-
stealing was a fashionable pursuit on Exmoor ;
and at Brendon Forge (see *Lorna Doone*, chapter
lxii.) the conversation was divided between the
hay-crop and "a great sheep-stealer"—apparently
not the same individual whose hanging set up
strife between the manors of East Lyn, West
Lyn, and Woolhanger on account of his small
clothes, since he is described as "a man of no
great eminence" (*Lorna Doone*, chapter lv.).   Be
that as it may, Jan was a daring sheep-stealer,
and yet, in his way, a public benefactor.   Often,
during a hard winter, he would bring into Exford
stolen mutton, which he retailed at twopence a
pound, and at such times the inhabitants were

fairly kept alive by him. His *modus operandi* was to go and gather the sheep—his own and others—on Kitnor Heath and Old Moor into Larcombe Pound at the entrance to his farm, where there was a convenient avenue or grove of beech-trees. Having brought them so far, he would kill the strange sheep, and turn out his own again over the allotments.

Jan played this trick so often that old Farmer Brewer determined to take him, if possible, in the act. With this object in view he "redded" his sheep, and as he could stand in his farm and observe the manœuvres, saw Glass driving among the sheep some red ones. With all speed Brewer made his way across, but by the time he reached Larcombe, Glass had killed and skinned the sheep that were not his own.

In the meantime Betty had not been idle. She had dipped the skins in hot water, so that the wool had come off as easily as from a lamb's tail, and had given the skins to the dogs.

What had become of the wool? Farmer Brewer, anxious to ascertain, glanced around and spied a large pot. Lifting the cover, he found the fleeces, and, turning to the disconcerted woman, exclaimed :

"Aw, fy, Betty! Here's the wool!"

This led to Glass's conviction, and he was sentenced to seven years' transportation. He had certainly had a wonderful career. He did not confine his attention to sheep, but was quite as notorious for stealing colts. Not being able to keep her from her foal, he had been known to kill the mare and throw the carcass into the pond. His thefts of sheep from "Squire" Knight alone

used to average fifty or sixty a year.   He would
gallop into a flock, pick up one of the sheep, as
a hawk or a raven would pick up a small bird,
and carry it home on the top of his saddle.   It
may seem strange that he was permitted to
indulge in these malpractices so long, but he
lived in a very out-of-the-way place.   There were
no police in those days, sheep were gathered only
once or twice in the year, and the animal he
appropriated   might   possibly   be   crippled   or
diseased.   Anyhow, until Farmer Brewer interfered, nobody took any notice.

Glass lived to return after being transported,
and eventually found himself on a bed of sickness,
when he was visited by an old farmer, James
Moore.

" Jan," said he, " I yur thee art very bad, and
thee hasn't got nort to eat.   I've killed a sheep
and brought thee a piece of mutton."

" Aw, maister," answered the poor man, " I
thort thee'd a bin the last man to come to zee
me."

" What vur, Jan ? "

" Well, I don't know, maister, how I can
taste the mutton, for I've stole scores o' sheep
from thee at the time you lived to Thurn and the
time you lived to Ashit."

" Never mind, Jan, I freely forgive thee, and
I aup that God'll do the same."

Glass never got over the illness, but soon
after this touching interview gave up the ghost,
and was buried in Exford churchyard.

Betty Glass was just as resolute a thief as
old Jan, and, whilst at Larcombe, was very
intimate with Sally Bristowe (or " Bursta," as

the name was pronounced), at Rocks, an adjoining farm.   On one occasion, Betty paid a visit to Sally at harvest time, when young turkeys were about, and after she had been hospitably entertained, eating what she liked and drinking what she liked, she had the good taste to go out and steal a score of the aforesaid small turkeys. Shortly afterwards, Sally happened to open the door and found the heads of some of the birds lying in the yard, whereupon she set out in pursuit of old Betty, overtook her, and discovered the bodies of the turkeys in the old woman's apron, blood still flowing from them.

"Now, Betty," quoth the indignant woman, "however could'st thee steal my turkeys after I'd gi'd thee plenty to eat and drink."

"Aw, for goodness sake," was the reply, "keep dark.   I'll give thee a guinea.   Say nort about it."

Sally thereupon accepted the guinea, deeming it better to do so than institute proceedings. This was certainly a mistake, for a week or two later, when Betty was in company with Farmer Brewer, and three sheets in the wind, she remarked, "Hey, Jimmy, what's think of Sal Bursta's spot-faced yo?   D'ye think I be going to give her a guinea for nort?"

From which it was evident that she stole the ewe to make good the loss of the money.   Sal undoubtedly lost the sheep.

During a visit to Minehead, seeing nothing else on which she could conveniently lay hands, Betty appropriated two 7-lb. weights ; but she had not gone more than a mile or two from the town when she found the weights too heavy to carry, and dropped them beside the hedge.

At that time the Crown Inn, Exford, was kept by Nicholas and Mary Harwood. One day when Betty was on the spree, Mrs Harwood entered the house and looked over the old woman's wardrobe. To her surprise she found three of her own dresses and several petticoats, which she brought down into the kitchen, and, spreading them out before old Betty, inquired how she came by them.

"Needn't make so much fuss about it," was the easy response, "for, if I'd sold 'em, you'd a had the coin."

As Betty was a good customer at the Crown, Mrs Harwood "kept dark" and condoned the offence.

On another occasion, Betty brought a bag into the "White Horse" and put it behind the settle. A man, called Mike Adams, was in the room, and mischievously turned the bag mouth downwards, so that when old Betty took it up, out fell the mutton—very likely a joint of Sal Bristowe's spot-faced ewe. On hearing the thud, Mike ran round the settle, and was immediately "squared" by Betty, who observed, " Say nort, and I'll sell it and spend the money."

Before her marriage with Jan, Betty had an illegitimate son, Jack Reed. In due time this boy was apprenticed to the husband of Sal Bristowe, who kept a farm and proved a rough master. Things grew so bad that at last the lad declared that, if he stayed there, he should be either transported or hanged. Luckily he had a warm friend in young Sally Bristowe. They had grown up boy and girl together, and shared each other's confidences. Privately, Sally made a collection for Jack, and amassed the large sum of sixteen shillings, which she placed in his hands.

The 'prentice had now to look out for a favourable opportunity of escape, and this offered when Farmer Bristowe went to Bratton Fleming Fair, since by running away at this time the boy was assured of a day's start. On going to bed, Jack ostentatiously bolted the door, but unbolted it "with the same," so that the old woman might not hear when he made his exit. The plan worked perfectly, and Jack ultimately settled down at Bristol.

The master of the Devon and Somerset staghounds (Mr R. A. Sanders) resides at Exford, and here are the kennels of the pack. The latter are substantial stone buildings with gable ends, and stand on the slope of a hill, close beside the road to Simonsbath. One enters first the "cooking-house," the lobby of which is hung around with antlered heads, brow, bay, and tray. Some heads are preserved on account of their peculiarities or misshapen forms ; and to each head is attached a plate setting forth the date and place of the capture of the animal. Advancing, one is conscious of a pungent odour, which is found to proceed from a chamber where a huge furnace is burning fiercely, and a seething mass of horse flesh is being boiled off the bones for the dogs. Some of this boiled flesh is in a large wooden trough, and, mixed with oatmeal, flour, or biscuit, is undergoing a process of solidification. In the adjoining room are two larger troughs, in one of which biscuit is soaking, whilst the other contains a quantity of oatmeal paste.   Both sorts of food are intended for the younger dogs.

The kennels of these hounds, situated at a short distance, are provided with an extensive boarded-in grass plot, which forms their exercise-yard. When heavy rain does not permit of a parade, they will be found on the bench.   A magnificent lot of dogs, containing the blood of the most celebrated hounds in the best packs, they are not much disturbed by the entrance of strangers. Some of them half step down from the bench, when you pat and stroke them; they do not attempt to bite, and are, in fact, exceedingly quiet, unless you are foolish enough to strike them.   Then you will see.   Although the hounds are so much alike, the huntsman has the name of each dog on the tip of his tongue, and when, he calls, the animal is back in his place in an instant—so absolute is his command.

As regards the older hounds, they are kennelled in the same fashion, reclining on a bench with a thick layer of clean straw.   They have had a season or two's "blooding," and during that time some of them, by their doings in the pack, have made a name for themselves.   A few years ago two of them had the honour of appearing on several public platforms in attendance on the huntsman, the late Anthony Huxtable, a merry dog himself, who, as he could troll a rattling hunting-song, was in great request at local concerts, and on such occasions brought the hounds with him as a bit of realism.

Another kennel houses the oldest hounds— dogs which have hunted for seven seasons or more, and are still fit.

WINSFORD (page 141).

It is a curious fact that nothing upsets hounds so much as thunder. A flash of lightning followed by a loud crash of thunder makes every dog spring to his feet and relieve his feelings by low whines and growls.

A Faggus incident (see below, chapter xiv.) is duly credited to Exford by Blackmore, who entrusts the telling of it to John Fry (*Lorna Doone*, chapter xxxix.). He appears, however, to have robbed the parish of a still more thrilling episode (see chapters xiv. and xvi.).

CHAPTER IX

FROM Exford to Simonsbath the road presents few points of interest. At White Cross enters the highway that leads from Spire Cross to Comer's Gate, and thence between hedges to Chibbet (always so spelt and pronounced, but query Gibbet?) Post, a rendezvous of the staghounds and other packs; and perhaps the spot where Red Jem hung in chains, but it is more than two miles from Dunkery. After White Cross we arrive at Red Stone Gate, where we alight or not as we choose. Red Stone, having been mentioned in the perambulation records as a landmark of the old forest, has some claim to be considered historic. Then we pass what is commonly known as Gallon House, a white-washed building with a porch, standing back from the road and formerly a public-house. Its proper name was the Red Deer, and it is said to have been called Gallon House from the fact that "drink" — beer is always or often thus described hereabouts—was sold only by the gallon. That may or may not have been the case, but, as regards intoxicants, Exmoor is still under restrictions. To ensure the respectability of the neighbourhood, the "Exmoor Forest" Hotel (late the "William Rufus") is limited to the sale of wine, no beer or spirits being obtainable. This rule was imposed by Sir Frederick Knight, and is maintained in full force by his successor, Lord Ebrington.

The proper name of Gallon House was the "Red Deer," but Blackmore was evidently acquainted with the other description. John Fry is led by a shepherd to a "public-house near Exford," where "nothing less than a *gallon of ale* and half a gammon of bacon" brings him to his right mind again (*Lorna Doone*, chapter xxxi.).

The associations of Gallon House and its vicinage are tragic, since it was in a cottage situated in the rear that William Burgess, in the fifties of the last century, murdered his little daughter. He then conveyed her body across the road and down into the valley, where he buried it; but, fearing detection, he again removed the poor child's corpse and threw it down the shaft of the disused Wheal Eliza, a copper-mine. Here it remained undiscovered for months, but at last, through the untiring exertions of the Rev. W. H. Thornton, then curate of Exmoor, it was found, and the unnatural father expiated his crime on the gallows.

In his privately printed *Reminiscences*, Mr Thornton has given a detailed account of the whole episode.

The Wheal Eliza appears to have been the original of Uncle Ben's gold-mine, so far as situation is concerned.

The next stage is to Honeymead Two Gates,

with Honeymead Farm[1] lying away to the left. "Two Gates" is quite an Exmoor term. We meet with it again in Brendon Two Gates, and it stands for an arrangement whereby on both sides of the posts are suspended separate gates, so hung as to fall inwards. These effectually prevent stock from getting either in or out of the enclosures *proprio motu*, whilst the farmer, by crooking back the near gate with his whip, and pushing his horse against the other, can pass through without having to dismount. To judge from the maps, Simonsbath is the hub of the moor. In some senses this is true and soothfast, but as one travels along the excellent highway and looks across the country, there is little suggestion of either moor or forest. The land is evidently poor, but everywhere one's glance falls on enclosed fields, and Winsford Hill harmonises much better with one's preconceived ideas of Exmoor than this eminently civilised region. Doubtless the landscape presented a very different aspect before Mr Knight's advent in 1818, and one hardly knows whether to thank him for his pioneer improvements or not. At all events, one would have preferred the dry-wall system that obtains in the North Forest, to fences that seem stable and permanent, though shivering sheep may be of a different opinion.

Cloven Rocks, the next point, has no obvious right to the name. Its situation, however, may be indicated by stating that it lies at a bend of the road, and a tiny stream trickles down through the bare turf. It may be needless to remind the

---

[1] A Dulverton farmer once remarked to me on the great size of Exmoor farmhouses, saying that it would be possible to put into one of them two or three average homesteads.

reader that Cloven Rocks is twice mentioned in
Lorna Doone as adjacent to the Wizard's Slough,
a perilous morass that has since been drained.
Whether the story which appears in chapter lviii.
of the romance is based on a real tradition, or is
the offspring of Blackmore's fertile imagination,
I am unable to say. It has, at any rate, a
genuine ring, and all Exmoor once teemed with
strange legends, which the present "more en-
lightened" generation has chosen to forget.

Which reminds me. The little stream above
referred to is called White Water, and joins the
Barle at Cow Castle, an old British camp, which
is situated on one of three hills. Cow Castle is
the name of the principal eminence as given in
the maps, and Cae Castle it is sometimes called
by the learned. To the natives, however, it is
known as Ring Castle, and is so described in a
delightful article contributed by the Rev. George
Tugwell, M.A., author of an excellent *North
Devon Handbook*, to *Fraser's Magazine* in 1857.
His delineations of the scenery are worthy of a
Blackmore or a Black, and would that I had
room for some of them! As I have not, I must
confine the quotation to the dialogue between the
wanderer and a peasant, carried on by the blaze
of the latter's peat fire.

"'Half an hour before we met you and little
Nelly, we discovered an old British camp—a real
discovery, an indubitable camp, with its line of
earthworks as perfect, gateway and all, as when
it was first piled—and to be found in no book or
antiquarian memoir in all the three kingdoms.
There it stood, a circular crown on the brow of
a lonely conical hill, washed on three sides by the

wanderings of the Barle, out of bow-shot from all the neighbouring heights, with plenty of water, and provisions in abundance, for three valleys trended from it in a triple direction, commanding a wide and glorious view of peak and ravine, centrally placed in the very heart of "the forest." In truth, those old Britons knew something of the art of fastnesses, if they were not well skilled in the art of war.   Did you ever see the strong-hold of your ancestors, friend Jan?'

" 'I'm thinking we're somehow about Ring Castle!' quoth Jan, with sly good humour in his eye.   'Camp indeed!   I don't know much about camps [we omit the Doric]; but all I know is, that it was something far different which built Ring Castle.'

" Hereupon, dropping his voice, he hurled up the broad chimney a whole series of mystery-betokening smoke cloudlets.

" 'Did you ever hear tell on Pixies?' quoth Jan again, after a pause.   'And fairy rings?' he added, as Nelly emerged from a dark corner, and nestled close to her father's shoulder.   We suggested that we had heard of the Devonshire fairies, a race of spirits peculiar for their diminu-tive size and perfect beauty, and for their friendly dealing with mankind.

" 'Well,' said John, 'this here be all about it.'

(And he proceeded to tell us so pretty a legend that we cannot refrain from translating it for the benefit of the uninitiated in the Devonshire dialect.)

" 'Ever so long ago, the Pixies were at war with the mine spirits who live underground all

THE HEART OF THE MOOR 127

about the forest and the wild hill-country around.
Now, the Pixies being perfectly harmless, and
withal good-natured to excess, weren't at all a
match for the evil-nurtured earth-demons, who
were always forging all kinds of fearful weapons
in their underground armouries, and overcoming
their poor little foes by all manner of unfair and
unexpected stratagems.   But the Pixie Queen of
those days being like all women, fertile in
resources, bethought her of a means of escape
from the unbearable tyranny of the oppressors.
Ever since the days of Merlin, running water,
the numbers three and seven, and the mysteries
of the emblematic circle, have been sure protec-
tions against the machinations of the foul fiend
and his allies.   And the fairy queen, like a wise
woman, recollected this fact, and, like a wiser
woman, applied it ; for she assembled all her
subjects, and bade them build on the summit of
this central Exmoor Peak that strange circle
which you have seen to-day.   But it was no
common building this, for with every stone and
turf that the builders laid, they buried the
memory of some kindly deed which the good
Pixies had done to the race of men ; and so,
when the magic ring was completed, the baffled
demons raved and plotted in vain around its
sacred enclosure.   Nor was this all ; for when
the grey morning broke upon that first night of
victory and repose, as the driving mists rolled
upwards and swept along the hill-tops like the
advance-guard of a victorious army [we are not
sure that this was Jan's own similitude], from
the summit of the fairy fortification there rose
ring after ring of faintest amber-tinted vapour,

and floated away in the brightening sky, each on its own mission of safety and peace.

"'For these tiny wreathlets wandered hither and thither all over the broad expanse of the Exmoor country, and wherever the grass was greenest, and the neighbouring stream sang most merrily, and the sunlight was purest, and the moonbeams brightest, there these magic circles sank down softly on the level sward, and left no trace behind them of what they had been, or whence they had journeyed.

"'But from each soft resting-place there sprang a ring of greenest grass, which flourished and grew year by year; and within those safe enclosures the Pixies danced on moonlight nights in peace and security, unharmed by the demon rout, who were never seen aboveground after that memorable morning. So you see that kind hearts and actions do not go unrewarded, even in other spheres than our own.

"'And so,' concluded Jan, 'that's my story about the building of the Pixie's camp; and wise folk may talk for a year and a day without making me believe that there's any other reason for fairy rings, at all events, hereabouts in Exmoor Forest.'

"Of course it would have been absolute cruelty, after so fanciful a legend, to have instilled any botanical ideas into Jan's head, with regard to the law of the circular increase of fungi and the like; so we 'left him alone in his glory,' and felt duly thankful for the pleasure he had given us."

Lower down the river is Landacre Bridge, where Jeremy Stickles had so narrow an escape

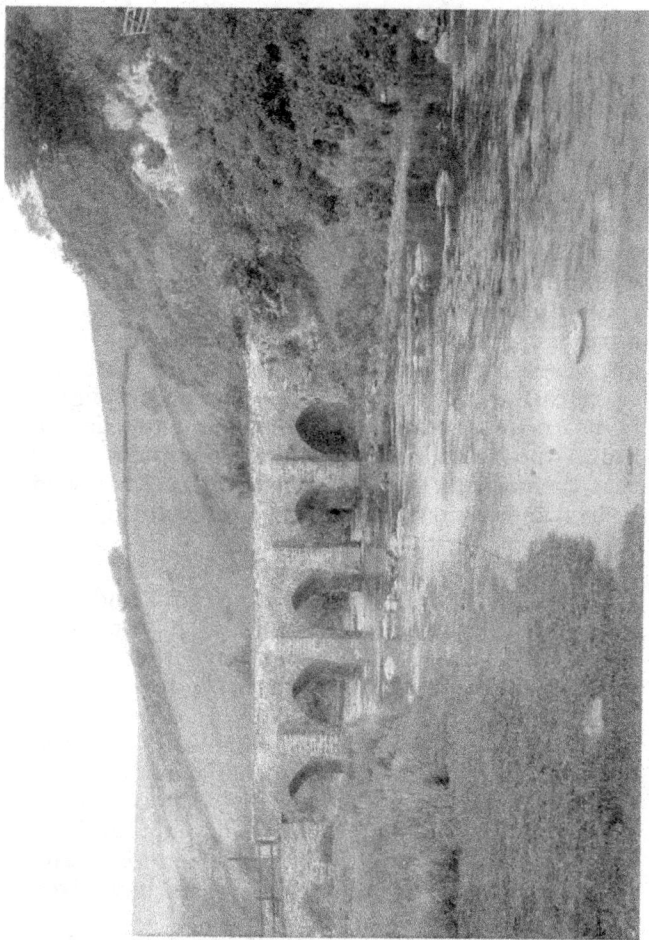

LANDACRE BRIDGE, EXMOOR.

from flood and foeman. (*Lorna Doone*, chapter xlvii.), and lower down still is the moorland village of Withypool. In summer, the water-meadows here, with background of brown moor, are lovely, but in rainy seasons Withypool is a wet place indeed, the little streams being even more to be dreaded that the raging of the Barle and Kennsford Water. In passing through the village a few years ago, I happened to hear that there are five wise men of Withypool, whose names were mentioned to me. One, I believe, was a follower of St Crispin, whom his neighbours, on account of his being at once "long-headed" and little of stature, called, Torney Mouse. Here also resides the renowned "Joe" Milton, a champion of the old wrestling days, in which he bore off many a trophy.

When the snow lies piled in impracticable drifts on the main Exford road, the Simonsbath people creep round to Dulverton and the world by way of Withypool. Let us proceed to the capital of Exmoor by this route. As we do so, it may be well to say something of the term "forest," as applied to Exmoor. To anyone who knows the country, such a description must inevitably suggest the famous etymology, *lucus a non lucendo;* except at Simonsbath, there is hardly a tree to be seen. But, according to legal usage the word does not of necessity connote timber; it indicates nothing more than an un-cultivated tract of country reserved for the chase. The term indeed is said to be identical with the Welsh *gores* or *gorest* (waste land), whence comes also the word "gorse," used alternately with "furze," as being a common growth on wastes.

R

From the earliest times, Exmoor was a royal hunting-ground, and so remained until that portion of it which still belonged to the Crown was sold, in 1818, to Mr John Knight, of Worcestershire. The Crown allotment comprised 10,000 acres; subsequently Mr Knight bought 6000 more, and so became owner of, at least, four-fifths of the forest.

Much has been written concerning those ancient denizens of the moor—the ponies. In my *Book of Exmoor*, I have dealt almost exhaustively with the subject as regards the pure breed; and every year experts in horsey matters favour the British public with accounts of those wary little animals in various periodicals. Sportsmen, however, have often put to me the question, "After all, what good are they?" That they are good for some purpose, is proved by the ready sales at Bampton Fair; but it is true, nevertheless, that the breed labours under a grave disadvantage in point of size, and those interested in the problem have often essayed to produce a serviceable cross.

Instead of treating once again those aspects of pony science which have been discussed *ad nauseam*, I propose to devote attention almost exclusively to Mr Knight's remarkable efforts in this direction, full particulars of which have never, so far I know, been embodied in any permanent work.

For some years previous to the sale of the forest, the price of the ponies ranged from four to six pounds, but the exportation of this class of live-stock, as well as sheep, did not always proceed on regular or legitimate lines. The Exmoor

shepherds, in defiance of the "anchor brand,"
took liberal tithe of them, and, at nightfall, passed
them over the hills to their crafty Wiltshire
customers.   On the completion of the sale the
original uncrossed herd was transferred to
Winsford Hill, where Sir Thomas had another
"allotment," only a dozen mare ponies being left
to continue the line.   At that time Soho Square
was as fashionable a quarter as Belgravia, and one
of its residents was the celebrated naturalist, Sir
Joseph Banks, who invited Mr Knight to a
dinner party.   Bruce's Abyssinian stories were
then all the rage, and the conversation chanced to
fall on the merits of the Dongola horse, described
by the "travelling giant" as an Arab of sixteen
hands, peculiar to the regions round about Nubia.
Sir Joseph consulted his guests as to the
desirability of procuring some of the breed, and
Lords Hadley, Morton, and Dundas, and Mr
Knight were so enamoured of the idea that they
handed him there and then a joint cheque for one
thousand pounds to cover the expense.

Over and above their height, the Dongola
animals had somewhat Roman noses, their skin
was of a very fine texture, they were well chiselled
under the jowl, and, like all their race, clear-
winded.   As regards their action, it was of the
"knee-in-the-curb-chain" sort, whilst their short
thick backs and great hindquarters made them
rare weight-carriers.   As against all this, the
"gaudy blacks" had flattish ribs, drooping
croups, rather long white legs, and blaze fore-
heads.   Perfect as *manège* horses, the dusky
Nubian who brought them over galloped them
straight at a wall in the riding-school, making

them stop dead when they reached it.   Altogether
ten or twelve horses and mares arrived, of which
the Marquis of Anglesey observed that they
would "improve any breed alive." Acting on
his advice, Mr Knight bought Lord Hadley's
share, and two sires and three mares were at
once sent to Simonsbath, where the new owner
had established a stud of seven or eight
thoroughbred mares, thirty half-breds of the
coaching Cleveland variety, and a dozen twelve-
hand pony mares.   The result of the first cross
between these last and one of the Dongolas was
that the produce came generally fourteen hands
two, and very seldom black.   The mealy nose, so
distinctive of the Exmoors, was completely
knocked ; but not so the buffy, which stood true
to its colour, so that the type was not wholly
destroyed.

The West Somerset pack often visited
Exmoor to draw for a fox, and on such
occasions the services of white-robed guides were
usually called into requisition ; but the half
Dongolas performed so admirably that this
practice gradually fell into disuse.   They
managed to get down the difficult hills so
cleverly, and in crossing the brooks were so close
up to the hounds, that nothing further was
necessary.[1]

The cross-out was intended for size only, not
for character.   No sire with the Dongola blood

---

[1] According to one writer, that mighty hunter,
Katerfelto, earned huge glory both for himself and for his
owner, a lusty farmer, by taking the bit between his teeth
on the Barkham Hills, and carrying him bodily over a
twenty-foot gap in an old Roman iron-mine.

was used, and such mares as did not retain a good proportion of the Exmoor type were immediately drafted. The first important successor of the Dongola was Pandarus, a white-coloured son of Whalebone, fifteen hands high, who confirmed the original bay, but reduced the standard to thirteen hands or thirteen and a half. Another sire was Canopus, a grandson of Velocipede, by whom the fine breeding as well as the Pandarus bay was perpetuated.

Meanwhile the colts were wintered on limed land, and thus enabled to bear up pretty well against the climate. Later, however, the farms were let by the late Sir Frederick (then Mr F. W.) Knight—a course which necessitated the withdrawal of the ponies to the naked moor, where, if the mares with the first cross could put up with the fare and the climate, they grew too thin to give any milk. On the other hand, those which were only half bred stood it well with their foals. About 1842 the whole pony stud was remodelled. The lighter mares were drafted, and from that time Mr Knight resolved to stick to his own ponies and the conventional sire. For many years this was strictly observed, and apart from the chestnut Hero, a horse of massive build sprung from a Pandarus sire, and the grey Lillias, of almost unalloyed Acland blood, no colour was used but the original buff.

An able judge who visited the moor in 1860, included in his report the following remarks, which are worth quoting :—

"The pony stock consists of a hundred brood mares of all ages, from one to thirteen. The mares are put to the horse at three, and up to

that age they share the eight hundred heather
acres of Badgery with the red deer and the
blackcock, protected on all sides by high stone
walls, which even Lillias, the gay Lothario
of the moor, cannot jump in his moonlight
rambles. . . .

"The bays and the buffy bays (a description
of yellow), both with mealy noses, are in a
majority of at least three to one. The ten sires
are all wintered together in an allotment until the
1st of May, apart from the mares; but Lillias,
who has more of the old pony blood than any of
them, twice scrambled over at least a score of six
feet walls, and away to his loved North Forest.
It is a beautiful sight to see them jealously
beating the bounds, when they are once more in
their own domains; and they would, if they wore
shoes, break every bone in a usurper's skin. The
challenge to a battle royal is given with a snort,
and then they commence by rearing up against
each other's necks, so as to get the first leverage
for a worry. When they weary of that they
turn tail to tail, and commence a series of heavy
exchanges, till the least exhausted of the two
watches his opportunity, and whisking round,
gives his antagonist a broadside in the ribs,
which fairly echoes down the glen. In the
closing scene they face each other once more, and
begin like bull-dogs to manœuvre for their
favourite bite on the arm. The first which is
caught off his guard goes down like a shot, and
then scurries off with the victor in hot pursuit,
savagely 'weaving,' while his head nearly touches
the ground, and his 'flag' waves triumphantly
in the air. With the exception of Lillias, the ten

are generally pretty content with their one
thousand acres of territory, and like Sayers and
Heenan, they are ultimately 'reconciled' in
November.

"The percentage of deaths is comparatively
small, and during last winter, when many of the
old ponies fairly gave in on the neighbouring
hills, Mr Knight's ponies fought through it, but
five or six of them died from exhaustion at
foaling, or slipped foals at ten months. Their
greatest peril is when they are tempted into
bogs about that period by the green bait of the
early aquatic grasses, and flounder about under
weakness and heavy pressure till they die. The
stud-book contains some very curious records.
'Died of old age in the snow,' forms quite a
pathetic St Bernard sort of entry. 'Found
dead in a bog' has less poetry about it. 'Iron
grey, found dead with a broken leg at the foot
of a hill,' is rather an odd mortality comment on
such a chamois-footed race; while 'grey mare
c.22 and grey yearling, missing; both found,
mare with a foal at her foot,' gives a rather
more cheery glimpse of forest history."

The "forest mark," with which the foals are
branded on the saddle-place, was changed by
Mr Knight from the Acland anchor to the spur,
which formed part of his crest, and is burnt in
with a hot iron, just enough to sear the roots of
the hair. No age eradicates it. Should a dispute arise concerning a wandering pony, the hair
is clipped off, and once it happened that after a
white sire had been lost for three seasons he
was discovered in this manner by the head
herdsman's brother. The spur has only one

heel, and the brand can be affixed with a rowel
pointing in four directions, on each side of the
pony, beginning towards the neck.   It thus
coincides with a cycle of eight years, and is
available as a guide if the footmarks are pre-
maturely worn out.

The hoof-marks are of two kinds—that of the
year of entry on the off hoof, and the register
figure of the dam on the near.   In the second
week of October the Dominical letters of their
year are placed on the yearlings, and the registered
hoof-marks renewed on the mares.   The foal, of
course, is not marked on the foot, but an exact
record is taken of his dam and all his points.

Until 1850 the ponies were sold by private
contract.   Sales were then established, and in
1853 an auditory of two hundred persons
assembled at Stony Plot, the knoll with its belt
of grey quartz boulders where now stands the
church.   The following autumn 'the venue was
altered to Bampton Fair.   There is a curious
story or legend—I hardly know what to make
of it—that after one of the Simonsbath sales a
Mr Lock, of Lynmouth, roasted an Exmoor pony
for his friends, who, if they ever partook of the
repast, must be credited with fine Tartar taste.

According to one version the original Exmoor
ponies, with their buffy bay colour and mealy
nose, were brought over by the Phœnicians
during their visits to the shores of Cornwall to
trade in tin and metals ; and ever since that time
the animals have preserved their characteristics.
We do not propose to go so far back into the
recesses of history, but will return for a moment
to the now rather distant date, 1790, before

BAGWORTHY VALLEY (page 141).

which hardly anything is known of Simonsbath.
At that period there are said to have been only
five men and a woman and a girl on Exmoor.
The girl drew beer at the Simonsbath public-
house, and the customers were a decidedly rough
lot. Doones indeed there were none—their day
was past—but the illicit love of mutton was
universal in the West country, as was also a
partiality for cheap cognac. Smugglers slung
their kegs across their "scrambling Jacks" at
night, and hid their treasure in the rocks, or left
it at a certain gate till the next mystic hand in
the living chain gave it a lift on the road to
Exeter. When they did not care to do this,
there were always friendly cellars under the old
house at Simonsbath. The ale was decent, the
landlady wisely deaf, and who can doubt that
the old ingle, where the date 1654 still lingers on
a beam shorn or built into half its length, heard
many an exciting tale of contraband prime
brandy and extra parochial liberties which would
have extorted blushes from an honest beadle and
groans from a conscientious exciseman?

Simonsbath having been formerly so insig-
nificant, it is not to be wondered at that Blackmore only refers to it as the abode of a "wise
woman," by which he means a witch (*Lorna
Doone*, chapter xviii.).

CHAPTER X

SIMONSBATH is the centre of several converging roads, all of them waiting to help the traveller out of Exmoor before he is well in it. A drive from Lynton or some other fairly populous or fashionable resort, followed by a lunch at the Simonsbath Hotel, is many people's conception of the proper method of "doing" Exmoor; but, while pleasant enough as an excursion, such a mode of exploration permits of only scanty guesses and imperfect glimpses of the inner fastnesses, which seem for the most part far away.

If the excitement of the chase be not too distracting, possibly the best way of acquainting oneself with the country is by following the staghounds; but should that be impracticable, the most useful advice the writer can offer is to follow the watercourses. Any one of these, if patiently traced, will usher the pilgrim into Nature's mysterious solitudes, which, if he be at all of a contemplative turn of mind, will awaken in him many a pleasant or pensive reverie. In any case, one must get away from the roads, the very

185

excellence of which is evil, as tempting to sloth.

I cannot, however, send forth an innocent person into the wilds without referring to the bogs. Personally, I have a considerable respect for Exmoor bogs, as I have for "they Hexëmoor vogs," which are equally treacherous, and make one wet through as sure and as fast as any rain ; nor is it so many years ago that Sheardon Hutch and similar names were sounds of terror in my ears. Familiarity breeds contempt, and therefore those at home in the district—some of them, at all events—are apt to disparage these man-traps, which are not by any means confined to the low lands, but are found on the summits of hills, especially the notorious Chains. In many places black decayed vegetable matter has been accumulating for ages to a depth of several feet, and as the rocks beneath are of the transition class, impervious to water, the rain is retained and saturates the bog-mould. After much wet weather, there are spots that will not bear the weight of a man, let alone a horse, and in riding over the moor, they constitute so real and serious a danger that great care should be exercised to avoid getting into them. Otherwise it may prove an impossible task to extricate the devoted "mount." There is one consolation—heather will not grow on those deep bogs, and wherever its purple bells show, the ground is safe.

The Exmoor hills are variously configured. Sometimes they take the form of a bold foreland sometimes of a continuous ridge, sometimes of an isolated cone or orb. A very intelligent moorman reminded me, somewhat superfluously, when I looked in upon him on a September evening, that all the hills have names, and queer names some of them are—*e.g.*, "Tom's Hill," "Swap Hill," "Scob Hill," etc., etc.   The meaning of not a few is anything but plain, but one "termination," if the phrase be permitted, speaks for itself.   I allude to the expression "ball," which is frequent on Exmoor, and much more likely to be derived from visual impression than any long-descended traditions of Baal, to which a late friend of mine, out of regard for the Phœnicians and their hill-altars, was anxious to assign it.   Thus we have Cloutsham Ball (famous as the scene of the opening-meet of the Devon and Somerset Stag-hounds), Ware Ball, Ricksy Ball, Ferny Ball, and, as a gloss, Round Hill.   The intersecting valleys have somewhat the character of huge corridors leading in and out of each other, and the smaller "combes," running up into the hills, may be likened to stairways of providential appointment, for the Exmoor "sides" are not quite perpendicular.   The hill-tops and slopes are dotted with sure-footed Exmoor horned sheep and Cheviots, beautiful long-tailed ponies, and a few red cattle. The grass is of two sorts—a short, close variety found in the drier parts, and tall sedge grass on wet ground, where it grows rankly.   Sheep are fond of the former when it comes up green and fresh after the annual "swalings," which take place in February or March.   Exmoor sheep have faces like those of the native deer, being free from wool, while the sharp-pointed nose resembles that of a fox.

Simonsbath village is in a sheltered position on the left bank of the Barle, and, thanks to the care of the late Sir Frederick Knight and his father, it is further protected against the keen winterly gales by ample plantations of fir and other trees. Hence we again mount the hills, this time in the direction of Brendon Two Gates, where the " forest " ends. After a time we gain a point from which a good view is obtained of the Prayway (or Prayaway) Meads. There are no hedges here, and, with the inconsistency of human nature, one misses them. It seems so odd to stand and gaze over a grassy expanse that has never been enclosed, and yet has much the look of ordinary meadow. Through the midst flows the Exe, here quite a baby-stream ; we are, indeed, not far from its source. To those who are familiar with its lower reaches, and call to mind the river as it appears (say) at Cowley Bridge, the sight is inexpressibly absurd. The absence of trees and shrubs makes Prayway seem bare and forsaken. The high sloping banks are like deserted ramparts or—but the name may have some influence—the nave of a vast natural cathedral haunted by the ghosts of dead Britons. Continuing our route, we arrive at a gate, inside which is a sort of quarry known as Black Pits. The gate opens into a common, at the other end of which is Brendon Two Gates. The origin of this term has been explained ; it may be well to add that at present it is a misnomer.

We now for the first time catch sight of Bagworthy, lying over on the right, and Bagworthy, as the reader may happen to remember, was, or has been imputed to be, the stronghold of the savage Doones. This is, in a sense, the parting of the ways. The traveller may either quit the beaten track for the carpet of sward in quest of a shepherd's cot, whence he may easily proceed to the traditional site of Doone Castle and down the Doone valley, along the Bagworthy Water, to Malmsmead, where the Bagworthy water unites with the East Lyn, and so by Cosgate or Brendon to Lynton ; or he may stick to the road, which will take him by a shorter cut to the same destination, by Farley and Cheriton and the aforesaid Scob Hill. It may be that, like the mythical churchmen of old, when asked to state which see he preferred—Bath or Wells— the latter-day pilgrim may elect for "both." I will assume, however, that his immediate objective is the famous valley, and that, once there, he will pursue without faltering the longest way round.

Technically we are no longer on Exmoor. Bagworthy, Badgworthy, or Badgery—all are permissible forms—is in the parish of Brendon and the county of Devon. In ancient times the wood is said to have covered a much greater area, and a century ago some of the older shepherds could point out its former limits. Within their recollection and since their time, its dimensions steadily contracted, until the disappointment with the valley, to which visitors so often and freely own, became explicable.

Now it must be admitted that in *Lorna Doone* there is a large spice of exaggeration, and this quality is naturally reflected in the illustrations with which the goodlier editions are adorned. Such deviations from the literal have brought it to pass that nowhere is Blackmore in so little esteem as among the hills he pictured so lovingly. Even the humble writer of the present volume probably enjoys on Exmoor a greater measure of esteem as a more trustworthy historian of the neighbourhood. But, sensible people will agree, the writer of a romance must be in a large measure a law unto himself, and he is under not the least obligation to consult the feelings of plain folk incapable of sharing his flights of imagination. It is a question of the light "borrowed from the youthful poet's dream," and I am inclined to apply the phrase in a somewhat distinct and definite sense. A romance—this romance in particular—may be regarded as a fairy-tale raised to a higher plane of evolution, and Blackmore seems to have possessed the godlike faculty of reflecting in his pages the shining images of his boyish fantasy, when, to copy Kingsley, every goose was a swan and every lass a queen. On this point I shall say no more, but return forthwith to the matter-of-fact. This includes the deep pool and the waterslide, but the reality of Doone Castle, or its remains, cannot for various reasons be taken for granted.

The first printed notice regarding these male-factors occurs in Mr Cooper's *Guide to Lynton*, published in 1851, and runs as follows :—

"The ruins of a village long forsaken and deserted stand in an adjacent valley, which, before the destruction of the timber, must have been a spot exactly suited to the wants of the wild inhabitants. Tradition relates that it consisted of eleven cottages, and that here the ' Doones ' took up their residence, being the terror of the country for many miles round. For a long time they were in the habit of escaping with their booty across the wild hills of Exmoor to Bagworthy, where few thought it safe or even practicable to follow them. They were not natives of this part of the country, but having been disturbed by the Revolution from their homes, suddenly entered Devonshire and erected the village alluded to. It was known from the first to the inhabitants of the neighbouring villages that this village was erected and inhabited by robbers, but the fear which their deeds inspired in the minds of the peasants prevented them from attacking and destroying it. The idea is prevalent that before their leaving home they had been men of distinction, and not common peasants. The site of a house may still be seen on a part of the forest called the Warren, which is said to have belonged to a person called 'the Squire,' who was robbed and murdered by the Doones.

"A farmhouse called Yenworthy, lying just above Glenthorne, on the left of the Lynton and Porlock road, was beset by them one night ; but a woman firing on them from one of the windows with a long duck-gun, they retreated, and blood was tracked the next morning for several miles in the direction of Bagworthy. The gun was found at Yenworthy, and was purchased by the Rev. W. S. Halliday. They entered and robbed a house at Exford in the evening before dark, and found there only a child, whom they murdered. A woman servant who was concealed in an oven, is said to have heard them say to the unfortunate infant the following barbarous couplet :

> ' If any one asks who killed thee,
> Tell 'm 'twas the Doones of Bagworthy.'

BRENDON, NEAR OARE (page 150).

"It was for this murder that the whole country rose in arms against them, and going to their abode in great haste and force, succeeded in taking into custody the whole gang, who soon after met with the punishment due to their crimes."

This excerpt represents the legend of the Doones which Blackmore inherited, and which it is absurd to designate as his invention. What he did was to add colour and definition to an already existing, though faded, tradition. How much of the substructure of *Lorna Doone* is due to his imaginative genius, is a fascinating problem, which, it is to be feared, it is beyond the wit of man to solve satisfactorily. In the above quotation, for instance, no mention occurs of the heroine, but it does not follow that she found no place in the local tales, and Blackmore, quite as good an authority as the writer of the guide, and on this particular subject even better, expressly affirms the contrary.

As to the time of the Doones, Mr Cooper, it will be noticed, says "after the Revolution." This is altogether opposed to Blackmore's account, which sets back their advent to a date long anterior to 1688. Mr Edwin J. Rawle, whose valuable *Annals of the Royal Forest of Exmoor* entitles him to a very respectful hearing, is absolute in rejecting any historical basis for the tradition, the mere existence of which he tardily acknowledges. Mr Rawle's theory is that "Doone" really stands for "Dane," the sea-wolves in the olden times having harried the neighbourhood pretty severely. I do not know what philologers may say of this suggestion, but

T

the vagaries of the local dialect suggest a far more plausible explanation.   In the romance John Fry speaks of his "goon," meaning his "gun."   Now "Dunn" is a fairly common patronymic in the West Country, and I am informed that the natives formerly pronounced the vowel in an indeterminate manner consistent with either spelling.

Blackmore, however, evidently regarded the name as identical with the Scottish "Doune," and his assertion of a high North British pedigree for the robbers has been wonderfully seconded of late by the publication of Miss Ida Browne's *Short History of the Original Doones*, which, if correct in every particular, proves amongst other things how extremely imperfect and untrustworthy are many of the records on which the scrupulous historian is wont to rely.   Mr Rawle will not have that it is correct, and her pleasant and plausible narrative is the object of a fierce onslaught in his brochure, *The Doones of Exmoor*. Personally, I have always favoured the notion that the rogues were a similar set to the Gubbinses and Cheritons, little communities of moorland savages, and that their rascalities, handed down from generation to generation, were magnified and distorted in every re-telling.   This solution has the advantage of being easily reconciled with Mr Rawle's demand for authentic evidence of their monstrous doings and Blackmore's and Miss Ida's Browne's insistence on their Scottish nationality.   To me, however, it seems like beating the air to attempt any final settlement of the question on our present information, and if I again refer to the lady's booklet—already I have

given the substance of it in my *Book of Exmoor*
—it is not so much from the belief that it casts
any certain light on the actuality of the Exmoor
marauders as on account of the possibility—which
she notes—that Blackmore by some means
obtained access to the evidence now in her
possession.

This consists of a manuscript entitled "The
Lineage and History of our Family, from 1561
to the Present Day," compiled by Charles Doone
of Braemar, 1804; the Journal of Rupert Doone,
1748; oral information, and certain family heir-
looms. Assuming these to be genuine, there is
obviously much likelihood, in view of the numerous
points in common, that Blackmore succeeded in
getting hold of the written testimony of the
later Doones; and, indeed, the circumstance may
have been the factor which led him to elaborate
the romance on a scale transcending that of his
other stories, since he must have realised that
here he had struck an entirely original vein of
historical fiction.

Before quitting this part of the subject, it is
desirable to present the views of the Rev. J. F.
Chanter, who has given much attention to the
problem, and whose long and intimate acquaintance with the district invests his opinions with
exceptional importance. In a letter received
from him, he remarks :—

"I may say that, as far as I am concerned,
I accept as genuine the main facts of Miss
Browne's story, but not its details, *i.e.*, the
relationship between Sir Ensor and Lord Moray,
or even Sir Ensor being a knight. The title
'Sir' was given at that date to many who were

neither knights nor baronets, *e.g.*, the clergy always; and as I find in rural districts, even to this day, a lady of the manor is spoken of, and written to, as Lady so-and-so. Mr Rawle's criticism is entirely negative; his position seems to be this:—Miss Browne's paper states that Sir Ensor was twin brother of Lord Moray. Now Lord Moray had no twin brother; therefore the whole claim falls to the ground."

To this I answer:

" 1. If the claim of Charles Doone of Braemar, as to the ancestry of his family, is wrong, it is absurd to say he had no ancestors. We are all apt to claim as ancestors people who were not really so, and many of the published pedigrees do this, claiming as ancestors some of the same name, though there is no evidence of the link.

" 2. The peerage is no evidence that Lord Moray had not other brothers, though not twins. There is, for instance, evidence that Lord Moray had a brother mentioned in no peerage I ever saw, one John Stuart who was executed for murder in 1609.

" 3. There may have been merely a tribal connection between the Doones of Bagworthy and the Stewarts of Doune, and a tribal feud caused them to fly to a remote spot; and they were recalled on a later Lord Moray wanting every help when he fell from Royal favour.

" Be this as it may, Miss Browne's story fits in so wonderfully with Blackmore's romance that I cannot conceive he had not heard of it. This I can vouch for—Miss Browne did not invent it.

" Now as to Miss Browne's documentary

evidence, I had the original of Charles Doone's family history, and it was undoubtedly a genuine document of the age it purported to be. I made a full copy of it. Of other documents I only saw copies. The originals she stated to be in the possession of a cousin in Scotland, and promised to get them for me as soon as she could. I have, however, not seen them as yet. The relics also seem to me genuine."

It must not be supposed that these were Blackmore's only sources of information—they deal in the main with merely one side of the story. Other material, both written and oral, was available on the spot. Mr Chanter observes on this point : "I myself can perfectly recall that, when I first went to a boarding-school in 1863, there was a boy there from the Exmoor neighbourhood who used to relate at night in the dormitories blood-curdling stories of the Doones." That boy, it is interesting to know, is still alive. At any rate, he was alive in July 1903, when he addressed to the *Daily Chronicle* the following letter in answer to a sceptical effusion from a correspondent signing himself "West Somerset." "'West Somerset' could never have known Exmoor half so intimately as was the case with myself during my boyhood, youth, and early manhood, or he must have heard of the Doones. During the 'fifties' and 'sixties' of last century I lived on Exmoor, knew it thoroughly, and rarely missed a meet of the staghounds. The stories or legends of the Doones were perfectly familiar to me. They varied much, but the germs of the great romance were so well known and remembered by me that when it was issued, one of its many charms was the tracing of the writer's embroidery of the current tales. I have hardly been in the district since 1868, but my memory is sufficiently good to remember the names of several from whom I heard the traditional annals. Among them were John Perry, the old 'wanter' or mole-catcher of Luccombe; Larkham, the one-armed gamekeeper of Sir Thomas Acland, and above all, Blackmore, the harbourer of the deer.[1] The name of another old man, who allowed me on two occasions to take down Doone stories at the inn at Brendon, has escaped me. So familiar were these stories to me when I was a boy that I used to retail them with curdling embellishments of my own in the dormitory of a West-country boarding-school. The result of this was that a room-mate of mine, either just before or just after he went to Oxford, wove my yarns (he had not himself then ever visited Exmoor) into a story, which he called 'The Doones of Exmoor.' This tale was eventually published in some half-dozen consecutive numbers of the *Leisure Hour*. My copy of it has long been lost, but I remember that, though it was delayed some time by the editor, it appeared three or four years before *Lorna Doone*. Moreover, I had a letter from Mr R. D. Blackmore, soon after his immortal work was issued, wherein he acknowledged that it was the accidental glancing at the poor stuff in the *Leisure Hour* that gave him the clue for the weaving of the romance, and caused him to study the details on the spot. I have never been across Exmoor

[1] The original of "Red Rube" in Melville's *Katerfelto*.

since *Lorna Doone* was published, but I am sure that I could at once find my way either on foot or horseback to the very place that I knew so well as the stronghold of the Doones, either from the Porlock or the Lynton side."

I am permitted to quote also a passage from a private letter of Miss Gratiana Chanter (now Mrs Longworth Knocker), author of *Wanderings in North Devon*, who is a firm believer in the Doones.

"I wish you could have a talk with old John Bate of Tippacott [he is dead]; he gave me a most exciting description one day of how the Doones first 'coomed in over.' No dates, of course; you never get them. He said there was a farmhouse in the Doone Valley where an old farmer lived with his maidservant. 'Twas one terrible snowy night when the Doones first 'coomed.' They came to the house and turned the farmer and his maid out into the black night. Both were found dead—one at the withy bank and the other somewhere else. He said, 'They say, Miss, they was honest folk in the North, but they took to thieving wonderful quick.'

"Bate, and one John Lethaby, a mason, were both at work at the building of the shepherd's cot in the Doone Valley, and had tales of an underground passage they found that fell in, and that they took a lot of stones from the huts for the shepherd's cot."

To return to Mr Chanter, we learn that, even before those nightly entertainments in the dormitory, he had read about the Doones in an old manuscript belonging to his father, and he adds

that there were to be found at that period in
North Devon several such manuscripts, which,
he thinks, had a common origin, and might be
traced to the tales of old people living in and
around Lynton seventy or eighty years ago.
In range of information and power of memory
none might compare with a reputed witch, one
Ursula Johnson, who, though now practically
forgotten, can be proved from the parish register
to have been born a Babb in 1738—not forty
years after the exeunt of the Doones.   The
family of Babb were servants to Wichehalses,
and one may recall the circumstance that in
chapter lxx. of *Lorna Doone* John Babb is
represented as shooting and capturing Major
Wade.   Ursula was not so ignorant as many
of her gossips, and upon her marriage to
Richard Johnson, a "sojourner," could sign her
name—a feat of which the bridegroom was
incapable.   Her long life reached its termination
in 1826, when she was, so to speak, within sight
of ninety.

Seven years later a locally well-remembered
vicar, the Rev. Matthew Murdy, came to Lynton,
and being keenly interested in the old lady's
stories, began a collection of them.   Subsequently two friends of his, Dr and Miss Cowell,
entered into his labours by "pumping" Ursula
Fry, a native of Pinkworthy on Exmoor, and
Aggie Norman.   Both were tough old creatures,
the former dying in 1856, at the age of ninety,
and the latter in 1860, when she was eighty-
three.   In Mrs Norman, who passed a good
deal of her time in a hut built by her husband
on the top of the Castle Rock, in the Valley of

NICHOLAS SNOW'S FARMYARD GATE (page 159).

Rocks, Lynton, Mr Chanter identifies the
original Mother Meldrum.

Mr Mundy reduced the tales to something
like literary shape, and they were then transcribed
by the older girls in the National School, whose
mistress, Miss Spurrier, saw that the copies were
properly executed. An old lady residing at
Lynton possesses one of the documents, dated
1848, of which the contents include a description
of the neighbourhood, reference to Ursula Johnson,
and three "legends": those of De Wichehalse,
the Doones of Bagworthy, and Faggus and his
Strawberry Horse. In the *Western Antiquary*
of 1884, part xi., may be found an excellent
account of the manuscript by the late Mr J. R.
Chanter, who quotes the following observations
by the editor :—

"The recent introduction of candles into the
cottages of the neighbouring poor has tended
greatly to produce the most lamentable decay of
legendary lore : the old housewife, crouching over
the smouldering turf, no longer enlivens the
tedious winter evening with well-remembered
tales of the desperate deeds of the outlaws or the
wonders wrought by the witches or wisemen, and
many of the curious legends are in danger of
being consigned to utter oblivion, unless immediately collected from the old peasants, who are
falling fast : their children being by far too much
engrossed by the Jacobin publications of the day,
to pay any attention to these memorials of the
days of yore. From these causes much has
already been lost."

That R. D. Blackmore obtained a sight of
one of these MSS. is, on the face of it, extremely

probable, but for certain elements of the story he might well have been indebted to his grandfather, the Rector of Oare. Such are the account of the great frost, the mining and wrestling incidents, and the tales of the Doones, in chapters v. and lxix., which the notes pronounce to be authentic, and which differ from other versions.

I come now to the facts of the Wade episode mentioned in chapter lxx. of *Lorna Doone*. In this same parish of Brendon is a hamlet called Bridgeball, and on a hill just above the hamlet is Farley farm, where a comparatively new house occupies the site of an older structure pulled down in 1853. It was on this farm that Major Wade, one of the leaders in the Monmouth Rebellion, was captured after the battle of Sedgemoor. Driven ashore in an attempt to escape down the Channel, he succeeded in concealing himself for several days among the rocks at Illford Bridges, and made a confidante of the wife of a little farmer named How, who lived at Bridgeball in a house of which he was the owner, while the field behind it and a portion of land near the present parsonage were also his property. The good woman provided him with food so long as he continued in his rocky hiding-place, and interceded for him with a farmer at Farley named Birch, who consented to harbour him for a time. Situated on the verge of Exmoor, no refuge could have appeared more secure than this isolated spot, but the event proved that Wade might have been as safe, or safer, in a great and populous centre. To his credit it must be recorded that, after obtaining his pardon, the gallant gentleman did not forget his benefactress,

on whom he settled an annuity. The particulars
of his capture have been preserved in the
Lansdowne MS., No. 1152, which contains the
following rather dramatic reports :—

"*To the Right Hon. the Earl of Sunderland,
Principal Secretary of State.*

"Barnstaple, *y*ₑ 31*st July* 1685.

"My Lord,—I here enclosed send your Lop.
an account of yᵉ apprehending of Nathaniel Wade,
one of ye late rebells. I came to this towne
to-day, and can, therefore, only give yʳ Lop. wᵗ
relation I have from yᵉ apothecary and chirurgeon
wᶜʰ they had drawn up in a letter designed for
Sir Bourchier Wrey ; their examination of him is
enclosed in yᵉ letter, to wᶜʰ I refer your Lop.
He continues very ill of a wound given him at
his apprehending sixteen miles hence, at Braundon
parish in Devon. I designe to examine him as
soon as his condition will permitt, he promising
to make large and considerable confessions ; and
herein, or if he dye, I humbly desire your Lop.'ˢ
directions to me at Barnstaple, and shall herein
proceed as becomes my duty to his Majesty and
your Lop.—My Lord, yʳ Lop.'ˢ most humble
Servant,   Richard Armesley."

"*To the Honourable Sir Bourchier Wrey, Kᵗ.
and Bart., in London.*

"Brendon, 30*th July* '85.

"Honʳᵈ Sir,—This comes to give you an
account of one, not yᵉ least of yᵉ rebells, who

was taken up last Monday night at a place
called Fairleigh in y⁰ p'ish of Brundun, by
Jno. Witchalse, Esq., Ricᵈ Powell, Recᵗ of y⁰
same, Jno. Babb, servᵗ to Jno. Witchalse and
Rob. Parris.   They haveing some small notice of a
stranger to have bin a little before about yᵗ village,
came about nine of y⁰ clock at night to one Jno.
Burtchis house.   As soon as they had guarded
y⁰ house round, they heard a noise.   Watching
closely and being well armed, out of a little back
door slipt out this person within named, and two
more as they say, and run all as hard as they
cold.   Babb and Parris espieing them, bid them
stand againe and againe.   They still kept running,
and they cockt their pistols at them.   Parris his
mist fire, but Babb's went off, being chargᵈ wᵗʰ
a single bullett, wᶜʰ stuck very close in y⁰ rebells
right side ; ye entrance was about two inches
from y⁰ spina doris.   Y⁰ bullett lodged in y⁰
under part of y⁰ right hypogastrind, wᶜʰ we cut
out.   Y⁰ bullett past right under y⁰ pleura ; from
the orifice it entered to y⁰ other, wᶜʰ we were
forced to make to extract y⁰ bullett (having strong
convulsions on him) : it was in distance between
six and seven inches.   He was very faint, having
lost a great quantity of blood.   Y⁰ orifice we
made (y⁰ bullett lying neere y⁰ cutis) was halfe
an inch higher yⁿ y⁰ other.   It begins to digest,
and his spirits are much revived, only this day
about 10 of y⁰ clock he was taken with an aguish
fitt, wᶜʰ I suppose was caused by his hard diet
and cold lodging ever since y⁰ rout, he leaving
his horse at Illfordcomb. _ Ever since Tuesday
last in the afternoon, Mr Ravening and myself
have bin wᵗʰ him, and cannot wᵗʰ safety move

from him. We desire to know his Maties pleasure w^t we shall due wth his corps, if he dyes, wch if he does before ye answer, we think to embowell him. We will due w^t possible we can, for he hath assur^d us, y^t as soon as he is a little better, he will make a full discovery of all he knows, of wch this inclosed is part, by wch he hopes to have, but not by merrits, his pardon. Here is noe one y^t comes to him y^t he will talk soe freely wth as wth us; if you will have any materiall questions of business or p'sons to be askt of him, pray give it in y^{rs} to us. We will be privat, faithfull, to o^r King, whome God long preserve. W^{ch} is all at present from them who will ever make it their business to be.—S^r y^r most humble Serv^{ts},

"NIC^s COOKE and HENRY RAVENING."

The addressee was Sir Bourchier Wrey, of Tawstock, Bart., son of another Sir Bourchier, and grandson of Sir Chichester Wrey, who married Ann, youngest daughter of Edward Bourchier, Earl of Bath.

Bagworthy and Farley are both in the parish of Brendon, but we must not forget that, as regards bodily presence, we are still in the Doone valley, and not far from Oare, where, according to Rupert Doone's Diary, his ancestors, on quitting Scotland in 1627, first fixed their residence. They then removed to the upper part of the Lyn valley, on an estate bounded on one side by Oare and on the other by Bagworthy. The Doone valley, which used to be called Hoccombe, is a glen lying between Bagworthy

Lees and Bagworthy, and Mr Chanter expresses the belief that this name and that of "Lorna's Bower" were first applied to the small side-combes by his cousins, the Misses Chanter, soon after the publication of *Lorna Doone*. Ruins of the traditional "Castle," rectangular in form, are still to be traced, and consist of two groups. Unfortunately, stones were taken from them to build an adjoining wall, and now it is impossible to state the character of the buildings, some of which were probably houses, and others cattle-sheds. Miss Browne, indeed, is of opinion that they were all of the latter description, and that the real home of the Doones was in the Weir Water valley, between Oareford and the rise of the East Lyn. So far as Hoccombe is con-cerned, Blackmore has idealised it with a vengeance. The "sheer cliffs standing around," the "steep and gliddening stairway," the rocky cleft or "Doone-gate," the "gnarled roots," are all purely imaginary. As regards "Doone track" or "Doones' path," it directly faces the valley, and after crossing the Bagworthy Water, ascends the Deer Park and Oare Common, and so to Oare. Being covered with grass or hidden by heather and scrub, it is not easy to follow, but viewed at a little distance it presents the appearance of a broad terraced roadway, not improbably Roman, and connecting Showls-borough Castle, near Challacombe, with the coast. The site of the house where the "Squire" was robbed and murdered by the Doones is still visible in the part of the forest known as the Warren (*Lorna Doone*, chapter lxxii.).

Exmoor was once a paradise of yeomen,
thrifty sons of the soil, who owned their own
farms. They consisted of two classes: those
who did the work themselves, with the assistance of their family and jobbing workmen,
to whom they paid good wages; and the
owners of large farms, where labourers were
constantly employed at a shilling a day.
The former sort is entirely extinct. Many of
their descendants have been merged in the
mass of common labourers; a few have risen
to the rank of large farmers; others have
emigrated.

The more substantial class of yeomen is still
represented in the district. The late Mr W. L.
Chorley, Master of the Quarme Harriers, was
an excellent specimen of the order, but the
most relevant example is that of the Snows,
whom Blackmore treats somewhat unfairly.
The family may not have been rich in what
Counsellor Doone described as the "great
element of blood," but a genuine yeoman of the
type in question would hardly have been dubbed
"Farmer Snowe," and he certainly would not
have perpetrated such an awful lapse as
"pralimbinaries." I have been informed by a
correspondent that Blackmore apologised to the
family for his painful caricature, which was only
just, in view of their actual status and the esteem
in which they are held by their neighbours.
About the year 1678, two-fifths of the manor of
Oare belonged to the family of Spurrier, and
passed by marriage at the beginning of the
eighteenth century into the possession of Mr
Nicholas Snow, who left it to a son of his own

name.   The latter, in 1788, purchased the other
three-fifths, and, at his death in 1791, bequeathed
the manor to his youngest son, John Snow, who
died without issue, leaving the property to his
nephew, Nicholas Snow—the "Farmer Snowe"
of *Lorna Doone.*

It will be noticed that the Snows did not
become landowners at Oare until long after the
period of the story.   As for the Ridds, or Reds,
the only mention of the name in the parish
register occurs in the year 1768, when John Red
was married to Mary Ley.   The real Plover's
Barrows was Broomstreet Farm, in the
neighbouring parish of Culbone ; at any rate, a
John Ridd was resident there.   A John Fry,
no mere farm-servant, was churchwarden of
Countisbury, of which Jasper Kebby was like-
wise a parishioner.   Plover's Barrows has been
identified by Mr Page with Mr Snow's residence
—"according to Blackmore, anciently the farm
of the Ridds."   But in *Lorna Doone* (chapter
vii.) the two farms are represented as adjoining, and Plover's Barrows is evidently further
upstream (see *Lorna Doone,* chapter xiv. : "In
the evening Farmer Snowe *came up.*")   The
same writer speaks of the Snows as having
been seated at Oare since the time of Alfred.
Can Mr Page be thinking of John Ridd's
boast to King Charles (*Lorna Doone,* chapter
lxviii.) ?

Oare Church, where the elder Ridd lay buried,
where his son stole the lead from the porch to
his subsequent shame, and where the brute
Carver shot Lorna on her bridal morn, has
received an addition in the shape of the chancel

OARE CHURCH.

since the last disastrous event—which, as things
are, rather falsifies the narrative. Graced with
ash and sycamore, the little cemetery is as
Blackmore describes it, "as meek a place as
need be."

CHAPTER XI

THE MOUTH OF THE LYN

THE scenery of the district described in many excellent guide-books may not tally in every particular with the superb word-portraiture of *Lorna Doone*, but that it possesses charms of supreme merit will be admitted by all who know the country, whether as residents or visitors. Almost before R. D. Blackmore was breeched, the poet Coleridge testified : "the land imagery of the north of Devon is most delightful"; and his brother-in-law, Robert Southey, is equally emphatic.

"My walk to Ilfracombe," he says, "led me through Lynmouth, the finest spot, except Cintra and Arrabida, that I ever saw. Two rivers [*i.e.*, the East and West Lyn] join at Lynmouth. You probably know the hill streams of Devonshire. Each of these flows through a combe, rolling over huge stones like a long waterfall; immediately at their juncture they enter the sea, and the rivers and sea make but one noise of uproar. Of these combes, the one is richly wooded, the other runs between two high, bare, stony hills. From the hill between the two is a prospect most magnificent, on either hand combes,

and the river before the little village—the beautiful little village—which, I am assured, by one
who is familiar with Switzerland, resembles a
Swiss. This alone would constitute a view
beautiful enough to repay the weariness of a
journey; but, to complete it, there is the blue
and boundless sea, for the faint and feeble outline
of the Welsh coast is only to be seen, if the day
be perfectly clear."

Inland, it is certain, the moorland streams—
Lancombe, Bagworthy Water, the East and
West Lyn, etc.—and all that they imply, are
paramount attractions; and Miss Gratiana
Chanter both truly and happily observes that,
"to follow one of these tiny streams from its birth
to its end, is a dream of delight to those who
love to be alone with nature and her many
marvels." Another reason why we should seek
the "founts of Lyn" is, that there Jeremy
Stickles gave his pursuers "a loud halloo" on
feeling himself secure (see *Lorna Doone*, chapter
xlvii.).

The name "Lyn" is said to be derived from
the Saxon word *hlynna*, signifying a torrent.
The East Lyn, rising above Oare, John Ridd's
birthplace, flows in a north-westerly direction to
Malmsmead, where it unites with the Bagworthy
Water, which at this point is the richer for two
or three tributaries, including Lancombe (or
Longcombe) stream and its waterslide. From
the bridge and the thatched cottages that define
this spot, the river pursues its course past
Lyford Green and Lock's Mill, where it encounters a weir, to Millslade and its meadows,
and the blacksmith's forge, "where the Lyn

stream runs so close that he dips his horse-shoes in it," *Lorna Doone*, chapter lxii.), and thence through woodlands to pretty Brendon. Here the Farley Water, arriving from Hoar Oak by way of Bridgeball and Illford Bridges, joins the East Lyn, and their confluence is known as Watersmeet, a poetical description not belied by the rare beauty of the scene.

Meanwhile, from the hills around Woolhanger the water gathers into two streams, which are trysted at a place called Barham, whilst at Cheribridge another brook, hailing from Furze-hill, helps to swell the current. Passing Barbrook Mill and Lynbridge, the West Lyn weds the East Lyn in private grounds at Lynmouth, and then the combined torrent eddies tumultuously into the sea. Nothing can excel the cataracts of the West Lyn, dashing athwart huge boulders and down a chasm of grey rock, in an incline stated to be "one in five." Clothing the sides of the ravine are oaks and beeches and thickets of underwood, while ferns of the most exquisite sorts fringe the banks.

> " Here are mosses deep,
> And thro' the moss the ivies creep,
> And in the stream the long-leaved flowers weep,
> And from the craggy ledges the poppy hangs in sleep."

It must not be forgotten, however, that the road *via* Brendon, Illford Bridges, and Barbrook was that taken by John Ridd and Uncle Reuben on their visit to Ley Manor (*Lorna Doone*, chapter xv.).

All who are fond of quaint authors will find a congenial companion in old Thomas Westcote,

whose *Survey of Devon*, written in the reign
of James I., or during the early years of
his successor, is stored with all manner of
gossip, set forth with many a stroke of arch or
naïve humour. In his book, at all events, he
approaches Lynton by much the same route
as we have followed, and then spins us an
amusing yarn about the finny visitors and a
certain parson.

" For our easier and better proceeding, let us
once again return to Exmoor. We will, with an
easy pace, ascend the mount of Hore Oak Ridge ;
not far from whence we shall find the spring of
the rivulet Lynne, which, in his course, will soon
lead us into the North Division, for I desire you
should always swim with the stream, and neither
stem wind nor tide. This passeth by Cunsbear,
alias Countisbury, and naming Lynton, where
Galfridus Lovet and Cecilia de Lynne held
sometime land, and, speeding, falls headlong with
a great downfall into the Severn at Lynmouth ;
a place unworthy the name of a haven, only a
little inlet, which, in these last times, God hath
plentifully stored with herrings (the king of
fishes), which, shunning their ancient places of
repair in Ireland, come hither abundantly in
shoals, offering themselves (as I may say) to the
fishers' nets, who soon resorted hither with divers
merchants, and so, for five or six years, continued
to the great benefit and good of the country,
until the parson taxed the poor fishermen for
extraordinary unusual tithes, and then (as the
inhabitants report) the fish suddenly clean left
the coast, unwilling, as may be supposed, by
losing their lives to cause contention. God be

thanked, they begin to resort hither again, though not as yet in such multitudes as heretofore. Henry de Lynmouth, after him Isabella de Albino, and now Wichals, possesseth it. A generous family : he married Pomerois ; his father, Achelond, his grandfather, Munck."

Concerning the " generous family " more anon ; we have not quite done with the sign of Pisces. Originally Lynmouth was a little village—Blackmore speaks of it as " the little haven of Lynmouth " (*Lorna Doone*, chapter xxxix.)—whose inhabitants dwelt in huts and depended for a livelihood on the curing of herrings, which was carried on in drying-houses. From the beginning of September to the end of October shoals of these fish frequented the shore, and sometimes their number was so great that tons of them were thrown away or used as manure. In 1797 the herrings deserted the coast, and the peasantry attributed their conduct to the insult just referred to. The common duration of truancy was computed at forty years—a calculation which seems to hold true of the period between 1747 and 1787. The following decade consisted of fat years, when the sea at Lynmouth yielded rich autumnal harvests, and masses of herrings were sent to Bristol, whence they were shipped to the West Indies. From 1797 to 1837, and indeed longer, the fish fought shy of the place, but not entirely. On Christmas Day, 1811, there was an exceptional and very abundant shoal of herrings, and the inhabitants were called out of church in order to take them out of the weirs. A similar gift of fortune marked the year 1823. Practically, however, the fishermen's avocation was gone, and they had to look elsewhere for a livelihood. Happily, they did not look in vain. Pastured on the surrounding hills were large flocks of sheep, and in the neighbouring towns there was a constant demand for yarn. This was of two kinds—one for the woof, consisting of worsted, which was supplied by the Yorkshire mills; the other for the warp, which was of softer texture, and then made by hand. The latter industry became the chief—almost the sole—prop of Lynton and Lynmouth, where the good people diligently applied themselves to spinning, and by this means kept the wolf from the door.

The sea-fishing is not altogether unconnected with the history of the De Wichehalses, since the original fishermen are stated to have been Dutch Protestants forced by religious (or irreligious?) persecution to emigrate from their homes by the Zuyder Zee. The names Litson, Vellacot, etc., still borne by local families, are quoted as evidence of Dutch extraction. A trade in cured herrings sprang up with Scotland, and the Dutchmen not only had commercial transactions with Scotch sailors and traders, but married, many of them, braw Scotch lassies who came to buy their herrings. The possible bearing of this intercourse on the problem of *Lorna Doone* will not escape attention. It was at Lynmouth that old Will Watcombe, the great authority on the "Gulf Stream," lived and sought to be buried (*Lorna Doone*, chapter xii.).

Now as to the Wichehalses, whose name Blackmore spells with a supererogatory "h"— Whichehalse. The Protestants of the Low

Countries had often attempted, by petition and remonstrance, to bend the stubborn will of their master, Philip II., and not a few of the Gueux or Beggars—a sobriquet bestowed on the Huguenot conspirators who met at Breda—left the country in despair. In 1567 the Spanish despot dispatched to the ill-fated land the Duke of Alva with an army of 20,000 men, and the latter signalised his arrival by instituting a " Council of Blood," which resulted in the execution of 18co patriots, while 30,000 more were reduced to abject straits by the confiscation of their property. Hordes of terrified Dutch folk fled to England, in the wake of the nobles, and a certain number of them settled, as we have seen, on the north coast of Devon.

Hugh de Wichehalse belonged, strictly speaking, to neither class of fugitives. The head of a noble and wealthy family, which had early become converts to the principles of the Reformation, he continued to struggle for his beliefs until the fatal day of Gemmingen, when, escaping the clutches of the vindictive Spaniards, he crossed the channel with his wife and children. The bulk of his property had already, by a timely precaution, been removed hither.

Such is the tradition which has to be reconciled with the pedigree of the family in the visitation of 1620. This shows three generations, and, to say the least, would be consistent with a much longer settlement in the county. The following is a copy :—

JUNCTION OF LYN AND BAGWORTHY WATER (page 163).

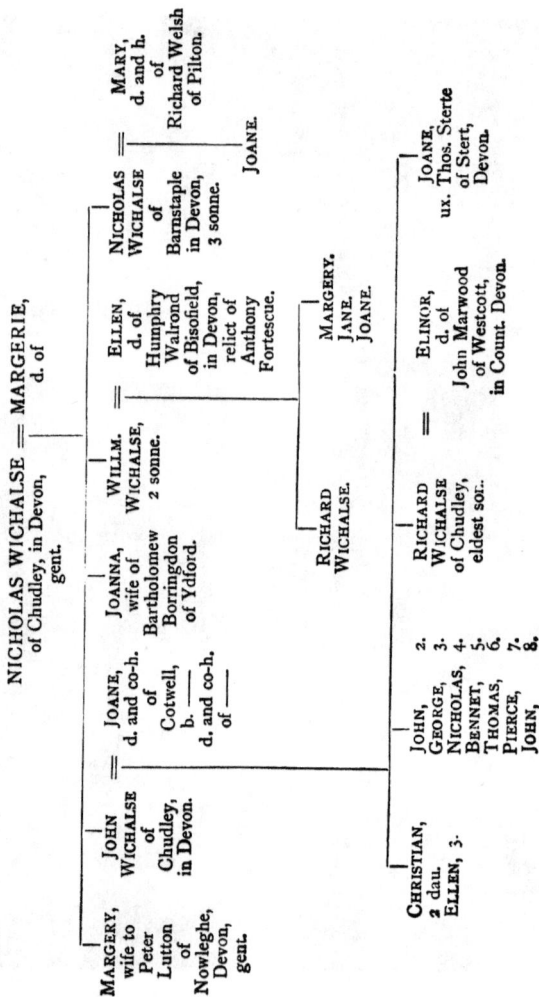

NICHOLAS WICHALSE = MARGERIE,
of Chudley, in Devon,   d. of
gent.

MARGERY,
wife to
Peter
Lutton
of
Nowleghe,
Devon,
gent.

JOHN
WICHALSE
of
Chudley,
in Devon.
=
JOANE,
d. and co-h.
of
Cotwell,
b. ——
d. and co-h.
of ——

JOANNA,
wife of
Bartholomew
Borringdon
of Ydford.

WILLM.
WICHALSE,
2 sonne.

ELLEN,
d. of
Humphry
Walrond
of Bisofield,
in Devon,
relict of
Anthony
Fortescue.
=

NICHOLAS
WICHALSE
of
Barnstaple
in Devon,
3 sonne.
=
MARY,
d. and h.
of
Richard Welsh
of Pilton.

JOANE.

RICHARD
WICHALSE.

MARGERY.
JANE.
JOANE.

CHRISTIAN,
2 dau.
ELLEN, 3.

RICHARD
WICHALSE
of Chudley,
eldest son.
=
ELINOR,
d. of
John Marwood
of Westcott,
in Count Devon.

JOANE,
ux. Thos. Sterte
of Stert,
Devon.

JOHN,
GEORGE,
NICHOLAS,
BENNET,
THOMAS,
PIERCE,
JOHN,
2.
3.
4.
5.
6.
7.
8.

Y

On one point there is no possible doubt—
namely, that the Wichehalses were once owners
of a manor-house at Lynton, standing on the site
of the handsome residence known as Lee Abbey.
Traces of the old structure were to be seen in
an intermediate building, and gave indications of
much splendour, while, as could be easily
recognised, the adjacent fields and orchards
formed part of the erstwhile pleasure-grounds.
Just above Lee Abbey is Duty Point, famous for
its beautiful views—northwards, the belt of silver
sea, southwards the heathery hills, eastwards the
Valley of Rocks, and westwards the grey oaks of
Woody Bay ; famous, too, as the scene of
romantic tragedy. The principal personages of
the story were old Wichehalse, his daughter
Jennifried, and cruel Lord Auberley. One
evening the lovelorn maiden fell or threw herself
over the terrific precipice ; and, hungry for
revenge, her father met and slew the false suitor
at the battle of Lansdown, near Bath—one of the
memorable encounters of the Great Civil War.
It is needless to recapitulate the details of the
narrative. The story has been told by Blackmore
in his *Tales from the Telling House ;* and before
that, it was told very pathetically by Mr Cooper
in his *Guide to Lynton.*

On the south wall of Lynton Church, close to
the west window, is the following inscription on
the monument of Hugh Wichehalse of Ley, who
departed this life, Christide Eve, 1653, æt. 66.

" No, not in silence, least those stones below
That hide such worth, should in spight vocal grow.
Wee'l rather sob it out, our grateful teares
Congeal'd to Marble shall vy threnes with theirs.

This weeping Marble then Drops this releife
To draw fresh lines to fame, and Fame to greife :
To greife which groanes sad loss in him t' us all,
Whose name was Wichehalse—'twas a Cedar's fall.
For search this Urn of Learned dust, you'le find
Treasures of Virtue and Piety enshrin'd,
Rare Paterns of blest Peace and Amity,
Models of Grace, Emblems of Charity,
Rich Talents not in niggard napkins Layd,
But Piously dispenced, justly payd,
Chast Sponsal Love t' his Consort ; to Children nine
Surviving th' other fowre his care did shine
In Pious Education ; to Neighbours, friends,
Love seald with Constancy, which knowes no end.
Death would have stolne this Treasure, but in vaine—
It stung, but could not kill ; all wrought his gaine.
His Life was hid with Christ ; Death only made this
   story,
Christ cal'd him hence his Eve, to feast with him in
   glory."

The subject of this epitaph would have been
the hero of the legend. One may observe, in
passing, the play upon words, the Scotch elm
being often termed the *wych* elm. This suggests
a possible, and indeed probable, derivation of the
name. The reader should compare Blackmore's
account of the family, and especially his portrait
of Hugh Wichehalse, in chapter xv. of *Lorna
Doone*.

According to the folklore of the district it was
intended to build the church at Kibsworthy,
opposite Cheribridge, on the Barnstaple road,
and day after day the workmen brought materials
to the spot. Each morning, however, it was
found that they had been carried away during
the night to the present site—it was supposed by
pixies ; and finally, those little gentlemen had
their way. Obviously, little dependence can be

placed on folklore where questions of fact are concerned. A small volume, entitled *Legends of Devon*, printed at Dawlish in 1848, contains another story about a church equally void—the story, and the church, too—of foundation. In the middle of the twelfth century, it is said, Lynton Castle was the abode of a family named Lynton, in whom the Evil One, from the year 500, had taken a malicious interest. Reginald of that ilk then resolved to erect a church at Lynmouth in honour of his God, and chose for it the site of an old abbey. This devout undertaking ended the long and dreadful spell. "'The castle fell, the cliff heaved as if in pain, and the terrible convulsion formed the valley of rocks. The devil was seen scudding before the wind; he had lost his hold on the House of Lynton." Unfortunately, there never was a castle at Lynton, nor an abbey or church at Lynmouth. Moreover, one learns from Hazlitt, that, according to the popular belief, the rocks represent persons caught dancing on a Sunday, and so, like Lot's wife, transformed into stone.

The "Valley of Rocks," is not the primitive name of this singular and romantic spot. The Devon peasantry knew it of old as the "Danes" or "Denes"—a term probably connected with the word "den," and signifying "hollows." Prebendary Hancock, in his estimable *History of Selworthy*, shows it to be a commonplace name in this corner of the world. One is tempted to inquire—who christened the locality the "Valley of Rocks?" The problem is perhaps insoluble, but the *London Magazine* for 1782 contains a poem on the "Valley of Stones," in a note on which it is stated that the place owed this name to Dr Pococke, Bishop of Upper Ossory, who had visited it "some years since" with Dr Mills, the Dean of Exeter.

Some have found fault with the name "Valley of Rocks" as too ambitious, but attempts to belittle the grandeur of the spot would have received small support from Southey, who wrote about the scene in the language of ecstasy.

"Imagine a narrow vale between two ridges of hills somewhat steep ; the southern hill turfed ; the vale which runs from east to west covered with huge stones and fragments of stone among the fern that fills it ; the northern ridge completely bare ; excoriated of all turf and all soil, the very bones and skeletons of the earth ; rock reclining upon rock, stone piled upon stone ; a huge, terrific mass—a palace of the pre-Adamite kings, a city of the Anakim, must have appeared so shapeless, and yet so like the ruins of what had been shaped after the waters of the Flood had subsided. I ascended, with some toil, the highest point ; two large stones inclining on each other formed a rude portal on the summit. Here I sat down. A little level platform, about two yards long, lay before me, and then the eye immediately fell upon the sea far, very far below. I never felt the sublimity of solitude before."

Southey evidently referred to the "Castle Rock" on the right. On the left is the pile of stone which marked the abode of Mother Melldrum (see *Lorna Doone*, chapter xvii.). Blackmore mentions two names by which the place was known—the "Devil's Cheese-ring"

and the "Devil's Cheese-knife," which he states
to be convertible; but there appears to have been
a third—the "Devil's Cheese-press."

At one time the valley was the fitting haunt
of a herd of wild goats, but the animals had to be
destroyed—they butted so many sheep over the
adjoining cliffs.

It would be pardonable to imagine that
Lynton is indebted for its popularity as a water-
ing-place to *Lorna Doone*, but this would betray
ignorance of its history. I have spoken of the
spinning industry formerly carried on by hand;
when that ceased owing to the introduction of
machinery into the towns, the dealers, who had
employed people to work up the wool or bought
up the poor folk's yarn and taken it to larger
markets, found their occupation gone. What
was to be done? Mr William Litson, one of the
persons in this predicament, hit upon the idea of
opening an hotel. This was at the beginning of
the last century, but already visitors, hearing
reports of the rare and beautiful scenery, wended
their way to Lynton, although not in large
numbers. For their accommodation Mr Litson
acquired the "Globe," and furnished also the
adjoining cottage. Among the first to patronise
his establishment were Mr Coutts the banker, and
the Marchioness of Bute. From that time the
tale of visitors rapidly grew until, in 1807, the
enterprising Mr Litson was encouraged to build
the "Valley of Rocks" Hotel. The ball had
now been fairly set rolling; hotels, lodging-
houses, and private residences multiplied, and in
the middle of the last century—years before a
line of *Lorna Doone* had been written or so much

THE CHEESEWRING, VALLEY OF ROCKS.

as meditated—Lynton and Lynmouth were in all essentials the same as they are now.

To the lover of nature and the simplicity of country life this conversion of scenery into shekels, and Exmoor into Bayswater, represents by no means pure gain, albeit the lover of humanity may decide otherwise—on the principle of the greatest happiness of the greatest number. Both sorts, however, may unite in casting curious glances at the old Lynton which courted neither aristocratic nor democratic favour, and actually had a revel. This began on the first Sunday after Midsummer Day, and lasted a week. When the congregations emerged from the parish church, there awaited them near the gate a barrel of beer, and the majority of them were speedily "at it," quaffing a glass or discussing revel-cake —a special confection made of dark flour, currants, and caraway seeds. The principal feature in this, as in all revels, was the wrestling, in anticipation of which big sums were laid out in prizes. Silver spoons, for instance, were sometimes an incentive to competition. However, what with the drunkenness and the collusion that characterised too often the annual festival, the custom became obsolescent, and then obsolete, having incurred the taboo of the "respectable inhabitant" and the genuine sportsman alike.

In chapter xv. of the *Maid of Sker* mention is made of the practice of singing hymns at funeral processions on the Welsh side of the Bristol Channel. The same practice obtained on the North Devon side. One of the singers gave out the words verse by verse and the dirge was chanted to peculiar music reserved for such occasions. The first two or three verses were sung on the removal of the coffin from the house before the procession started, and the rest at intervals *en route* to the church. The following is a hymn used at the funeral of a grown-up person :—

"Farewell, all my parents[1] dear,
  And, all my friends, farewell!
I hope I'm going to that place,
  Where Christ and saints do dwell.

"Oppressed with grief long time I've been,
  My bones cleave to my skin ;
My flesh is wasted quite away
  With pain that I was in.

"Till Christ his messenger did send
  And took my life away,
To mingle with my mother earth,
  And sleep with fellow clay.

"Into thy hands I give my soul ;
  Oh! cast it not aside ;
But favour me and hear my prayer,
  And be my rest and guide.

"Affliction hath me sore oppressed,
  Brought me to death in time ;
O Lord, as thou hast promised
  Let me to life return.

"How blest is he who is prepared,
  Who fears not at his death ;
Love fills his heart, and hope his breast,
  With joy he yields his breath.

---

[1] Subject to variation, *e.g.*, "children."

"THE WATERSLIDE," LANCOMBE (page 163).

"Vain world, farewell! I must begone,
   I cannot longer stay ;
 My time is spent, my glass is run,
   God's will I must obey.

"For when that Christ to judgment comes,
   He unto us will say,
 If we his laws observe and keep,
   'Ye blessed, come away!'"

A friend of mine wrote to Blackmore respecting the harvest-song in *Lorna Doone* (chapter xxix.), being under the impression that it might be a true farmhouse ditty such as were common until a comparatively recent date. The romancer, however, admitted that the composition was his own.

CHAPTER XII

WEST of Lee Abbey and Duty Point lies much that is interesting, but this is also true of the country to the east of Lynton. For the moment we mount the coach with the intention of making a circuitous return to Dulverton. The writer does not forget his first experience of North Devon coaching. The placards showed four noble steeds, full of fettle and the joy of life; but "galled jades" would better have described the aspect of the miserable brutes condemned to drag the trunk-laden vehicle up those frightful ascents. Once on the summit, however, the going was easy, and passengers resumed their seats with a safe conscience, so far as cruelty to animals was concerned.

The drive from Lynton to Porlock, and from Porlock to Minehead, over breezy commons or through entrancing sylvan scenery, is gloriously exhilarating, and might put heart into the most confirmed dyspeptic. Which reminds me that in the neighbourhood of Porlock and Minehead there used to be gathered from the rocks vast quantities of laver, which was pickled and exported to large centres, such as Bristol, Exeter, and London. This sea-liverwort was eaten at the tables of the rich as a great delicacy. The hills and heaths also minister to the palate, since they produce various sorts of wild fruit—the dwarf juniper, the cranberry, and the whortleberry. The last, a most delicious fruit, is often made into pies, and the writer, when staying in the neighbourhood, is always glad if he finds one before him, knowing that he can command instant popularity, especially with the fair, by suggesting a second helping. Other bipeds appreciate it no less, since it is the summer food of the black game, and the decrease in the number of the species on the Brendon and Quantock hills has been attributed to the great demand for this fruit in the large towns. The berries grow singly, like gooseberries, the little plants being from a foot to eighteen inches in height. The leaves are ovated, and of a pale green colour.

Porlock and Porlock Weir are both charming places. Perhaps the most memorable object at the former—if the epithet may be applied to an object rather than a speech or event—is the old Ship Inn at the foot of the hill. This quaint survival of an older day is closely associated with the poet Southey, who used to wander thus far from his home on the Quantocks; and in the parlour, on the right of the main entrance, is a nook still known as "Southey's Corner," where he is said to have indited his sonnets and other poetry on the landscapes he so warmly admired.

"Porlock, thy verdant vale so fair to sight
Thy lofty hills, which fern and furze embrown,
Thy waters that roll musically down,
Thy woody glens the traveller with delight
Recalls to memory," etc.

Then there is the church with its spire, which, if not beautiful, is at least peculiar, being faced with wooden shales. Opinions differ as to whether or not it was once of superior altitude, but tradition alleges that in the year 1700, a great storm arose and the tower suffered. Porlock tradition possesses unusual claims to respect, the reason being that it has been proved, in one instance at least, to be remarkably accurate. In the preface of his excellent *History of the Ancient Church of Porlock*, the late Prebendary Hook, alluding to the great monument, observes :" "There had always been a tradition handed down from sexton to sexton, that the effigies were those of Lord Harington and his wife, the Lady of Porlock. But neither Collinson, the historian of Somerset, nor Savage, in his *History of the Hundred of Carhampton*, knew anything of it, and the former speaks of it as the tomb of a Knight Templar, though he does not explain how a wife happened to be there! But investigation proved the truth of the tradition, as is shown in the beautifully illustrated volume entitled *The Porlock Monuments*, now, unfortunately, out of print."

It may be worth recalling that one of Miss Ida Browne's relics is an old flint-lock pistol, engraved midway between stock and barrel with the name "C. Doone," whilst on the reverse side is the word "Porlok." Miss Browne is in some doubt as to whether the weapon was purchased in the village, or a C. Doone resided there, but she inclines to the latter opinion.

Porlock served as market town for the Ridds; indeed, it was in returning from Porlock market that Ridd's father was murdered (*Lorna Doone*, chapter iv.). There also dwelt Master Pooke, and there a lawyer made John Ridd's will.

Just off the road to Minehead, in the parish of Selworthy, stands Holnicote (pronounced Hunnicot), the Exmoor seat of the Acland family—a comparatively modern mansion, its predecessors having been destroyed by fire. In the widest sense, this old West-country race is best known through Mr Arthur Acland, late Minister of Education, and his father, the late Sir Thomas Acland, who was contemporary with Mr Gladstone at Oxford, and, like him, the winner of a "double first," and between whom and the distinguished statesman there was maintained to the very last a close and uninterrupted friendship. Locally, although the late baronet was always most highly esteemed, it is doubtful whether he was quite as popular as his sire, still referred to by the departing generation as "the *old* Sir Thomas." One of my childish recollections is lying in bed one dark night at Tiverton and listening to a muffled peal on St Peter's bells. It was the first muffled peal I ever heard, and I was much impressed when told that it was rung to mark the passing of a great county magnate, Sir Thomas Acland, tenth baronet, and for forty years a member of Parliament. This was in 1871.

When at Holnicote—the family has another seat, Killerton, near Exeter—the *old* Sir Thomas made it a rule to attend church twice on Sundays, and in the afternoon he usually brought with him two or three favourite dogs, which were shut up in Farmer Stenner's barn during the service.

The Acland pew was in the parvise over the
south porch, while in the west gallery the village
orchestra, comprising fiddle, violoncello, flute,
hautboy, and bassoon, was yet in its glory.
Animated by something of the feudal spirit, the
choir, on the first Sunday after the baronet's
arrival, invariably indulged in an anthem. On
one such occasion, back in the fifties, the Rev.
Edward Cox, rector of the neighbouring parish
of Luccombe, chanced to be officiating, and at
the conclusion of an elaborate performance, graced
by startling orchestral effects, was so unnerved
that he forgot his place in the service, and began
in a faltering tone the Apostles' Creed!
Naturally there was some confusion, which was
ended by Sir Thomas himself coming to the
rescue. Bending forward from his seat in the
gallery, he not only seconded the clergyman with
stentorian accents, but waving his hand
peremptorily, signed to the congregation to
repeat the creed over again. The command was
obeyed, and with such fervour that soon every
corner of the church was echoing with the
confession of faith. After the service Sir
Thomas waited for Mr Cox in the porch, and
slapping him on the back, remarked cheerily,
"Well done, well done! Whenever you are in
doubt, fall back on the articles of your belief, and
I'll support you!"

The pew occupied by Sir Thomas was
originally a priest's chamber, and was transformed
into a pew by the Hon. Mrs Fortescue, whose
husband was a pluralist rector of the old school,
and a rare lover of port wine. Her brother, the
Rev. Robert Gould, born in the rectory house at

Luccombe, was a remarkable fisherman and an equally remarkable shot. Once he is said to have caught such a quantity of fish in Bagworthy Water as to make his basket ridiculous, and he was forced to requisition a boy and horse to carry his spoil away. At another time he walked from Ilfracombe, where he resided, to Allerford, on a visit to his mother—most probably by way of Hangman Hill, Showlsborough Castle, Cheriton Ridge, and Bagworthy. However that may be, he was able to bring as a present to the old lady, forty snipe—a snipe for every mile, as he said. The same accomplished gentleman shot two bitterns in Porlock Marsh—a feat which, it is safe to assert, has never been repeated in that quarter or, perhaps, in England. The birds were stuffed, and passed into the keeping of his sister, Mrs Fortescue.

The Rev. W. H. Thornton avers that Mr Fortescue was in the habit of winking his eye and confessing that he had excellent cognac in his cellar. *Apropos* of this weakness, he reports these not quite "imaginary conversations."

" 'I found one morning that both my horses were gone,' he would say, 'but James Dadd (his coachman), James Dadd knew which way to search, and we found them loose in a lane beyond Exford, and there was a keg of this brandy left under the manger too. Will you try it?'

"Now, in all my intercourse with smugglers, illicit distillers, and such-like people, I have remarked the peculiarity that their wares either were, or were honestly deemed to be, of extra quality! Was it that the sense of irregularity added flavour to the dram, or were the smuggled spirits really particularly choice?   I do not know, but later in my life I sat by the deathbed of a very old smuggler, who told me how he used to have a donkey with a triangle on his back, so rigged up as to show three lanthorns, and how chilled he would become as he lay out winter's night after winter's night, watching on the Foreland or along Brandy Path, as he called it, for the three triangled lights of the schooner, which he knew was coming in to land her cargo, where Glenthorne[1] now stands, and where was the smugglers' cave. 'Lord bless ee, sir,' and the dying man of nearly ninety years chuckled, 'we never used no water. We just put the brandy into the kettle, and heated it, and drinked it out of half-pint stoups.'"

If it is to be a question of retailing smuggling stories, I also can tell one of Exmoor origin, only it relates to Minehead, whither our course now lies.   Many years ago—I fancy it was in the forties—there was a certain quay-lumper, who "caddled about" anywhere, away under Greenaleigh. His name was Moorman. Just about this time a French vessel was on her way with a cargo of smuggled brandy, but a fall-out between uncle and nephew, on account of the former refusing to lend money, led to information being given, with the result that one of Her Majesty's cutters was seen cruising up and down before Minehead. The whole town was in an uproar.

After a while the foreigner drew in under Greenaleigh, and discharged her cargo ; and

_____
[1] *Lorna Doone*, chapters ix., xlviii.

SHIP INN, PORLOCK (page 179).

Moorman, having been called to assist, was rewarded with a sum of money and a quantity of brandy. It was beautiful brandy, and Moorman's wife very kindly gave some of it to her neighbours, remarking as she did so, "My old man helped discharge the cargo." This observation was carried to the excise officers, who searched for Moorman, and insisted on his telling them where the spirit was concealed. As a matter-of-fact, it had been hidden in the sand ; but this was perfectly smooth, and Moorman, though he made a show of looking for them, declared he could not find the kegs. Just as they were about to give up in despair, one of the party hitched his foot in a rope, with which, it turned out, the kegs had been slung together. Several persons were arrested in connection with the affair, among others an old Mr Rawle, a farmer ; and some few were sent to prison. As for the cutter, she had been lying useless in Minehead harbour, in low water.[1]

It cannot be charged against Minehead that "the hobby-horse is forgot," and those mindful of him belong, for the most part, to the seafaring class. Early on May morning, they perambulate the town with the idol, a rough similitude of

[1] Blackmore refers to the subject in *Lorna Doone*, chapter xxxix. Speaking of Jeremy Stickles, he says that "his duty was first and most ostensibly to see to the levying of poundage in the little haven of Lynmouth and further up the coast, which was now becoming a place of resort for the folk whom we call smugglers, that is to say, who land their goods without regard to the King's revenue, as by law established. And indeed there had been no officer appointed to take toll, until one had been sent to Minehead, not so very long before" (see also *Lorna Doone*, chapter xii.).

the equine species, decked off with ribbons;
the "counterfeit presentment" being supported
on the shoulders of a man whose legs are concealed by the trappings, and who is responsible
for its motions.   Its progress through the streets
is heralded by the tap of the drum, and horseplay—seldom is the expression so apt—is the
order of the day.   For it may be taken for
granted that there is more than one performance,
and the worship of the beast is resumed at
intervals till vesper-time.   However, the custom,
which was formerly observed at Combmartin also,
is gradually dying out.

Probably one of the most sensational events
in the annals of Minehead, which do not appear
to be particularly rich in historic interest, is a
seventeenth-century episode, in which the chief
actors were the Rev. Henry Byam, rector of
Selworthy, and "another."   A notable man was
Henry Byam, who was born at Luccombe, in
1580.   Being a devoted Royalist, he attended
Prince Charles in his flight to the Scilly Islands,
and thence to Jersey.   Byam was in great esteem
as a preacher, and his sermons were edited by
Hamnet Ward, Prebendary of Wells, who states
that "most of them were preached before His
Majesty King Charles II., in his exile."
Perhaps, however, the discourse which will most
attract modern readers, is that entitled: "A
Return from Argier.—A Sermon preached at
Minehead, in the County of Somerset, the 16th
of March, 1627, at the re-admission of a Relapsed
into our Church."   It seems that a young Minehead man had been taken prisoner by the Turks
and compelled to embrace the Mohammedan

religion.   Having escaped, he returned to Minehead, where, clothed in Turkish attire, he had to
stand in St Michael's Church, whilst the rector
of Selworthy "improved" the occasion.   In one
part of the sermon, the preacher addressed
himself directly to the offender :

"You whom God suffered to fall, and yet of
His infinite mercy vouchsafed graciously to bring
you home, not only to your country and kindred,
but to the profession of your first faith, and to
the Church and Sacraments again ; let me say
to you (but in a better hour), as sometime Joshua
to Achan : 'Give glory to God, sing praises to
Him who hath delivered your soul from the
nethermost hell.'   When I think upon your
Turkish attire, I do remember Adam and his
fig-leaf breeches ; they could neither conceal his
shame, nor cover his nakedness.   I do think
upon David clad in Saul's armour.   How could
you hope, in this unsanctified habit, to attain
Heaven?"

But it is time that we set out for Dunster,
which is as rich in striking memories as the
seaport town is poor.   The two places, however,
are not altogether separable ; indeed, it must be
evident at a glance that small towns situated at
so short a distance from each other—two miles
and a half—will have been influenced, though in
varying degrees, by the same incidents and
accidents, and freaks of fortune.   If we go back
to the first quarter of the fifteenth century, we
find that a "shipman" of Minehead, called Roger
King, was employed in conveying provisions
from this part of the world to Normandy, where
war was then raging ; and his return cargo often

consisted of wine, which Lady Catherine Luttrell, of Dunster Castle, readily purchased from him. Once Sir Hugh Luttrell embarked on a vessel called the *Leonard of Dunster*, taking with him five live oxen and two pipes of beer for consumption during the voyage. His expenses, including repairs, amounted to the then considerable sum of £42, 3s. 1d.; but the master, Philip Clopton, having been paid £40, 10s. by certain foreign merchants for a freight of wine on the journey home, the lucky knight had merely to make good the difference—£1, 13s. 1d. In 1427, several Minehead fishermen, tenants of Sir Hugh, adventuring as far as Carlingford, were captured by a Spaniard named Goo, and having been conveyed to Scotland, were confined in Bothwell Castle, whence a special letter, addressed to the King of Scotland in the name of Henry VI., was necessary to procure their release.

In the Middle Ages, Dunster itself was a seaport, and, in the reign of Edward III., writs directed to the bailiffs forbade friars, monks, or treasure to quit the realm by that door. It is to be observed in this connection that the river Avill, before joining the sea, widens out at a place called the "Hone" or the "Hawn"—no doubt the site of the old *haven*, of which term its present name is a corruption.

To many, Dunster Castle is indissolubly associated with the family of Luttrell, and no wonder, seeing the ages that have elapsed since it was owned by persons of different descent. Its earliest lords, however, were Mohuns—a name which at once awakens recollections of Thackeray and the famous duel between Lord Mohun and

the Duke of Hamilton in Hyde Park, in 1712.
The first Mohun of Dunster was a gallant leader
called William the Old, who attended his name-
sake, the Conqueror, with a large retinue to the
field of Senlac, and received Dunster as a part of
that day's spoil.   The family had large posses-
sions in Normandy, and drew their name—De
Moion—from a village near St Lo.

The history of the English branch, or rather
branches, is by no means devoid of interest.   The
founder of Newenham Abbey (Devon), for
instance, was Reginald de Mohun, who died in
1246.   In recognition of his munificence, he
received from the Pope the gift of a golden rose,
and as such a present was made only to persons
of high rank, His Holiness dubbed him Earl of
Este (or Somerset).   The monkish chronicler
reports that Reginald had seen in a vision a
venerable man, who bade him make his election
between going with him then, in which case he
would be safe, or remaining until overtaken by
danger.   De Mohun at once accepted the former
alternative, but the old man would have him stay
till the third day, when the confessor saw in
another dream the same old man leading a boy
"more radiant than the sun, and vested in a robe
brighter than crystal," which boy, he heard him
say, was the soul of Reginald de Mohun.   The
chronicler further states that he was present when
Reginald's tomb was opened nearly a hundred
years later, what time the body was perfect, and
exhaled a most fragrant odour.

I now pass to the year 1376, when the Lady
Joan, relict of Sir John de Mohun, sold the right
of succession to the barony for £3333, 6s. 8d

to the Lady Elizabeth Luttrell, the receipt being still in the possession of the present owner, Mr G. F. Luttrell. It is worth remarking that Mr Luttrell is a descendant of the Mohuns of Beconnoc (the junior branch which produced the Lord Mohun before mentioned), through the marriage of his ancestor, John Fownes, with the heiress of Samuel Maddock, her mother having been the daughter and ultimate heiress of the third Lord Mohun of Okehampton.

The Lady Elizabeth Luttrell was the daughter of Hugh Courtenay, Earl of Devon, and Margaret, daughter of Humphry de Bohun, Earl of Hereford and Essex, who was styled "the flower of knighthood, and the most Christian knight of the knights of the world." Her husband was a less considerable person, being only a cadet of a younger branch of the baronial family of Luttrell of Irnham. Their son was the Sir Hugh Luttrell already referred to, who, in his time, was governor of Harfleur and Grand Seneschal of France—in fact, the right-hand man of Harry the Fifth. He rebuilt Dunster Castle in somewhat the form we find it to-day, and added a new gate-house. The alabaster effigies on the north side of the chancel of the conventual church are those of Sir Hugh and Lady Catherine Luttrell.

There are black sheep in every family, and among the Luttrells one black sheep was pretty clearly James, grandson of great Sir Hugh. The latter had a receiver-general named Thomas Hody, and it was probably his son—one Alisaunder Hody, at any rate—that drew up a complaint against James Luttrell which enables us to see what manner of man he was. First, it seems, Luttrell ascertained from Hody's unsuspecting wife where her husband was likely to be for the next three days, and then clapped one of his servants into Dunster Castle, where he kept him closely confined for a night, to prevent him from giving information. Luttrell's next move was to set out with a party of thirty-five followers, with bows bent and arrows in their hands, for the house of Alisaunder's father-in-law, Thomas Bratton, with the intention of murdering the object of his resentment.

In the course of another expedition, in which he was attended by twenty-four armed retainers, he fell upon John Coker, a servant of Hody, and beat and wounded him so that his life was despaired of. His greatest coup, however, was his attack on Taunton Castle, where he broke open the doors and searched for Alisaunder, confiscated seven silver spoons, five ivory knives, and other goods belonging to him, struck his wife, and threatened to kill her with their daggers. A servant, Walter Peyntois, was stabbed, almost fatally, while " Sir " Robert, Alisaunder's priest, was assaulted, dragged to the ground by the hair of his head, and beaten by the ruffians with the pommels of their swords.

Whatever his faults, James Luttrell was undoubtedly brave, and, taking part in the strife of the Roses, was knighted on the field after the battle of Wakefield. At the second battle of St Albans he received a mortal wound, and in the first Parliament of Edward IV. his property was forfeited to the Crown. The attainder was reversed on the accession of Henry VH.

Another fighting Luttrell was Sir John, who served in the Scottish wars of the mid-sixteenth century, won the name of a "noble captain," and was ultimately taken prisoner in the fort of Bouticraig. Among the treasures of Dunster Castle is preserved a painting of Sir John Luttrell by a Flemish artist, Lucas de Heere, dated 1550; and a very extraordinary painting it is.

In the great Civil War, the Luttrell of the period, whose Christian name was Thomas, espoused the side of the Parliament, and "Mistress" Luttrell commanded the men in the castle to "give fire" at sixty of Sir Ralph Hopton's troopers, who had come to demand entrance, but after this reception deemed it expedient to retire. In 1643 the owner, rather weakly, surrendered the place, of which Francis Wyndham now became governor. Two years later, Colonel Blake, with a Parliamentarian force from Taunton, began the investment of the castle, which finally capitulated on April 19, 1646.

In 1645, after the battle of Naseby, the Prince of Wales (afterwards Charles II.) was commanded by his father to take up his quarters at Dunster, in order to escape the plague, which was raging at Bristol. This was to jump from the frying-pan into the fire, as the contagion was so bad at Dunster that the inhabitants feared to venture into the streets. However, there is no doubt that the prince visited the castle, where a room leading out

MINEHEAD CHURCH (page 187).

into the gallery is called "King Charles's Room." The "King's Chamber," mentioned in the inventory of 1705, adjoined the gallery; but the evidence does not point conclusively to the traditional apartment, which, being very narrow, with no window and only a stone bench, might have done fairly well as a place of concealment, more especially as there is a secret door in one of the walls. But at this time the Royalists were in possession, and there was no obvious motive for selecting the incommodious lodging for a guest of princely blood.

To conclude this account of the Luttrells, the male line came to an end on the death of Alexander, in 1737. Ten years later, his daughter married Henry Fownes of Nethway, and from him the present owner, Mr George Fownes Luttrell, is descended.

From the lords of Dunster let us turn to the place which, in spite of inevitable changes, retains a greater variety of mediæval features than may easily be found within the same compass. A complete description of the castle and park is impossible here, but it may be mentioned that very full information is contained in Mr G. T. Clark's preliminary essay in Sir H. C. Maxwell-Lyte's standard work. One thing is certain—that the aspect of the castle has been considerably altered from what it was in mediæval times. During the eighteenth century sad liberties were taken with the buildings. Spurious Gothic windows were inserted, and a thoroughly incongruous chapel erected. The restoration undertaken by Mr G. F. Luttrell rectified these absurdities, but went much further.

2 B

The northern tower of the principal façade was pulled down and rebuilt, and a new wing was added.   The old Edwardian gateway has been left intact.

About the year 1775, through the caprice of the then owner, was erected the Conegar Tower, which is merely a hollow shell standing on a conical hill.   Owing to its commanding position it is a prominent landmark, rising amidst woods which in the summer season are a mass of foliage, whilst intersecting foot-paths form shady alleys in which it is a joy to wander.   It is pleasant to add that the master of this splendid domain has always observed a most generous and unselfish attitude to strangers desirous of inspecting his house and grounds.

But Dunster has other wonders hardly inferior to the castle itself.   One may instance the Yarn Market, with its broad, overhanging penthouses, manifold gables, and pyramidal roof, in one of the beams of which is a hole said to have been caused by a cannon shot fired from the castle in the time of the Civil War.   Such a ball, however, could not have passed the intervening woodwork leaving it uninjured, so that the story is, at least, doubtful.

Hard by is the Luttrell Arms Hotel—a perfect treasure-house of antiquities.   These comprise a gabled porch pierced with lancet holes for cross-bows, a façade of oak, elaborately carved, and an oak chamber, with an open roof of timber work, somewhat resembling that of Westminster Hall. In Room 13 are emblazoned the Luttrell Arms— *or, a bird between three martlets sable.*   With these are impaled *a chevron between three trefoils, slipped, proper.*

Says an anonymous writer : " In old times it was the custom of every gentleman to set up his family shield on the house in which he sojourned ; this served as a rallying-point to his followers, and, in my opinion, was the origin of the signs formerly displayed on houses of business of every kind, but now confined to inns only." In the present instance the suggestion is not particularly helpful, as there are reasons for supposing that the building once belonged to the Abbey of Cleeve. Nothing, however, is certainly known of its origin and history, and it is quite possible that it was at one time in the occupation of a cadet of the great family at the castle.

Room No. 12 boasts a far more notable feature—namely, an elaborate mantelpiece bearing two shields, one emblazoned with the arms of England, and the other with those of France ; also a poor bust of Shakespeare, two large Elizabethan female figures, and a central medallion showing a prostrate man, nude, and worried by three dogs, clearly intended for Actæon, who was torn to pieces by his hounds for looking on Diana whilst bathing.

The " Luttrell Arms " is mentioned in chapter xxvii. of *Lorna Doone*, which tells also of Ridd's mother's cousin, the tanner, and his bevy of daughters, all resident in the town.

Another architectural curiosity is a weather-tiled house on the north side of Middle Street. This is usually described as "the Nunnery"—a quite modern appellation, born of pure fancy. Even so late as the last century it was known as the "High House," while a yet older name was the "Tenement of St Lawrence." Yet another interesting old structure is "Lower Marsh," with rich Perpendicular oratory over its entrance porch.

Next, as to the church. At the entrance to the churchyard stands a quaint timber building which goes by the name of the Priest's House. The church itself is a magnificent specimen of its kind, and worthy of the name of a cathedral. The most ancient part of it is the Norman arch at the west end. The east end is Early English, and nearly all the rest Perpendicular, including the old and beautiful rood-screen of open work with fan tracery headings, over which are four rows of ornaments. The portion of the church to the west of the screen is called by the inhabitants the "Parish Church," while the eastern section is termed the "Priory Church." The reason is that this was formerly the chapel of the Priory of Dunster, which belonged to the Benedictine monks of Bath ; and shortly after the dissolution of the monasteries the priory was acquired by the Luttrells, who have long claimed the part of the church assigned to the monks by the award of the Abbot of Glastonbury and his colleagues, and erected therein a number of funeral monuments, yet remaining, in various states of preservation. To the north-west of the church are the ruins of the priory, the great barn in which the good monks stored their grain, and two great gateways that led into the priory precincts.

Every visitor to Dunster is admonished to make the ascent of Grabhurst (or Grabbist) Hill, on the southern slope of which there was in the

Middle Ages a vineyard—not, by the way, a
solitary example in the England of that distant
time. The view from the summit is extremely
beautiful. In the foreground are moors, in the
background the sea, and on the right and the left
hand towards Minehead and St Audries, varied
and charming landscapes. On one side of the
ridge may be descried a typical farmhouse,
nestling amidst bright, green meadows and
clumps of trees ; and over the deep, narrow valley
towers the massive form of old Dunkery and other
heights in shadowy perspective.

Still grander are the prospects to be obtained
from Dunkery Beacon itself—the most commanding landmark of the district. About eight miles
south of Minehead, Dunkery is a mountain large
and high, with a base about twelve miles in circumference and an altitude of 1700 feet. With the
exception of Cawsand Beacon, it is the highest
summit in the West of England. One approach
to it is from Wootton Courtenay, the distance
from the parish church to the top of the hill being
three miles ; another is from Cutcombe, in which
parish part of Dunkery lies. The hilly character
of the country is well illustrated by the name of
the hostelry at the corner, where the road to
Dunkery digresses from the " Minehead turnpike "—" Rest and Be Thankful."

The view from the beacon embraces an immense tract, the sky-line being quite five hundred
miles in circumference. To the south-west can
be discerned the tors near Plymouth ; northwards,
the Malvern Hills, in Worcestershire—regions
more than two hundred miles apart. North and
north-west, nearly a hundred and thirty miles of

the Bristol Channel, and behind it the coast of Wales from Monmouthshire to Pembrokeshire. Most of Somerset, Devon, and Dorset, with parts of Wiltshire and Hampshire, are included in a spectacle which premises a clear atmosphere and not too bright a sun, lest the prospect be obscured by haze.

On Dunkery top is a vast quantity of rough, loose stones of all shapes and sizes, and ranging from one pound to two hundred pounds in weight, together with the remains of three large hearths, built of unhewn stones, and about eight feet square. They compose an equilateral triangle, in the interior of which is another and larger hearth. More than two hundred feet lower, on the slope of the hill, and nearly a mile distant, are two other hearths, with the same accompaniment of loose stones scattered in large numbers around. These are undoubtedly ruins of old-world beacons which, in periods of civil commotion or when foreign invasion threatened, were used to rouse the countryside and pass the fiery message from one end of the realm to the other. According to *Lorna Doone* (chapter iii.), the marauders prevented this legitimate use by throwing a watchman on the top of it. Chapters xliii. and xliv. contain a vivid description of the firing of the actual beacon in Doone Glen.

For the neighbours the beacon is a huge barometer. Often it is covered with clouds, and this is regarded as an infallible sign of rain ; hence the saying :

> " When Dunkery's top cannot be seen,
> Horner will have a flooded stream."

A former inhabitant of Luccombe, with a nicer ear for rhyme, penned the following pretty song on Dunkery Beacon, evidently modelled on "Sweet and Low," but worth quoting all the same :—

> " Stern and black, stern and black,
>   Low lies the storm on the mountain track :
>   Black and stern, black and stern,
>   Hardly may we thy face discern
>   By the light westward—lurid and red—
>   And the thunder voices are overhead !
>   Where the lightning is never still,
>   Who'll now come with me over the hill?

> " Grey and sad, grey and sad,
>   With a rain-wrought veil are thy shoulders clad :
>   Sad and grey, sad and grey,
>   Weird is the mist creeping up to-day,
>   Ghostlike and white from the stream where it lay,
>   Hanging a shroud o'er the lone wild way ;
>   Hidden and still, hidden and still,
>   Who'll now come with me over the hill ?

> " Fair and bright, fair and bright,
>   Purple and gold in the autumn light,
>   Bright and fair, bright and fair ;
>   The butterflies float in the warm, soft air,
>   Float and suck 'midst the heather bells,
>   And green are the ferns in the dear-loved dells ;
>   Now who will, now who will
>   Come with me, come with me over the hill ? "

The "Minehead turnpike," as it is termed, dates from the reign of George IV. Before that period the road, after leaving Timberscombe, passed up the long steep ascent of Lype Hill. The present highway is a trotting road of undoubted excellence. Being cut through hanging woods in some sections, and along the banks of the Exe in others, it is perhaps the finest and most romantic drive of its kind in the kingdom.

NOTE.—Watchet, the burial-place of Lorna's mother— a rather forlorn little haven by the wash of the Bristol Channel, lies somewhat apart from our suggested route, but is easily accessible by the railway, by which it is half-spoilt. St Decuman's Church, alone on the hill, contains exceptionally fine monuments of the Wyndham family, with effigies.

DUNSTER CASTLE GATE, FROM THE OUTSIDE (page 193.)

CHAPTER XIII

WE have now returned to Dulverton, but our pilgrimage is not yet over, for we have yet to explore a territory which may be termed the joint property, or "debateable ground," of *Lorna Doone* and the *Maid of Sker*. The Devon and Somerset line, connecting as it does with the light railway to Lynton, and the London and South-Western branch from Exeter to Barnstaple, will be found extremely convenient for our purpose, although these "iron roads" do not in every instance land us at the precise spots where we would be. So, peradventure, it may be wisdom to set up our headquarters at Southmolton and Barnstaple in succession, and peregrinate from those centres at our discretion.

First, a word of explanation as to the title of this chapter. Far be it from me to give evil pre-eminence to Southmolton as a school for scandal, but in chapter xii. of *Lorna Doone* Blackmore distinctly states that it is "a busy place for talking." There is no going from that.

Southmolton, like Bampton, is subject to the

"slings and arrows" of outrageous criticism as a place where it is "always afternoon." If that be so, all I can say is that, personally, I invariably find the P.M. extremely pleasant, and nothing will induce me to cast a stone at a town so hospitable. Moreover, it is beyond question an important hub of Blackmore associations, and the faithful votary of the novelist *must* betake himself thither. Whether or not the fact be due to this circumstance, it seems certain that more visitors patronise the neighbourhood than formerly, and Mr Brown, the obliging chemist, informs me that he has developed negatives for Americans, from whom he has received flattering testimonials. Well done, Mr Brown! The following entry in the visitors' book at the "George" has an independent interest.

"July 3rd, 1888—Dr Walter B. Gilbert, of New York, U.S., who was saved by being thrown out of the window at the corner house opposite, during the fatal fire of July 1835."

This reminds one of an early incident in the life of a famous divine, who declared that "the world was his parish." It was certainly Dr Gilbert's.

On one occasion when I stayed at the "George," where, it may be remembered, Master Stickles filled his little flat bottle with "the very best *eau de vie*" (*Lorna Doone*, chapter xlvii.), the fair was in full swing, and I recollect that, among other attractions, there was a negro marionette of large size, with aggressive, red lips. A young man indulged in an entertaining dialogue with him as a prelude to the sale of quack medicine. Now, the proletariat is master at Southmolton,

and the Corporation dare not remove from the
Square the shooting-galleries, ginger-bread stalls,
confetti tents, and other encumbrances connected
with this event. It was whispered to me that at
the time of an Agricultural Show, when the band
of the Plymouth division of the Royal Marines
was to perform in the market, the Mayor offered
£10 for an hour and a half's suspension of the
strident and powerful tones of a steam-organ,
but in vain. This mechanical purveyor of
popular airs represents the combined snort of a
tornado of galloping horses fitted to a roundabout of the most modern type. In the old-style
roundabout a boy worked a turnstile, and in
doing so sometimes slipped or fell, when he
received pretty severe contusions. This arrangement was succeeded by a cog-wheel in charge of
a man.

At fair time, East Street is blocked with
Exmoor sheep and North Devon cattle, and *à
propos* of this, you may notice over the entrance
to the market three carved rams' heads. On the
first day of the fair, a white sheepskin glove is
projected on a pole from a ring on the side of a
" Star." Locally, this is supposed to signify the
"hand of welcome," which accounts perhaps for
the nosegay. Another and less romantic version
declares it the "hand of authority."

Let us stroll through the town in search of
adventures. Naturally, our steps will be directed,
in the first instance, to the parish church, of
which the inhabitants are extremely proud. Well,
it is handsome, very handsome—sumptuous, if
you like—but the interior is nearly all brand-new.
As to that, however, there are exceptions, and

I will undertake to affirm that the amazing
gargoyle on the north side of the chancel arch,
albeit there are gargoyles on the Town Hall and
gargoyles on the "George," is not of our time.
Apparently, it is the face of a craftsman, and,
quite possibly, that of the master-builder of the
church. The pulpit also is ancient; the four
evangelists' flattened countenances and noses
sadly out of repair proclaim a reckoning with
time. The font is ancient and goodly. The
tower is a fine one, as is also that of Northmolton; but if you would see what North Devon
can show in the shape of church towers, away
to Chittlehampton. There is a local proverb:
"Southmolton for strength; Chittlehampton for
beauty," and tradition states that the tower of
the fane of St Heriswitha was erected by a pupil
of the man that built Southmolton tower.

For my own part, I find Southmolton churchyard, with its walled and paved avenues, more
stimulating than the church. The margins of
four banks were, it appears, planted with lime-
trees in 1735-6, and twenty-five years later the
New Walk was adorned with similar trees.
These in 1866 were rooted up by a "fanatical
iconoclast," but others took their place, and so
there is at present not much occasion to find
fault.

I remember one September evening standing
in this churchyard and talking to that worthy
man, the sexton, when he mentioned to me
casually that it was the scene of a desperate
battle. Particulars he had none to give, and for
the nonce I had forgotten my history book, so
we stood and gazed in silence, with a sense of

vague respect and profound mystery, at the home
of the dead, on which the shades of evening were
rapidly falling. Too late to enlighten him, I
recalled the abortive rising of the Cavaliers in
1655, when Sir Joseph Wagstaffe, aided and
abetted by a couple of Wiltshire squires, Hugh
Groves and John Penruddock, and a force of
loyal Cornishmen, proclaimed Prince Charles
king at Southmolton, after a rather discreditable
fiasco at Southampton. Cromwell's troops were
soon on their traces, and in a bloody fight,
mainly in the churchyard, the Royalists were
hopelessly defeated. Wagstaffe and a few of his
officers escaped by jumping their horses over the
north-west portion of the churchyard wall (on
which some forty years ago a lime-house was
built), and, crossing Exmoor, arrived at Bridge-
water. Groves and Penruddock, with twenty
others, were captured and conducted to the
castle at Exeter, where they were arraigned for
high treason, found guilty, and executed. The
leaders were beheaded and the rest hanged, the
drawing and quartering, ordinarily a feature in
such ceremonies, being omitted.

Comedy, as well as tragedy, may claim
Southmolton churchyard for her own, for here
Bampfylde Moore Carew, the famous King of the
Gipsies, wreaked dire vengeance on the local
bellman, who had insulted him, by appearing in
the likeness of Infernal Majesty, and chasing the
affrighted officer among the tombs. The fact
that the ghost of an old gentleman not long
deceased was reputed to walk the churchyard
probably made this characteristic revenge more
easy.

A ruinous building, to which no stranger uninitiated would direct more than a passing glance, stands back from the road on Factory Hill. Once it was a celebrated academy, at which nearly all the youth of Southmolton, and doubtless many boys of the neighbouring parishes, received their education. In this now abandoned seat of learning there were two departments—an English school and a Latin school—for which there were separate halls. The place wears a horrible appearance of neglect and desecration, but some of the old fittings yet remain, and when I inspected it, there were even some loose forms amongst the miscellaneous lumber. The founder was one Hugh Squier, a lesser Peter Blundell, who left injunctions that his portrait should be hung in what is now the sitting-room of a cottage, but was then, no doubt, the master's house, and that there, as if he were bodily present, his trustees should dine once a year. The portrait has been removed to the Town Hall. There is also a beautiful miniature of Squier attached to the mayor's chain of office, which is probably at his worship's.

Southmolton has been a great place for poets, the best of them being perhaps Richard Manley, a journeyman saddler, who died in 1832. The following lines are taken from a poem after Gray, entitled *Recollections of Schoolboy Days*, and supposed to be written in front of Squier's Free School, where the author had been taught reading, writing, and arithmetic :—

> "Ah! it was there, where yon green trees are bending,
>   And waving gently to the sunny air,
> Where schoolboys dally, anxiously contending
>   For empty honours in their sports—'twas there

Young life to me with hope and joy was beaming;
   Its sun in brightness rose, in sweetness set;
And childhood's happy hours were spent in dreaming
   Of future bliss and happier moments yet:
And now those dreams are vanisht and forsaken
By childhood's hopes: to manhood I awaken."

Personally, I must confess, I should not have appreciated the pathos of the scholastic derelict but for my good friend, the late Mayor of Southmolton, who offered his services as cicerone. Mr Kingdon was formerly associated with the firm of Crosse, Day, and Crosse, solicitors, and he recollects Blackmore coming into their office, his object being to look over some documents relating to the Manor of Oare. On leaving, he complained that he had not found much to the purpose; but Mr Kingdon is not so sure.

Speaking of Mayors—and we must not forget that Master Paramore was a high member of the town council (see *Lorna Doone,* chapter xii.) —the chief magistrate of Southmolton is noted for the splendour of his official retinue—doubtless a legacy from the days when corporations were wont to insist more than they do now on outward show and ceremony. Mr Mills, a local historian, gives an excellent account of the old style, founded in part on his own recollections:

"The Bailiff's livery is a coat and vest of cerulean colour, with red facings, velveteen breeches, and a gold-laced, three-cornered hat. This functionary formerly, as part of his livery, wore red stockings, but on the appointment of Mr Philip Widgery about sixty years ago (1892), he besought the Corporation to provide him with gaiters—alleging as a reason that his legs were the same shape as German flutes. His petition was granted, and he and his successors have had their legs encased in drab gaiters. The Sergeants at Mace have three-cornered hats and ample blue cloaks—both hats and cloaks being trimmed with gold lace.

"Prior to the Municipal Corporations Reform Act, 1834, these three officers always proceeded with the Mayor and other members of the Corporation to the Parish Church every Sunday morning. All the members wore robes; those who had passed the office of Mayor wore scarlet gowns, the other members were robed in black. A posse of the borough constables always preceded this procession, carrying blue staves with the borough arms in gilt letters on the upper end. These staves were about six feet long, and are preserved at the Guildhall. As soon as the second lesson had been read, the four took their staves in their hands, and holding them aloft, marched sedately out of church, to pay visits to the public-houses, in order to see if any person was tippling in them during Divine Service. The first place of call was the 'Ring of Bells,' adjacent to the churchyard, where, knowing the exact time their visit would be paid, the landlord had four half-pints of ale in readiness for their delectation as soon as they arrived. A similar visit was next paid to the 'King's Arms,' and similar treatment awaited them there. Generally by the time these two visits had been paid, the congregation at the church had been dismissed, and the vigilant constables retired to their respective homes to preside over the family dinner, and to

SQUARE AT SOUTHMOLTON (page 204).

say grace, after eating it, as good churchmen should do."

We are now to travel back three centuries and more, to the reign of Queen Elizabeth.

Leaving Southmolton for a time, we set out in the first instance for an ancient manor-house about three miles distant, in the parish of Bishop's Nympton. In doing so, we pass two old factories, which formerly gave employment to three hundred combers, etc. One of them is now a grist mill, while the other is turned to account as a collar factory, in which a score or two of women imitate the "little busy bee." As for the men who once worked in the mills, on the break-up of the industry some transferred their services to Mr Vicary, of North Tawton, while others migrated to Yorkshire.

A well-remembered character at Southmolton, Chapple, the parish clerk, was seated as usual at the foot of the pulpit, when the late rector, Mr King, being momentarily at a loss, whispered down to him, "What do they make at the factory?" Chapple replied in an audible tone, "Serge." Whereupon the preacher resumed, "I am informed," etc., drawing an illustration from the fabric.

Through winding lanes and some rough fields, which Leland would probably have described as "morisch," lies the approach to Whitechapel, and were it not for the railway, with its "level crossing," the spot would be rightly described as sequestered, and such as could hardly be excelled as the scene of a tragedy or perhaps a romance. The house stands on the slope of a green hill, against which its white walls stand pleasantly outlined. It has

two courtyards, the inner being entered by a
gateway flanked by tall brick pillars surmounted
by huge globes. It is said that on this inner
platform were mounted cannon—a battery of five
pieces of ordnance. About fifty years ago the
original mullioned windows were removed by a
farmer-tenant, and deposited in a cellar, where
they were lately discovered. Some of them have
been re-inserted in the right end of the building.
In the rear the remains of an old hearth have
been found, showing that cooking was carried on
outside the house proper. The interior is
remarkable for a splendid oak screen. The
place is now in thoroughly good hands, but it has
naturally suffered from having been so long a
farmhouse, the occupiers of which were profoundly
indifferent to its contents and history. The
present owner, Captain Glossop, when I met him,
was bringing taste and energy to bear on the old
mansion, although portions of it were beyond
repair.

Working backwards, I find that at the beginning of the last century the property was in
Chancery, and sold by the order of the Lord
Chancellor by public auction. The purchaser
was a familiar figure in Southmolton, a Mr
Sanger, who occupied Whitechapel till his death.
He made it his boast that he cut down and sold
enough timber on the estate to pay the whole of
the purchase money. At one time the property
belonged to an ancestor of Sir John Heathcoat-
Amory ; and during the Civil Wars it was the
residence of Colonel Basset, one of Prince's
"Worthies." Blackmore clearly remembered this
circumstance when he introduced Sir Roger

Bassett into his work (*Lorna Doone*, chapter xlvi.), and allowed him to be victimised by the joint cunning of lawyers and outlaw.

According to Prince, the place was the original home of all the Bassets; and the walls, as they now stand, were built during the reign of Elizabeth by Sir Robert de Basset, on the site of an earlier structure, and in the fashionable shape of an E. A few years later the knight lost his wife, and having had the good fortune to win the heart and hand of Mistress Beaumont of Umberleigh, removed to her mansion, standing where once had stood King Athelstan's palace. Umberleigh was afterwards the property of John o' Gaunt, from whom it passed to a relative—a fact to which old doggerel lines bear witness:

> "I John o' Gaunt, do give and grant,
>   From me and mine, to thee and thine,
>   The barton fee of Umberlee."

Sir Robert de Basset not only bade adieu to Whitechapel, whither he never returned, but shortly before the death of Queen Elizabeth, he made another change, and for the sake of his wife's health, took up his residence at Heanton Court, she having brought to him the manors of Sherwill and Heanton Punchardon. Situated on the right bank of the Taw, about three miles below Barnstaple, Heanton Court is now only a picturesque farmhouse, but sixty years ago, according to an eye-witness, the walls were still worse, and resembled a dilapidated factory. This place, as will be shown more plainly hereafter, was the original of the Narnton Court of the *Maid of Sker*.

Now Sir Robert and his wife were both descended from the Plantagenets — his wife certainly, and Sir Robert himself, if there was any truth in the allegation that his great-great-grandmother was the illegitimate daughter of Edward IV. Be that as it may, the knight saw fit to join himself to the inglorious company of claimants to the vacant throne of the Virgin Queen, two hundred in number ; and, on the accession of King James, he had, in consequence to escape down the river Taw and sail into the open sea *en route* for the Continent. Two years later an edict was promulgated, assuring the pretenders that, on dutiful submission, they would be allowed to escape with a fine. So the Bassets came back, and on bended knees craved King Jamie's forgiveness. Mrs Basset of Watermouth Castle is said to be the possessor of the embroidered silk apron worn by Lady Basset on this memorable occasion. The monarch used rough language, intimating to the male suppliant that he was a big bird, and that he must clip his wings—no idle threat, since he imposed a fine necessitating the sale of fifteen manors. The title also was annulled.

The next station to Umberleigh on the London and South-Western line is Burrington, where Mrs Shapland was discovered (*Maid of Sker*, chapter lxiv.).

About three miles and a half west of Southmolton lies the parish of Filleigh, in which is situate Castle Hill, the beautiful seat of Earl Fortescue, with its park of over eight hundred acres, a feature of which is an avenue of trees nearly a mile long, leading to a triumphal arch.

The name Castle Hill is actually a misnomer, as the mansion is not of the old baronial type ; but the top of the wooded eminence, on whose slope it stands, has an artificial ruin, serving to keep the description in countenance.   From the terrace the ground drops away to an ornamental lake, and what with the clusters of trees, the shrubbery, and the rare garden, Castle Hill may be fairly commended as a domain worthy of the ancient family by which it is owned.   One old building which has now disappeared, was called the " Hermitage."   This was the subject of a poem by Mr Badcock, a native of Southmolton, in the *London Magazine* for 1782, but I have been unable to discover much about it, save that it bore the inscription : " I have seen an end of all perfection, but Thy commandment is exceeding broad "—a suitable text, one may think, for a hermitage.

The grounds of Castle Hill were remodelled by Hugh Fortescue, Lord Clinton, created Earl Clinton and Baron Fortescue in 1746.   He died without issue in 1751, when the earldom became extinct.   The barony passed to his half-brother Matthew, who died in 1785, and was succeeded by his son Hugh.   In 1789 the latter was created Earl Fortescue and Viscount Ebrington, the second title being derived from his Gloucestershire seat, Ebrington Hall.   He was followed by his son, also called Hugh, who had taken an active part in the debates on the Reform Bill in the Lower House, and was appointed Lord-Lieutenant and Custos Rotulorum of the County of Devon.   An interesting episode in this noble-man's career was a visit to Napoleon in December

1814, of which he published a vivacious description.

The present earl was born in 1818. As is well known, he has long suffered from an affection of the eyes, brought about by a conscientious discharge of public duty. Viscount Ebrington, his eldest son, now occupies the honourable position so ably filled by his grandfather.

For a full history of the Fortescue family in all its branches, the reader is referred to the late Lord Clermont's large and handsome volume on the subject, of which it contains an exhaustive account. Here it may be observed that the name, which is a little remarkable, is traced to an incident in the battle of Senlac, when Richard le Fort saved the life of William, Duke of Normandy, by protecting him with his shield from the blows of his assailants. From that time, and for that reason, he was known as Richard le Fortescue, or Strong Shield. Such, at least, is Holinshed's story. Tradition further states that after the Conquest Richard returned to Normandy, where his descendants through his second son, Richard, continued to flourish till the eighteenth century. The eldest son, Sir Adam, who had also fought at Senlac, remained behind in England, and was the ancestor of all the English Fortescues.

Among the benefactors of Southmolton occurs the name of Lord Fortescue of Credan, who left £50 to the poor of the parish. A Justice of the Common Pleas, and descended from an offshoot of the Castle Hill branch (which, by the way, is not the senior), the *Conveyancer's Guide* preserves the following amusing anecdote

respecting him.   The baron was the possessor of
one of the strangest noses ever seen, much
resembling the trunk of an elephant.   " Brother,
brother," said he to the counsel, "you are handling
the case in a very lame manner."   " No, no, my
lord," was his reply, " have patience with me, and
I will make it as plain as the nose on your
lordship's face."

CHAPTER XIV

THE FORGE OF FAGGUS AND THE CURE OF CHOWNE [1]

A "TOWN" by courtesy (though Blackmore shows it no courtesy, dubbing it "a rough rude place at the end of Exmoor"), Northmolton is an inconsiderable village—that is, as regards size and population; very pretty, however, and romantic. Despite its comparative unimportance some of the inhabitants of the larger Molton cherish respect for its smaller neighbour as the seat of ancient tradition. I remember talking to a tonsorial artist — one does not speak of "barbers" nowadays—and a native of South-molton, who referred with bated breath to the Court Leet and Baron held in the sister parish, and the strange customs connected with such tribunals; and he evidently considered the Southmolton Town Council a mere mushroom institution of scant interest compared with the feudal juries. I determined to look into the matter.

There are two routes between South- and Northmolton—one the present highway along

---

[1] These worthies are coupled by Blackmore in the *Maid of Sker* (chapter lxviii.). "Since Tom Faggus died, there has not been such a man to be found, nowhere round these parts."

WHITECHAPEL BARTON (page 209).

the richly wooded valley of the Mole ; the other, doubtless more ancient, over the hill to the right, from the summit of which is obtained an excellent view of the village situated on the opposite ridge.

Northmolton is known far and wide as the birthplace of the renowned Tom Faggus, who from being a smith turned highwayman. It is only a few years ago since the forge at which he is supposed to have toiled was pulled down. It stood at the bottom of the square, next to and facing the " Poltimore Arms " ; and picture post-cards, showing what it was like, are on sale in the village. Just as I presented the reader with the pre-Blackmorian legend of the Doones, drawn from Mr Cooper's *Lynton*, so I reproduce from the same source the legend of Tom Faggus, as it existed before the publication of the romance.

Faggus and his Strawberry Horse.

Faggus was a native of Northmolton, and by trade a blacksmith, but being engaged in a lawsuit with Sir Richard Bampfylde, he was ruined, and obliged to leave his home.

He then turned a gentleman-robber, and for many years collected contributions on the highways, sometimes in company with a companion named Penn, but more frequently alone.

Many stories are told concerning his famous enchanted strawberry horse, and it was chiefly by means of this horse that Faggus escaped punishment for so long a time.

On one occasion a large party of farmers agreed to ride home together from Barnstaple Fair for the purpose of avoiding an attack from Faggus, who was supposed to be in the neighbourhood. However, when they arrived at the post on the top of Bratton-down, Faggus rode up, a cocked pistol in each hand and the reins lying on the neck of his strawberry horse; he threatened them with instant death, if they did not deposit their purses at the foot of the post. The farmers obeyed him in silent awe, and Faggus rode off with his booty.

He was seized while sitting in the ale-house at Simonsbath, but at his shrill whistle his invaluable horse, having broken down the stable door, rushed into the house, and after seriously maltreating the enemies of his master with his hoofs and teeth, bore him off in triumph. On another occasion he was recognised in Barnstaple and closely pursued to the bridge, where he was met by a party of constables, who blockaded the other end. Seeing all hopes of escape by the road completely cut off, he boldly put his horse at the parapet of the bridge. This he cleared, and swam off, to the great disappointment of his numerous assailants, who had considered his capture now as quite certain.

Intelligence being received at Exford that Faggus was to pass through that village on a certain day, a number of men were stationed in a certain part of the road to endeavour to seize him. They had not been long at their post, when Faggus rode up in complete disguise.

"Pray, my good friends," said he, "may I

ask for what purpose you are waiting here in such numbers ? "

On being answered that they were waiting for Faggus, he replied that he knew him well for a great rascal, and volunteered his services in assisting to take him. After a little more conversation he asked what firearms they had ; four or five guns were produced. He proposed that they should be discharged and reloaded, to secure their going off when required, as the dampness of the morning might have injured their priming. This was agreed to, and when his advice had been taken and the guns put for a moment *hors de combat*, he produced his pistols, and having declared his name and robbed his terrified adversaries, galloped away.

It being discovered on another occasion that Faggus had taken refuge in a house at Porlock, the whole of the inhabitants assembled ; some seized the rusty arms which had long hung neglected over their chimneys, or been emptied only in inoffensive war against the timid wildfowl ; others armed themselves with scythes, pitchforks, and other rustic weapons. They surrounded the house in a formidable array, shouting aloud, "Faggus is taken!" "Faggus is taken!" But they were mistaken. The door suddenly opened, and he rushed forth mounted on his strawberry horse, dashing through the crowd. Regardless of the blows and shots aimed at him from all sides, he disappeared, leaving them astonished and confounded at his daring and good fortune. He was at length captured in an ale-house at Exebridge, in the following curious manner.

One of the officers, equipped as an old beggar woman, entered the tap-room where Faggus was. With his usual kindness he ordered the supposed vagrant some food and liquor, and sat down near him. At a preconcerted signal the disguised constable, rising quickly, pulled the chair from under Faggus, and being thereupon joined by others who were concealed in the room, instantly fastened a rope to Faggus' feet and hoisted him up to the bacon rack. The shrill whistle Faggus gave, as was his custom when in difficulty, was given in vain, for the poor horse had been shot in the stable at the very moment the attack was made upon his master. All was now over with poor Faggus. He was tried and hanged at Taunton at the ensuing assizes.

Through his whole career not one act of cruelty was ever laid to his charge, while numerous are the acts of kindness and charity to the sick and the distressed that are recorded of him. Like the celebrated Robin Hood, he seems to have taken from the rich to give to the poor, for it required but little to supply his own immediate wants, living as he did in the most frugal manner.

On my last visit to Northmolton I was fortunate in making the acquaintance of Mr Dobbs, who represents the oldest firm of auctioneers in the district, his father and grandfather having wielded the fateful hammer before him. From this informant I learnt that over forty years ago, long before he set eyes on *Lorna Doone*, he gathered many particulars regarding Tom Faggus from Harry Lake, the parson's boy, who possessed a history of that half or wholly fabulous hero, which he was in the habit of reading whilst seated on the vicarage steps, waiting for his master and in charge of his Bucephalus. Harry afterwards emigrated to America, taking his book with him, but Mr Dobbs is able to recollect that Faggus had a relative living in Milk Street, Exeter—a poulterer. One anecdote in the book, which is mentioned also in *Lorna Doone*, was to the effect that once when Sir Robert Bampfylde, who had ruined Faggus and occasioned him the loss of his house, was riding to Barnstaple, he met the highwayman, who made him give up his purse. The next moment he threw it back, saying, "There is a rule among robbers not to rob robbers."

It is worth while to observe that if Faggus lived at the period to which Blackmore assigns him, the head of the family would have been, not Sir Robert, but Sir Coplestone, Bampfylde, one of Prince's "Worthies." As for the tale of tyranny, it is somewhat improbable; but, if true, is the more deplorable, in that the Bampfyldes themselves had endured pecks of financial trouble—a fact candidly and explicitly set forth on the great monument in the church, where mention is made of "diuturna litigia et graves impensas," which had nothing whatever to do with poor Faggus, but were undertaken for the object of regaining possession of their estates.

The two chiefs—Amias, to whom the monument was erected, and John, by whom it was erected, "pietatis ergo"—were both endued with the bump of philo-progenitiveness. The former was the father of twelve sons and five daughters, and the latter of eight sons and seven daughters. The sculptor has made a brave attempt to introduce as many figures as possible into his imposing work of art, but there was evidently scope for a sort of human ant-hill. From the way the numbers are paraded, the Bampfyldes, like the Hebrews of old, manifestly regarded a large family as a merit, or, at least, a blessing. "Happy is the man that hath his quiver full of them." Apart from the monument, the most striking feature of the church is the gorgeous display of carved oak in the chancel. The insertion of modern work in the old oak pulpit was a most wretched inspiration, whoever may have been responsible for it.

The Bampfylde family acquired the property by marriage with a coheiress of the St Maurs ; and in the course of centuries their honourable name has undergone almost every possible variety of spelling. Bamfylde, Bampfylde, Baumfield, Bampfeild, are some of the forms I have met with, but I will not answer for it that the list is exhaustive. The first baronet was Sir John Bampfylde, who received the title in 1641. The sixth baronet, the Right Hon. Sir George Warwick Bampfylde, was raised to the peerage in 1831 as Baron Poltimore, that being the name of another estate belonging to the family near Exeter. The present Lord Poltimore was born in 1837. He owns not only Court Hall, a fine old mansion standing to the east of the church, and almost hidden by trees, but Court House, an ancient ivy-covered structure, formerly the residence of the Parkers, the Earl of Morley's ancestors.

There lived in the village in those days a

charitably-disposed old lady, one Mrs Passmore, a dressmaker; and at Christmas-tide the dear old soul had always ready basins full of coppers, threepenny-bits, sixpenny bits, etc., to be distributed in the shape of doles. The Lady Morley of the period is said to have taken it into her head that this amiable custom detracted, in some measure, from the honour and reverence due to herself; so she suggested to Mrs Passmore that, as no doubt their charities overlapped, and some people had more than their share, while others had nothing, it might be well to entrust her with the combined funds, and allow her to act as almoner.

"No, my lady," was the reply, "I don't think I will. You know they come and say, 'Thankee, Lady Morley!' and 'God bless ee, Lady Morley!' but if I give away my own money, I shall have all the God bless ee's mysel'."

An apprentice of Mrs Passmore was the rather noted Mrs Treadwin, who wrote a book on lace, and from whose shop on the north-east side of Exeter Cathedral were supplied the wardrobes of generations of queens and princesses, including the wedding-dress of Queen Victoria.

The almshouses, the inmates of which live rent free and receive fourpence a week, were originally Parker property; and on the panelling round the chancel of the parish church may be detected the initials "T. P.," supposed to refer to one of the family—*not* to the well-known editor and Parliamentarian.

The Court Leet and Baron is held at the Poltimore Arms. In the bar-parlour of this hotel is a curious object—namely, a fire-back of

cast-iron, bearing the inscription, " ¹⁶ H S I ⁸⁰."
The purpose of the utensil is to throw the fire
forward and prevent it from burning the bricks.
The venue of the Court Leet, however, is not the
bar-parlour, but the large state-room on the right,
where a feast, to which Lord Poltimore contributes
thirty shillings and a hare, is held once a year.
The *personnel* consists of sixteen jurymen, twelve
of whom form the king's jury, and four that of
the manor.   The presiding officer is the Portreeve
(commonly known as the " Mayor "), and his
subordinates include a Bailiff, Ale Tasters, and
Searchers of the Market.   The Court Leet
possesses copper cups used as measures, but it
may be mentioned, parenthetically, that the
Searchers have not been round lately, as they
found on a certain occasion that their own
weights were not just.   Mr Dobbs's father
served for a long time as Bailiff, the only pay
he received being a dinner, while Mr Dobbs
himself has been Portreeve, and though now
quit of the office, is chaffingly greeted as " Mr
Mayor."   This jest has been doing duty for at
least half a century, but somehow the humour
does not grow stale, and nobody is so foolish as
to object.

The most colossal witticism attaching to
Northmolton concerns a certain Peter, which
appellation is, or used to be, in great favour in
the village.   The Peter in question was taken ill
and died, whereupon a district visitor, or somebody of the sort, called to condole with the widow.

" So you have lost your good man ? "

" Iss," replied Betty, " Peter's gone to Belze-
bub's bosom."

TOM FAGGUS'S FORGE, NORTHMOLTON (page 217).

"Pst!" said the visitor, "you don't know what you'm talking about."

"P'raps I don't," answered Betty, placidly, "Peter and me never could mind the names of great folks."

Five miles from Northmolton is the village of Charles, so long the home of the Rev. Richard Blackmore, the uncle of the novelist. During his incumbency a Northmolton man, fond of lifting his right arm, called on business at the rectory, and was immediately taken in hand by the rector's wife.

"Did you notice any wood-stacks as you came along?" she inquired.

"Yes, ma'am—a good many."

"And did you see any pigs?"

"Pigs, ma'am? Yes, I ran up against one."

"Ah, well; do you know why there are so many pigs at Charles?"

"No, I don't," replied the man, puzzled.

"Then I will tell you—because there is no public-house here," concluded the lady, triumphantly.

Almost due north of Charles is the parish of High Bray, where is a farmhouse called Ludcote, Liddicot, or Lidcote. The last is Sir Walter Scott's spelling of the name, which is, after all, a secondary matter. What is of more importance is the imputed connection with the place of Amy Robsart and her family. Chapter xii. of *Kenilworth* commences as follows: "The ancient seat of Lidcote Hall was situated near the village of the same name, and adjoined the wild and extensive forest of Exmoor, plentifully stocked with game, in which some ancient rights belong-

2 F

ing to the Robsart family entitled Sir Hugh to pursue his favourite amusement of the chase." On the faith of this statement it has been generally assumed that the unhappy Amy sprang from a good old Devonshire stock. Reference to the standard authorities, however, has failed to discover the slightest trace of such a family, and one or two antiquaries of repute, whom I have consulted, confess themselves utterly at a loss to explain the allusion. It is a suspicious circumstance that in neither his introduction nor his notes does the author throw any light on the Devonshire connections of his heroine, and for all these reasons combined I am disposed to regard this portion of his narrative as wholly imaginary.

As the topic is literature, I may here allude to a contemporary writer, whose portrait I purchased in a shop opposite the Poltimore Arms. At the time I was quite ignorant of his precise claim to celebrity, and the silk hat, frock coat and walking-stick were too conventional to suggest genius, though the face, perhaps, was not strictly normal. However, experience told me that no man would figure on a picture post-card unless possessed of unusual gifts, and it turned out that Mr Richard Slader was a poet and a solitary, whose recreations—to borrow a hint from *Who's Who?*— consist in keeping a hundred head of poultry and selling nuts and blackberries at Southmolton Fair. About forty-five years of age, and careless of appearances, he might be taken, as somebody expressed it, for an "old tramp," but he belongs to a respectable family; indeed, the name occurs in the Blackmore pedigree. Moreover, it is known that his father left him a good round sum of money. Slader talks broad Devonshire, and "Rachard and his pigs" have passed into a proverb. Swine have been a source of infinite worry to him. Certain of the species owned by his sister at Pixyweek became infected with anthrax, and were ordered by the police to be destroyed. This annoyed Mr Slader, and he gave vent to his indignation in a poem. On another occasion he was summoned for allowing his own pigs to stray on the highway, convicted, and fined. Resentment at this petty tyranny led to his penning an effusion, which was printed and circulated in leaflet form.

Like all poets, Mr Slader has his critics and detractors. In a counter-leaflet put forth by some "snake in the grass," he is reviled as the "silly old man of Northmolton," but the hiss of these ignoble stanzas is as far beneath his polished verse as it is possible to conceive. It is proper to add that Mr Slader indited pathetic and very pious compositions on the deaths of his mother and sister, so that his graceful muse is not always wedded to satire.

"With various talents, variously we excel," and as at Molland Cross we are not very far from Molland parish, in which Tom Faggus had land (*Lorna Doone*, chapter xlvi.), I am tempted to make a passing allusion to another family represented in the Blackmore pedigree — the Quartlys of Champson. When the Quartlys first sprang into fame as cattle-breeders, I cannot precisely state, but as such they certainly enjoyed a high reputation at the commencement of the last century, and they attained perhaps the acme of distinction during the reign of George IV., when their red kine were never shown at Smithfield without winning first prizes. The best animal painters in England visited Champson to inspect the stock, and among the rest came H. B. Chalon, animal painter to the king, who drew a sketch of two cows, afterwards engraved by Raddon for Mr White, of Pilton House, and dedicated to Mr T. W. Coke, M.P. for Norfolk.[1]

The Quartlys no longer reside at Champson, the death of the late Mr John Quartly on the railway, a few years ago, having led to the severance of a connection which had lasted for generations.[2]

The parish of Molland is associated with that of Knowstone. For centuries they have been consolidated as one benefice, and formed the original of Blackmore's "Nympton-in-the-Moors." Here, I must improve on this precedent by including a third parish, Lapford, which lies in a southerly direction. The reason is as follows. A reader of the *Maid of Sker*, who is also familiar with North Devon, must be struck with the, no doubt, intentional looseness of the geographical references. From a perusal of the romance, it would be natural to conclude that "Nympton-in-the-Moors" is much nearer Barnstaple and the coast than is actually the case,[3] and that no considerable town like

[1] See Note I., p. 280.   [2] See Note II., p. 280.
[3] True, in chapter liii. Blackmore speaks of the place as five or six leagues distant from Heddon's Mouth ; still, Chowne's frequent appearances at Barnstaple and beyond, and such indications as the fate of the Sherwill girl (chapter xlvii.), produce the opposite impression.

Southmolton is interposed between them. Southmolton is ignored also in favour of Tiverton, for, although "Nympton" is in the rural deanery of the former town, it is to the old church of St Peter, Tiverton, that Chowne is appointed by his bishop to bring his young people to a "noble confirmation" (*Maid of Sker*, chapter liii.). The name "Nympton" is common in Devon, where there are four or five villages so called, and distinguished from each other by some addition like "King's," "Bishop's," "George," etc. Besides these there is the form "Nymet" (apparently contracted in the first syllable of "Nympton"), which is found in Nymet-Roland, near Lapford, which, by virtue of the watercourses, stands in more direct relation to Barnstaple than the parishes before named. Still, I do not deny that on the whole, Blackmore intended by "Nympton-in-the-Moors" Knowstone-cum-Molland, of which the Rev. John Froude ("Parson Chowne"), who died in 1852, was incumbent for forty-seven years. It is distinctly stated that "Parson Chowne happened to have two churches" (*Maid of Sker*, chapter xxviii.), but it appears to me that, for certain purposes, he blended with them the parish of Lapford, of which his nephew, the notorious John Radford ("Parson Rambone"), was rector.

It was at Nymet-Roland that the "naked people," who bulk so largely in the *Maid of Sker*, lived in semi-nudity and utter savagery, in an old cottage of clay, of which one wall had given way, so that in their only room grass grew on the earth floor. They stole what clothes they required, and continually got into trouble with the police, one of whom was felled to the ground by a girl of the family. Contrary to Blackmore's account, they were finely built, muscular, and strong. The patriarch of the race died at Whitstone, having spent his declining years in a cider cask; and about 1860 the family was dispersed. These people were called Cheriton, and as they lived on their own freehold, could not be interfered with, until financial difficulties arose, which compelled them to give up possession.

Froude's real "lambs" were not of this description, but ordinary village folk. With these his word was law, and no matter how extravagant his commands, they were obeyed to the letter. Though a man of unquestioned ability, the parson hardly possessed the diabolical cunning of Chowne, but it is to be feared that he had no small share of his cruel malice, and he carried buffoonery to a pitch utterly inconsistent with his cloth and calling. His moral character was such that his relations, some of whom I know, regard him as outside the pale of apology; while old labourers, who remember his white hat, though perhaps none too good themselves, are shocked to recall such conduct in a "minister." Froude never issued instructions directly; he preferred oblique methods. Thus he would be riding along where a group of men were at work, and begin to mutter, "I'm certain sure Farmer Besley's fuzz-brake will be burnt—I know 'twill." The nearest man would prick up his ears, and, having accomplished the prophecy, would return to the spot, where he would find a sovereign on the gate-post. At another time, Froude would say to a follower severely, "Look here, John, don't you cut off that donkey's tail"—pointing to an animal on the other side of the hedge. The next day the unfortunate animal would be found minus its appendage. Froude's "lambs" were staunch to him, and years afterwards one of them, called Peagram, who lived at Southmolton, refused to divulge anything of their relations.

Parson Chowne was a marrying man—having, it will be recollected, three wives in succession ; Froude was twice married, his second wife being Miss Halse, daughter of "Squire" Halse, a yeoman farmer of Pulworthy. Tradition says that he officiated at the lady's christening, and, at the convivial party given in honour of the event, observed that, if the girl baby lived to grow up, he would marry her. From another source I have heard that, when he was courting her, he and her father would stay up late, drinking, and Froude, by no means so abstinent as the terrible Chowne, generally got into a condition which rendered it necessary for him to be "personally conducted" to Knowstone by one of the men, who would ride behind him, buoy him up in the saddle, and lift him from his horse at the end of the journey, and make himself responsible for his safety. Sad to say, Froude was neither civil nor grateful, and although consciously incapable, heaped all kinds of profane and opprobrious epithets on his companion. "You only do it for your guts' sake. Go back—go back, or I'll yaw (thrash) tha." Bragg did not dare to dismount, knowing that if he showed signs of fear Froude would be as good as his word, and give him a good horse-whipping.

Froude could be a perfect gentleman if he chose, and, when in his capacity as master of hounds, he entertained sportsmen like Lord Portsmouth to dinner, he acquitted himself with surprising ease and some amount of refinement. But he was always relieved when such ordeals were over and he had attended the last of his guests to the door. He would then turn to a boon companion with the remark, "Thank Heaven, George; I've been a gentleman long enough. Come into the kitchen, and have some grog."

Radford was nothing like so prominent a character as Froude, but he was, if possible, even more disreputable. He was tall and well built, and his favourite recreation was fighting. As to time and place, he was not at all particular, and was often seen in the boxing booths at South-molton Fair giving an exhibition of his powers. Radford seems to have had quite a mania for pugilism. Once he invaded a gipsy encampment, and offered a sovereign to any of them who could beat him. The best man was picked, but proved of no use against the parson, who thereupon offered to fight the next, and eventually went through about a dozen of them, each new opponent being buoyed up with the hope that Radford was getting worn out with his exertions. But the hope turned out delusive.

In the same way, when the railway was being cut between Exeter and Barnstaple, Radford appeared among the navvies, issuing challenges

CHANCEL, NORTHMOLTON CHURCH (page 222).

right and left, and, as they were accompanied with offers of money, his gages of battle were eagerly taken up. The navvies, as a rule, fared no better than the gipsies, but one man named Tolly, who was afterwards a stationmaster on the line, was credited with the proud distinction of having beaten the redoubtable rector.

The Hon. Newton Fellowes, afterwards Lord Portsmouth, used to drive a four-in-hand, and occasionally experienced trouble with lazy carters, who did not make room for him as fast as he could wish, and whom he punished with a slash of his whip. One day Radford got himself up as a carter, and, lying down inside the cart, pretended to be asleep. On came Newton Fellowes, who, finding the carter deaf to his commands, flew into a perfect fury and began to flourish his whip. At the first touch up jumped Radford, and administered to his lordship the worst drubbing he ever had in his life.

As I have said, however, Radford was by no means Froude's equal, and as the Parson Rambone of the romance, rightly holds a secondary place. Radford, not Russell, was the original of the character, since Blackmore himself told Mr Bryan, of Southmolton, that the former was his model. Froude's redeeming virtue was his success as a sportsman, and the following article from the *Sporting Magazine* for 1821 shows in what esteem he was held by the hunting community.

Close of Mr Froude's Season in North Devon.

Experience teaches us that happiness is unattainable without reciprocity. I do not mean

2 G

that in all our actions we are to look out for an equivalent; reason and Scripture equally denounce such selfishness; but if in our amusements and recreations we are partially dependent on others, some attention must inevitably be paid to the feelings and predilections of our fellow-mortals. The galling yòke of feudalism is long ago removed; and it is better to be loved than dreaded. The rod of iron may chastise, but cannot win the affections, nor repress resentment; which, if not cancelled by kindness will, sooner or later, burst forth with the devastating fury of an avalanche. When a perfect understanding is established between sportsmen and farmers, game is seldom wanting, and every facility is afforded in following the hounds. A more harmonious feeling of unanimity and respect I never beheld, than at a hunting feast the other day at the house of Mr Froude, the master of a crack pack of harriers in the North of Devon. I may say *the* crack pack; in which Nimrod will, I think, agree, as he has signalised some of the hounds in your magazine, particularly old Guilty. We need not refer to Buffon for arguments to prove the sagacity of the canine species, as old Guilty has given abundant proof of it. The efficient number of the pack is about twenty-five couples; the hunting days are Mondays, Wednesdays, and Fridays: Guilty, though kept at a farmhouse nearly three miles distant from the kennel, always attended of her own accord on hunting mornings. If too late, one of the servants had only to point to her the direction the hounds went, and she invariably joined them without the aid of a compass.

At the end of a hunting season it is a custom with many masters of hounds to invite the yeomen and farmers over whose land they hunt, to dinner, thereby verifying the old adage, *finis coronat opus.* The other day I was present at one of those dinners or hunting feasts given by Mr Froude, where there were from fifty to sixty persons enjoying the good things of life, and where

"The story ran in such familiar strains,
With so much humour and so little pains."

On such occasions particular customs are strictly observed. The host resigns his domestic sovereignty into the hands of his guests, who appoint a Tapster from their own body, a Sword to enforce fines, and a Judge to settle disputes and to keep up ancient customs, who, in this instance, executed his office with the impartiality of a Rhadamanthus, particularly in seeing that his Sword performed his duty with justice in the sconcing department. On a table were huge flagons of foaming old October, with four magnums, or, as the classics say, *magna,* of spirits, surrounded with drinking cups, horns, and glasses, marked with hunting devices. Among other toasts, "the King" was drunk, while standing, at *one draught,* in tolerably large tumblers : and those who were not particular in doing so were fined, as his Judgeship said, for cutting His Majesty in two—such being the established rule handed down from their fore-fathers. At all events the toast was a loyal one, and I wonder King Charles had it not inserted among his golden rules. Youngsters on their first introduction had to pledge the Judge in a glass of neat spirits; and after this matriculating ceremony was over they were considered as efficient members.   One of the initiated gave us a hunting song; and his memory having failed him in three or four instances, the inexorable Judge fined him a wineglassful of brandy for each omission; and ere he finished his melody, his head reclined on the mahogany, and he softly reposed himself in the arms of Morpheus.   I was excused fines, not being a member of the club.

> " It always has been thought discreet
> To know the company you meet;
>   And sure there may be secret danger
>   In talking much before a stranger.
> Agreed: what then? then drink your ale,
> I'll pledge you, and repeat my tale."

His Lordship the Judge now stood up to propose THE TOAST—viz., " Success to the merry harriers and their worthy master! Whoever does not preserve game, and allow him to follow his hounds wherever he pleases, is a craven, *et cetera, et cetera!* "—(what the *et ceteras* are I must beg leave to be silent)—which was received with tumultuous applause.   The contents of the cups disappeared with such a magic rapidity that Macbeth's words, " Damn'd be he who first cries hold! enough!" would have been an exceedingly appropriate motto.   I did not see the finale; but I saw quite enough to convince me that a little attention timely applied has gained Mr Froude the goodwill of all his neighbours.   Our English yeomen are composed of too tough materials *to be driven;* they require as much management as a restive horse; however, with a little tact they can *be easily led.* A rough, generous, and hospitable yeoman is a perfect epitome of JOHN BULL. Who can read Sir W. Scott's description of Dandy Dinmont without a feeling of admiration? The neighbouring poor also partook of the entertainment; and the day is always looked upon as a jubilee by the villagers.

Mr Froude is generally allowed to be one of the first hare-hunters in the West of England. One glance of his is sufficient to find out the good and bad points of a dog. His first instructions he received at the hands of the late Mr Karslake, and it may be justly said of him that he was bred up at the feet of Gamaliel. The moment his leading-strings were thrown aside, he set about organising a pack of harriers, to which he has ever since devoted the greater part of his time. Hounds are kept by many for the sake of effect and parade, by way of getting a name in the Sporting World; but it cannot be said so in this instance. Sportsmen being so few in the neighbourhood of Knowstone, the field mostly consists of persons staying at the Vicarage, a few surrounding friends, and an occasional wandering lover of the chase, attracted by the fame of the Knowstone pack. The hounds, in size, shape, and colour, bear a wonderful similarity to each other. I recollect once, on meeting the Tivy-side Hunt on the Welsh Hills, my remarking that one of the hounds bore a strong similarity to Mr Froude's breed of hounds, which I found on inquiry came from Devonshire—so strong is the family likeness through the whole pack. When a man's principal attention has for years been devoted to the breed of hounds, it must ultimately arrive at the maximum of perfection, particularly if the person, like Mr Froude, understands his business well. The prominent points of his hounds are :—height nineteen inches, considerable length of back, immense strong loins, with firm and well-shaped haunches, productive of speed and durability : they are particularly quick in all their movements : one should have the flying arrow of Ababis to follow them ; and their note is sharp and cutting. A friend of mine used to say that "a deep-mouthed Southern hound" sounded well in poetry, but it always reminded him of a cathedral bell. The deep and solemn tone of Great Tom is very well at Lincoln ; but the sharp and cheering cry of harriers is much more invigorating to the spirits on a raw and cold morning on the bleak hills of Devonshire.

Had Nimrod time during his Devonshire Tour to call on Mr Froude, he would have had many amusing anecdotes. One of those whose minds are chiefly devoted to the admiration of their pretty selves happened once to join the Knowstone pack, and kept on in spite of hints, though pointedly given, clearing banks and furze bushes to the manifest danger of the dogs' lives. A hare at last was started ; off went the parson and the dandy side by side until they came to the margin of a bog. His reverence instantly tightened one of his bridle-reins, and continued to spur his nag, which gave it the appearance of shying. The dandy went in neck and crop ; and thus the nuisance was got rid of by "his own act and deed," as the lawyers say. However, he was soon landed, and had every attention paid him. This I had from the late poor Jack Harvey, who was a tolerable master of the laconic style. The late Marsh, Fauntleroy & Company used to be his bankers. I recollect when he wanted the needful to go to Warwickshire, his addressing Mr Marsh thus : " Dear Agent, send me some coin. I am yours, etc." When his house in Devon was burnt, he acquainted his guardian with the accident thus : " Dear Nunky, I have no *domus :* ditto is burnt." His brother, who was then studying at St John's, Cambridge, offered him his purse : for his kind offer he was answered thus : " Dear George, I thank you for your Balm of Gilead letter ; send me fifty pounds." Coulton himself could not have improved on this.

Mr Froude has hunted the fox more frequently for the last two years than he used to do, and has bred two couples of hounds out of a favourite harrier bitch of his own by a clever foxhound from the celebrated blood of George Templar, Esq. : these are reserved expressly to go with the harriers, when drawing for a fox, to keep them steady to the varmint. Here instinct is clearly shown on the drag ; and when the pack is well settled to the line of scent, the quickness and vivacity of the merry harrier are quickly apparent. They have this season, I hear, had some brilliant runs, an animated account of which has been given in our provincial papers by a gentleman from the neighbourhood of Exeter, attracted to visit the pack by common fame, like the Queen of Sheba, when she paid a visit to Solomon.

The hunting season is now over ; the horn is replaced in its case ; the whip is suspended from the nail, denoting a suspension of field sports

The fox and the hare are allowed to revel un-
molestedly over hill and dale, secure from the
thrilling " tally-ho " and " gone away " of the keen
and determined sportsman.   A straggling hound
may now and then steal unperceived to remind
them of their implacable foes.   However, the
period will arrive

" When bright Aurora shall unbar the morn,
    And light discover Nature's cheerful face ;
The cracking whip and the loud-sounding horn
    Will call blithe huntsmen to the distant chase.

" Eftsoons they issue forth a goodly band,
    The sharp-tongued hounds with music rend the air,
The fiery coursers strike the rising sand ;
    Far through the thicket flies the frighted hare.

" Froude the honour of the day supports,
    His presence glads the woods, his orders guide the
    chase."

—LEEK.

ASHFORD CHURCH, NEAR BARNSTAPLE.

CHAPTER XV

To Barnstaple, capital of North Devon, and capital also of the *Maid of Sker*, or such portions of the story as relate to the county, proceed we now. Already we have winged brief flights to the neighbournood in connection with Heanton Court and Ashford, one of Blackmore's early homes described so lovingly in the above-named romance. The scenes appear very real, and would have been still more so but for the construction of the railway, which shuts off from the view the house and the old boat-stage (*Maid of Sker*, chapter xxxix.). The true name of "Deadman's Pill," which was opposite Ashford, is Fremington Pill or Penhill, a creek in which there was a sort of dock, where the larger vessels anchored, and received or delivered cargoes.

Barnstaple is a place on which it would be a pleasure to bestow many a page of garnered lore, and the district around is no less delightful to the lover of the past. This being the case, it may be well to premise that my hope is, in a subsequent volume on the Kingsley country, to amplify the account here given, and this must excuse seeming deficiencies.

The recollections of old inhabitants are always interesting, and it may be laid down that, next to our own, no age attracts like that immediately preceding it, out of which we are sprung, and in which Blackmore flourished. Therefore I account it a fortunate accident that made me for a short time an inmate in the house of Mr Parminter, one of the makers of modern Barnstaple, who drew my attention to a remarkable fact—that in the old days the town was provided with iron gates, which were closed at night, to keep out tramps and travellers. Mr Parminter remembers two—those in High Street and Cross Street. Boutport Street, where Parson Rambone challenged all and sundry, must also have had its gate.

A great support of old Barnstaple was the shipping industry. Vessels of one hundred to two hundred tons were built here and owned by Barnstaple men, amongst whom was Mr Bament, father of Mrs Carruthers Gould, who was also a tanner. The ships were employed in different services, and known as London traders, Liverpool traders, Bristol traders, etc., according to the port of arrival. Their cargoes were of all kinds—groceries, draperies, and general merchandise. There was also a considerable traffic in Scotch herrings. The quays, of which there were four —three above Barnstaple Bridge—were at right angles to the river. At present, ships are barred from coming up beyond a certain distance by the railway bridge. Below this, however, is the Rolle Quay (so called after the Rolle family, to whom it belongs), which is still accessible, and where much business is done. When in

Barnstaple recently, I watched a sailing ship from
the opposite bank, and her action in entering
curiously resembled that of a mouse stealing into
its hole. One of the services of the Barnstaple
vessels was as emigrant ships, and Mr Bament
helped to export hundreds of sturdy colonists to
the Antipodes. In the *Maïd of Sker* (chapter
xxx.), the "Tawton fleet" of brown-sailed lighters
is referred to; the river is navigable for barges
and small craft to about three miles above the
town.

Mr Parminter has many appetising reminiscences of parliamentary elections, which in days
of yore were in the hands of the freeman. This
position was esteemed a valuable privilege, since
it carried with it other rights, not merely that of
voting. Mr Parminter, for instance, as a
freeman, was able, when building a chapel at
Ilfracombe, to convey all the material by sea
without paying quay dues. As to politics,
however. Adjoining the North Walk is a
mansion called the Castle, in the grounds of
which is a raised mound, on which in former times
guns were mounted for the defence of the river
passage. This house was occupied for many
years by Mr Brembridge, M.P. for the borough
(commonly known as "Dick Brembridge"), who
was pitted against Lord Ebrington, the present
Lord Fortescue, on one occasion, and, together
with his colleague, unseated for bribery. His
lordship, however, was unable to occupy either of
the vacant places, as one of his own agents was
convicted of corruption, to the tune of £10. This
was really a modest amount, seeing that in 1841
as much as £80 was paid for a single vote.

There were other modes of gaining or retaining support, and amongst these may be reckoned a champagne breakfast at the King's Arms, which Mr Parminter recollects attending when quite a boy, with his father. A famous contest was that in which Messrs Hudson and Gore, the former a wealthy brewer, succeeded in ousting the Hon. John Fortescue, brother of the present Earl, and Sir John Palmer Chichester ("Arlington Jack"), representing two of the oldest local families.

All the world has heard of Mr F. Carruthers Gould, the renowned caricaturist, but all the world may not know that, although not a resident in the town, Mr Gould is a thorough Barnstaple man, and his wife, as we have seen, is a Barnstaple lady. The Goulds are an old Barnstaple family. The grandfather of F. C. G. was a lime and slate merchant, and his father, Mr Richard David Gould, a very clever architect, in large practice, who designed the market and many private residences, including the house in which Mr Parminter lives and I lodged. Prior to this my excellent landlord occupied the Castle, an hotel which he built for himself in the street of the same name, where he had Mr R. D. Gould himself as a paying guest. In his youth Mr Carruthers Gould was a clerk in the Old Bank, and, whilst in that position, presumed to caricature old Trewin, the jailor — a terrible personage, with a great capacity for holloaing. The sight of the picture enraged him beyond measure, and it is said he was almost for murdering the daring young artist.

For many years Barnstaple has known no

such benefactor as the late Mr W. F. Rock, who, I believe, started in life as a linen-draper and lived to found the North Devon Athenæum, which originated in a debating society. He was the author of a dialogue in the North Devon dialect, and took an interest in many other things besides literature. For instance, he gave a most useful stimulus to the slumbering artistic taste of the townspeople; and the wonderful development of Barum ware and cabinet work may be attributed, directly or indirectly, to the seed sown by this wise and patriotic townsman.

From this gossip of recent days I turn to severer researches, suggested in part by points that have already cropped up—for instance, the matter of the castle. When Barnstaple Castle was first erected, whether by King Athelstan or some other Saxon ruler, cannot be accurately stated. This much is certain—that there was ample reason for such a fort in Anglo-Saxon times, since the berserker Hubba appeared in the neighbourhood, and at the mouth of the Taw is the so-called Hubba-stone, supposed to mark his grave. Two other Norse chieftains, Crida and Putta, are reputed to have given their names to Croyde and Putsborough. The castle was rebuilt or considerably extended by Judhel de Totnes, a favourite of William the Conqueror, to whom he, William, granted the borough of Barnstaple, and who occasionally resided there. He also repaired the town walls. Judhel was afterwards banished, and the barony and castle, after passing through a number of different hands, came at length to Sir John Chichester, who in 1566 conveyed the entire manor, with the exception of the castle, to the corporation, in whom it is still vested. For some reason the fortress attracted the jealous attention of the Government, and in the reign of Henry III., A.D. 1228, a precept was directed to the Sheriff of Devon, commanding him to reduce its walls to a height not exceeding ten feet. According to Fuller, it was in the following century the principal residence of the worthy Lord Audley, but in Leland's time (1542) it was already a ruin.

"The town of Berdenstaple," he says, "hath been waulled, and the waulle was in compace by estimation half a myle. It is now almost clene faullen. The names of the four gates by east, west, north and south, yet remain, and manifest tokens of them. There be manifest ruines of a great castelle at the north-west side of the towne, a little beneath the towne bridge, and a place of dungeon yet standeth."

The next notice of the castle is found in the Journal of Philip Wyott, Town Clerk of Barnstaple from 1586 to 1608 : "1601, nineteenth day of December, at night, some of the castle walls was blown down and blown into the Castle, and did no harm, saving some ravens were found dead, and belike sat within the wall." Elsewhere the Journal tells how two hundred trained soldiers were reviewed in the Castle Green, and, how, in October 1606, a great flood "threw down the whole house wherein James Frost did dwell, whereby himself was slayne, and two children. lying within bed was slayne, with the falling of the walls, and all the walls between that and the Castle fell."

The aforesaid mound, and some remains of two

or three massive walls incorporated with the Castle House, alone are left to mark the site of the once proud river-fort. With regard to the mound, time was when it was surmounted by a small keep or watch-tower, and it is supposed that part of a wall on one side of it is a remnant of the ancient building. This had plainly vanished in 1727, when trespassers on the mound were put on their trial at Exeter.

Next, as to shipping. Barnstaple was one of the subsidiary Cinque Ports, and, as such, assisted in repelling the Spanish Armada. The local contribution to the English fleet amounted to five ships out of a total number of 197. Old Philip Wyott says briefly : " Five ships went over the bar to join Sir Francis Drake at Plymo," but Stow, in his *Annals*, supplies the names of three of them—the *Tiger*, the *God Save Her*, and the *Galleon Dudley*. On the dispersal of the dreaded Armada, letters of marque were issued by the English Government, and piracy having become both legal and respectable, Barumites engaged in it with considerable energy and success, the reprisal ships bringing in freights of gold, ivory, and wine. The *White Hart*, the *Blessing*, the *Prudence*, the *John of Braunton*, and the *Mayflower* were the names of some of these Barnstaple vessels, and in the case of the two last, complete lists of the "governors" and crews in 1612, together with inventories of the fittings, are yet extant.

One of the sights of Barnstaple is Queen Anne's Walk, with its convenient colonnade, in which one may see old men, who have borne the burden and heat of the day, resting placidly and watching the stream of traffic surge past them. Originally the building was intended as an exchange or merchant's walk, and did not acquire its present name till 1708, when it was restored by the Corporation, with the help of some noblemen ; and the statue of Queen Anne, in the costume of the period, was presented by Mr Rolle, of Stevenstone.

Not far away is Barnstaple Bridge, with its many arches, spanning the river Taw—the scene of one of Tom Faggus's exciting adventures. Westcote has a quaint tale concerning the origin of this stately bridge, which, he declares, was due to two maiden ladies, sisters, who were spinsters in both senses. Not only did they spin themselves, but they taught young children the art, and with the proceeds of their industry brought about the completion of the first two piers. Nor was this all. They obtained a license to go a-begging among good and charitable people with a view to accumulating funds for the finishing of the structure.

A terrible episode in the history of Barnstaple was the visitation of the plague in 1646. This came direct from the Levant in a vessel laden with wool, and after decimating Bideford, extended its ravages to the larger town. There is a gruesome tradition on the subject, which is worth recording, and may possibly have some foundation in fact. It is as follows. Four brothers, sons of Thomas and Agnes Ley, were fishing on the banks of the Taw, when the tide floated up a bundle. This they drew to the shore, and discovered that it was simply bedding and rugs, which had no doubt been the property of a

BARNSTAPLE BRIDGE.

sailor, and had for some reason been thrown into
the sea.   The sequel rendered it well-nigh certain
that the poor man had died of the pestilence, with
which all four brothers became infected, and of
which they all died.   As a precaution against the
further spread of the disease, the corpses were
ferried across the river to the Tawstock bank, and
interred at high-water mark.   Here a monument
was erected to their memory, and an enclosure
formed by seven elms, which, through some
confusion, resulted in the spot being named the
"Seven Brethren Bank."   In 1791 a certain
Elizabeth Horwood made a copy of the inscription on the tombstone, which she described as
standing in Higher Pill Marsh, on the east side
of the gut that emptied itself into the Taw, a
little above the higher Tawstock marsh and bank.
The epitaph, apparently genuine, is stated to
have been :—

" To the memory of our four sweet sons, John, Joseph,
Thomas, and Richard, who immaturely taken from us
altogether, by Divine Providence, are Hear inter'd, the 17
August, Anno 1646.

"Good and great God, to thee we do resigne
Our four dear sons, for they were duly thine,
And, Lord, we were not worthy of the name
To be the sonnes of faithful Abrahame,
Had we not learnt for thy just pleasure sake
To yield our all as he his Isaack.
Reader, perhaps thou knewest this field, but ah !
'Tis now become another Macpelah.
What then ?   This honour it doth boast the more,
Never such seeds were sowne therein before,
W^{oh} shall revive and Christ his angells warne
To beare with triumphe to the heavenly Barne."

From   tragedy   to   romance.   Mr Charles

Cutcliffe, of Weach, a solicitor residing at
Bideford, is the narrator ; Madam Chichester,
daughter of the Rev. Charles Howard, and relict
of Arthur Chichester, of Hall, the lady implicated,
and the Rev. George Bradford, the eloping
parson.   The incident is succinctly related in the
following letters—with a rider.

"May 21, 1728.—There was a very great
storm at Pill last Friday.   I mean within
doors, for that morning ab^t one, the parson
of Tawton and Mad^m Chichester ridd away
together without a serv^t, in order to be married ;
but where the jobb was done, I don't yet hear
with certainty.   The parson yesterday made
a visit in his coach, and no doubt looks very
grand.

"June 9, 1728.—I think I wrote you that the
Viccar of Tawton had married Mad^m Chichester.
I must now acquaint you that Coz^n Moll
Chichester was married to Mr Waldron, her old
sweetheart, the Monday following, but not discovered till last week.   I had the pleasure
yesterday of bringing father and daughter
together at Pill, where all things were perfectly
reconciled, and am forthwith to prepare an
handsome settlement."

Tawstock Court, a long castellated building,
and Tawstock Church, which has been called the
"Westminster Abbey of the West," encompassed
with old woods, and so closely linked that they
may almost be regarded as one, are near
neighbours of Bishop's Tawton, the home of the
romantic vicar.   Their unity of interest may be
illustrated by an ancient custom depicted in a
print belonging to Sir Bourchier Wrey, and a

much valued heirloom. In the churchyard are
two ivy-covered pillars, the remains of a gateway
through which the family at the mansion walked
on their way to church, while behind them, in
solemn procession, marched their servants and
retainers.

A full account of the contents of this most
sumptuous church is beside my purpose, but
attention may be drawn to some of its more
important features. In the north transept is a
square wainscoted seat, which has a canopy
adorned with coloured bosses, and on the cornice
are Bourchier knots. The latter circumstance
suggests that it was the state pew of the
Bourchiers, Earls of Bath, though the opinion
has been hazarded that it was a confessional
box. The late Sir Gilbert Scott thought the
best piece of carving in the building the
little gallery leading into the belfry, the principal adornment being the vignette or running
decoration of leaves and tendrils. The bench-
ends also, with their alto-rilievo of rose, pome-
granate, and royal arms, are excellent specimens
of wood-carving.

The beautiful screen was erected by John
Bourchier, second earl, whose arms and quarter-
ings, impaling those of his countess, the Lady
Elinor, are to be seen on the outside of the church
over the priest's door.

The monuments are of almost unparalleled
splendour. The "goodliest of all," as Risdon
has it, is that erected to the memory of William
Bourchier, third earl, and his wife, Lady
Elisabeth Russell, daughter of Francis, Earl of
Bedford, whose armorial bearings are fully

blazoned. The recumbent figures of the earl and countess are life-size, and the colouring of their crimson robes, lined with ermine, is still perfect. The fifth and last earl, Henry, was honoured with a large sarcophagus, which is surmounted by "an elegant black urn," supported by four griffins. Beside it stands the marble statue of his wife, the Lady Rachel Fane, daughter of Francis, Earl of Westmorland. The work of Bernini, a famous Florentine sculptor, it is mounted on a decorated pedestal of circular form. A square canopy, built in memory of Lady Fitzwarren and her babes in 1586, adorns the south wall, and under an arch in the north wall of the chancel is the recumbent figure of a lady, *temp*. Edward III., carved in wood.

An ancient chest in a small room, to which access is gained by a flight of old oak stairs, preserves the remains of a collection of armour of the style worn by musketeers in the reign of Charles I., and till 1832 "as good as new." In that year a visitor requested permission to purchase it, but was informed that he was just too late—it had been sold to a Taunton man as old iron. And so nearly the whole of the morions, gorgets, back and breast-plates, wheel-lock guns and bandoliers, which were deposited in this chamber until comparatively recently, have been irrecoverably lost.

Another village within easy reach of Barnstaple is Landkey, the original home of the great Devonshire family of Acland. If, however, I allude to it here, it is on account of an extra-ordinary story, for which old Westcote vouches,

and which may as well be given in his own quaint
language.

"In this parish of Landkey are two towns
(indeed both will make but a pretty village were
they joined), named Easter and Wester Newlands ;
a thoroughfare much travelled, as being not passing two miles from Barnstaple. These are somewhat dangerous to be passed by strangers ; not
for thieves or such like, but to those whose
tongues are ushers to their wits, and walk before
them, such I mean as bring the cause with them ;
for if out of their blindness and boldness (for it is
no other), though they term it valour, they shall
cry out these words (I am almost afraid to
whisper them), "Camp-le-tout, Newland," held of
the good women very scandalous to their honesty,
they are instantly all up like a nest of wasps with
the first alarum, the streets are corded, the party
(or more, if more be in the company) beaten
down from his horse (if he ride) with stones, or
other dog-bolts always in readiness, so taken and
used at the pleasure of the good townswomen,
washed, shaved, and perfumed (and other like
dainty trimming, not for modesty to be spoken)
that he that travels that way a fortnight after
may smell what hath there been done ; and he
that hath made the trial will confess, by experience,
that it is folly for a wise man to anger a multitude
causelessly.

> "Believe what I set down for your behoof
> Or come that way and find it true by proof."

The great event in Barnstaple was, and
perhaps is, its fair, for which David Llewellyn

arrived just in the nick of time, establishing his
headquarters at the " Jolly Sailors " in Bear
Street.   I cannot find that any hostelry of that
name ever existed in this thoroughfare, which,
however, boasted the " Ebberly Arms," the
" Rolle Arms," and the " Northmolton Inn."
The importance of Barnstaple Fair is beyond
dispute, and formerly was much greater.   It is
still the largest in the county, both for business
and pleasure.   The opening ceremony is quaint ;
for a company assemble in the Guildhall, where
the Mayor provides a feast of mulled ale, toast,
and cheese.   On such occasions the civic plate
is displayed, including two massive silver flagons,
which are among the few Elizabethan municipal
drinking-vessels in the country ; and another
interesting piece is the punch-bowl presented
by Thomas Benson, who forgot to supply the
ladle, but afterwards repaired the omission, and
caused the latter to be inscribed " He who gave
the bowl gave the ladle."   Benson represented
Barnstaple in Parliament, but having cheated
the Government by sending convicts to Lundy
Island instead of abroad, was compelled to fly
the country.   Numerous speeches are made by
the Mayor and others, after which a procession is formed and wends its way to
the High Cross, where the Fair is formally
proclaimed.

The duration of the Fair is three days, the
first being devoted to the buying and selling of
cattle.   In the middle of the last century
£20,000, it is said, was often expended in the
purchase of live stock.   The cattle fair used to
be held in Boutport Street—the scene of

Rambone's swagger. On the second day was
the horse fair, and, in conjunction therewith, a
stag-hunt was held. The meet was on the
borders of Exmoor. The third day was given up
to sight-seeing and all manner of amusements.

CHAPTER XVI

THE SHORE OF DEATH

In relation to the *Maid of Sker*, the most important places in the immediate vicinity of Barnstaple
are undoubtedly Heanton Court, Braunton, and
Saunton. Heanton Court, as we have seen, is
only a memory. In the early part of the seventeenth century it was described as a "sweet,
pleasant seat"; and the account proceeded, "the
house is a handsome pile, well-furnished with
every variety of entertainment which the earth,
the sea, and the air can afford. A place, whether
you respect pleasure or profit, daintily situated on
an arm of the sea." A later notice speaks of it
as standing at the bottom of a park, very near the
river Taw, and acquaints us that it had a new
front of two storeys, each of which contained
eleven windows, and was ornamented with battlements, while at either end was a tower. Other
particulars have been given in a previous chapter
(see p. 211), and need not be recapitulated here.
The reader, however, may be assured of the
identity of Blackmore's Narnton Court with this
historic mansion.

Braunton is a village not easily forgotten.
The scenery is magnificent, and the great hills

TAWSTOCK CHURCH, NEAR BARNSTAPLE (page 250).

furnish admirable opportunity for climbing. On alighting at the railway station, the stranger will encounter an array of coachmen anxious to whisk him off without delay to Saunton Sands, but he will do well to resist their importunities until, at least, he has inspected the interior of Braunton Church. If he converses with the natives, somebody will be sure to tell him that three successive attempts were made to erect it on Chapel Hill, and that each time the building collapsed, the assumed reason being that the spot chosen by man was not the site approved and predestined by Heaven. He will learn also that in the panel work of the roof of the church, carved on one of the bosses, is the representation of a sow with a litter of pigs. This singular emblem is associated with St Brannock, the Irish missionary ; indeed, the very name of the place is said to have been originally Brannock's town, and it is averred that he founded a church on the site of the present one. As for the sow and her offspring, the legend is that St Brannock was commanded in a dream to rear a Christian temple on the spot where he should light on this vision of fecundity ; and it is added that he fetched the timber on a plough, to which he yoked the red deer of the adjacent forests, " who mildly obeyed him," while he milked the complaisant hinds. The old writer concludes summarily : " But to proceed no farther and to forbear to speak of his cow (which, being killed, chopped in pieces, and boiling in his kettle, came out whole and sound at his call), his staff, his oak, and his man Abel, which would seem wonders — yet all these you may see lively represented unto you in a fair glass window as this present, if you desire it."

Mr Z. E. A. Wade characterises this venerable tradition rather fiercely as a "senseless story," and proposes a symbolic interpretation which is certainly ingenious, and in the main not unlikely to be correct.

"Popular story says he tried in vain to build on a certain spot, but was bidden in a dream to rear his proposed church where he should encounter a litter of pigs.   He was to rebuild the work of earlier saints, the *pige* or *pigen*, female teachers, who had before his day fulfilled the promise of the Psalmist, 'The women that publish the tidings are a great host.' *Pige* is the Danish word for a maid; *piga* is the Anglo-Saxon form, hence the diminutive of Margaret. So Peg-cross is not unknown. . . .

"The cow or ox of sacrifice—also on an ancient church of Youghal—which finds place in his story, is suggested by the name of the place whence he came, Cowbridge, and by the covering of the boat in which he and his fellow-travellers came.   His staff and oak explain themselves. . . . The 'man Abel' in the story carries sticks; 'Isaac carrying wood represents Christ bearing the Cross,' said Bede in A.D. 677, a few years after Brannock's time. 'Under wood, under rood.'   This saint's man was 'the man Christ Jesus.'   The hart was one of the earliest types of the Christian, to be met with over and over again in the Catacombs, and on baptisteries, and the image of the 42nd Psalm is still used in sacred song.   It is said of monks in St David's school 'that they were required to yoke themselves to the plough and turn up the soil without the aid of oxen.' The harts at Braunton, like those on the sketch from St Andrew's, were converts."

At Braunton dwelt the fair Polly, after her days of service, and before she wedded old David (*Maid of Sker*, chapter lxiii.).

Now as to Saunton Sands, which are perhaps three miles in length, and viewed from the high ground at Braunton, form, with their grotesque hummocks, a weird background to the smiling landscape. Although efforts have been made to bind it by means of vegetation, sand continues to be blown inland, and Westcote states that in his time the wind drove it to large heaps near the house or court, by which he apparently intends Saunton Court, now a farmhouse. Between Saunton and Braunton the ruins of an ancient settlement have been seen amidst trees that have been "thrown down and overwhelmed." Westcote goes on to declare that a great quantity of the sand was removed every day to serve as manure for the fields, yet there was no diminution in the sum total, the wind constantly supplying the deficiency. On these grounds the old historian makes the name of the place "Sandton, *quasi* Sand-town."

To this Mr Wade demurs, his own derivation being "Sancton," a holy place. It seems that on Saunton Sands were chapels of St Sylvester, St Michael, and St Helen, as well as numerous palmer's crosses; and he suggests that since the Celtic missionaries set foot in the country in the sixth and seventh centuries, hundreds of acres have been submerged by the sands. This idea is

more than probable, and will remind the reader
of the early chapters of the *Maid of Sker*, which
contain realistic descriptions of similar visitations
on the coast of Wales.   In the same work
Blackmore frequently alludes to the Saunton
Sands, the scene of the fictitious burial of the
Bampfylde infants.

More famous than Saunton Sands are
Woolacombe Sands, chiefly owing to their
associations with the Tracys, some of which are
purely mythical.   There is a sensational story of
two brothers fighting a duel on Woolacombe
Sands for the hand of a waif who had been
rescued from the sea by their father; and a
notion exists that they were possibly Henry de
Tracy, who died in 1272, and his brother and co-
heir Oliver, who followed him within a year or
two after.   Dark hints are thrown out that one
of the duellists was rector of Ilfracombe from
1263 to 1272.

The most celebrated member of the family
came earlier, and he owes his celebrity to the fact
that he was one of the four assassins of Thomas
à Becket.   According to Risdon, who is decidedly
wrong, William de Tracy, after the commission
of the deed, lived in retirement at Woolacombe;
and on the south side of Morthoe Church is an
altar tomb, which Risdon and Westcote agree in
assigning to the murderer (or patriot).   The
Devonshire tradition is in flat contradiction to the
official version of the Church of Rome, which
imputes that William de Tracy died at Cosenza,
in Calabria, within four years of the sacrilege;
but other accounts testify that four years after
Becket's death Tracy was Justiciar of Normandy,

and that he survived his victim fifty-three years. These various stories are clearly irreconcilable, but one thing appears certain, that the altar tomb with the figure engraved on the grey marble and bearing the half-erased inscription, *Sqre [Guillau] me de Tracy [gist ici Dieu de son al] me eyt merci*, has absolutely nothing to do with any secular person. The figure is that of a priest in his robes, holding a chalice with both hands over his breast, and that priest was William de Tracy, rector of Morthoe, who died in 1322.

Blackmore does not say much of the Tracys, although he brackets them with the Bassets and "St Albyns" as an old West-country family. (See *Maid of Sker*, chapter lxvi.).

It is singular to find a remote spot like Woolacombe identified with political adventure, although it might have been, at one time, an apt place "to talk treason in." Odd to say, the Tracys of Woolacombe-Tracy have not been the only men to bring the great world, as it were, to these yellow sands. Already I have quoted the gossiping Cutcliffe; now I will quote him once more. In a letter of October 8, 1728, he writes :

"Last Sunday se'nnight, the Duke of Ripperda (who lately escaped out of the Castle of Segovia) was putt on Woolacombe Sands, out of an Irish barque; he had no one with him but the lady who procured his deliverance, the corporal of the guard, and one servant. He was handsomely treated at Mr Harris's, and last Tuesday went on to Exon."

The Mr Harris by whom the stranger was

entertained was John Harris, of Pickwell, in the parish of Georgeham, who was twice M.P. for Barnstaple, and died in 1768, aged sixty-four. Who was the Duke of Ripperda?

Protestant, Catholic, Mussulman, soldier, courtier, diplomatist, Dutchman, Spaniard, Moor —all these parts were supported (not, of course, at one and the same time) by the extraordinary character, who appeared momentarily, in his meteoric career, on the north-west coast of Devon. The whole of his chequered life cannot be recorded here. Suffice it to say that he was born towards the end of the seventeenth century, and came of a distinguished family in Holland. Having won his spurs as a soldier, he was sent on a diplomatic mission to Madrid, where he became the trusted minister of Philip V., and was created a duke. Incurring the hostility of the Spanish grandees, he was accused of treason and thrown in 1726 into the Castle of Segovia, whence, at the date of the above letter, he had just escaped. He next turned Mahomedan, and took service with the Emperor of Morocco, who appointed him commander in his army. His attacks on the Spaniards proving unsuccessful, he was imprisoned, and solaced his captivity by elaborating a sort of *via media* between the Jewish religion and Islamism. In 1734 he was ordered to quit the country, and found an asylum in Tetuan. He died in 1737.

The northern horn of Morte Bay is formed by Morte Point, with Morte Stone in close proximity. As the spot is unquestionably dangerous, there is no risk, I imagine, in accepting the ordinary and obvious etymology—Mort.

Morte Point and Morte Stone are as tragedy and comedy. Concerning the latter there is an ancient saw, "Would you remove Morte Stone?" and for centuries it has been held that no one can accomplish the feat save the man who can rule his spouse. Another tradition asserts that the stone can be moved by a bevy of good wives exercising sovereignty over their husbands. In this connection it may be noted that the old fable of Chichevache and Bycorn (the former a sorry cow, whose food is good women; and the latter fat and well-liking, owing to abundance of good and enduring husbands) is represented on the corbels of Ilfracombe Church amidst a menagerie of apes, mermaids, griffins, gnomes, centaurs, cockatrices, and other extinct hybrids too numerous to mention.

Morthoe has a bad record for wrecking operations, which brought much discredit on this coast, and of which it was one of the principal centres. Prayers are said to have been offered that "a ship might come ashore before morning." To facilitate this blessed consummation, a lantern was tied to some animal, and by this wandering light poor mariners were lured through the treacherous mist to their doom. Even women were to be found cruel enough to participate in this murderous trade, and the tale is told that one of Eve's daughters held a drowning sailor under water with a pitchfork. Another, a farmer's wife living at a certain barton, secured as a prize some chinaware, which was arranged on her dresser. One day a sailor's widow happened to enter, and recognising the ware as belonging to her late husband's craft, seized a stick and smashed it to atoms. The farmer's wife thereupon became a prey to remorse, and not long afterwards gave herself up to justice. A painful story regards the wreck of an Italian ship, when the only person on board to reach the shore was a young and beautiful lady, who bore with her a casket of precious family jewels, saved at the risk of her life. Utterly unmoved by her tears and entreaties, the savage wreckers carried her off to one of their vile haunts, and nothing was heard of her again. Many years after the event, the jewels, it was said, were still in the neighbourhood.

The last recorded instance of this shameful practice on the north-west coast of Devon occurred in 1846, at Welcomb, near Hartland, where a vessel and her ill-fated crew were ruthlessly sacrificed to the cupidity of heartless local wreckers. By the way, Blackmore's account of a wreck in the *Maid of Sker* is perhaps founded on the circumstance that at the commencement of the great war two transports from the French West India islands, laden with black prisoners, were driven ashore at Rapparee Cove, many lives being lost, whilst, afterwards, gold and pearls were washed about among the shingle.

Rapparee Cove is at Ilfracombe, which Blackmore describes as "a little place lying in a hole, and with great rocks all around it, fair enough to look at it, but more easy to fall down than to get up them" (*Maid of Sker*, chapter lxv.).

Historically, Ilfracombe has not much of interest save the escapades of the saint-like Cavalier, Sir Francis Doddington, who in

TOWARDS MORTE POINT.

September 1644 set the place on fire, but was beaten out by the townsmen and sailors, with the loss of many of his followers. Ten days later he returned, and, falling on the town with his horse, succeeded in capturing it. "Twenty pieces of ordnance, as many barrels of powder, and near 200 arms," were amongst his spoils. Ilfracombe was retaken for the Parliament in April 1646.

Sir Francis was no lukewarm partisan, for meeting one Master James, described as "an honest minister," near Taunton, he demanded whom he was for? "For God and His Gospel," was the other's reply, whereupon the enraged knight immediately shot him.

It was to Ilfracombe that Colonel Wade, Captains Hewling and Carey, and others fled after the battle of Sedgemoor, and here they left Ferguson, their chaplain, and Thompson, captain of the Blue Regiment, whilst they themselves, having seized and victualled a vessel, put out to sea. Being pursued by two frigates, they had to land at Lynmouth, as already narrated (see p. 154).

The great charm of the neighbourhood is its bold scenery and romantic walks, one of which will conduct the wayfarer to Hele, with its old earthwork, and thence to Chambercombe, concerning which Mr Tugwell has preserved a most delightful legend, worthy to be reproduced at length :—

Chambercombe is now a retired farmhouse in a beautifully wooded valley, through which saunters the little streamlet which shortly afterwards empties itself into the sea at Hele

Strand.   The inhabitants still show the Haunted
Room to the curious in such matters—a long,
low chamber in the roof of the house, from
which the flooring has been removed, and which
is now used only for the purpose of storing
away useless lumber.   There are many versions
of the legend which belongs to this house ;
the one which I shall give seems to have the
merit of a quaint originality, and is sufficiently
mysterious in its unexplained connection with
former days.

Many years ago, the burly, ruddy-cheeked,
well-to-do yeoman who owned this farm was
sitting under the shade of a tree in his garden,
enjoying in the cool of the summer's evening his
much-loved pipe of meditation and contentment.
After a time he exhausted his usual subjects of
reverie, the state of his crops, the rise or fall of
wages, the prospects of the next Barnstaple Fair.
What should he do?   He could not "whistle for
want of thought," because of his pipe—he
couldn't even indulge in the excitement of a
matrimonial "difference of opinion," because his
wife was gone into 'Combe to sell her last batch
of chickens.   Whatever should he do?

The evening was very still and warm, not
even a breath of wind stirring in the copse on the
hillside, where the last kiss of the sunset lingered
lovingly.   He was just dropping off into a doze,
and had nodded once or twice with much energy,
to the imminent danger of his "yard o' clay,"
when it suddenly occurred to him that he had
forgotten to see about some necessary repairs in
the roof of his house, and that his spouse had a
better memory for such things than himself, and

would not fail to remind him of the same on her
return.

So he roused himself, and facing his chair in
the direction of the house, began to arrange in
his mind the when and where of his intended
operations.   The hole in the roof was over his
wife's store-room, which accounted for her anxiety
in the matter, and as he did not expect to be
allowed to interfere with that sanctum, he settled
that he would get at the roof from the next
window, which opened into a passage, and had a
low parapet in front of it.   Then he rubbed his
eyes.   Certainly the passage was next to the
store-room, and the passage window was the only
window with a parapet to it, and therefore the
next window to the parapet must be the store-
room window, and consequently must have the
hole in the roof over it—ably argued and very
conclusive.   But, to his great perplexity, the fact
stared him in the face that the aforesaid hole was
over the window which was *next but one* to the
parapet.   Then he counted the rooms of the
house—"Our Sal's bedroom—passage — wife's
store-room—own bedroom—one—two—three —
four."   Next he counted the windows—"one—
two—three—four—*five.*"

There was one too many.   He repeated the
process with the same result.

Between the passage and the store-room,
which were next to each other, there was decidedly
a window—the window too many.

If a window, then a room—unanswerable
logic!

Now thoroughly aroused, he dashed his pipe
to the ground with a vast exclamation, and

rushed into the house at the top of his speed.   It was the work of a moment to call together half a dozen able-bodied serving-men, to arm them and himself with divers spades and mattocks, and to scale the creaking stairs which led to the parapet window.   There was no trace of a door, nothing but a flat, white-washed wall.   He sounded it with a hasty blow, and a dull, hollow sound rang through the house.

"Odswinderakins!" roared the farmer. "Down wi' un, boys! Virst o' ye thro' un shall ha' Dame's apern vull of zilver gerts.[1] Gi' it un, lads!"

Clash went the mattocks into the cob-wall; cling, clang rang the spades on the oak floor. A cloud of dust rolled through the staircase as the farmer's pick-axe went up to the head in the first breach, and the farmer's wife rushed up the stairs.   Half-choked, and wholly stunned by the din, she could get little information beyond a general statement that the Goodger[2] was in the house, which seemed self-evident.   Another five minutes' work, and the farmer dashed through the gap, which barely admitted his burly person, followed by his wife, whose curiosity mastered her rage and fright.

And what did they see?

A long, low room, hung with moth-eaten, mouldering tapestry, whose every thread exhaled a moist rank odour of forgotten years; black festoons of ancient cobwebs in the rattling casement and round the carved work of the open cornice; carved oak chairs, and wardrobe, and round table; black, too, and rickety, and dust-

[1] Groats.   [2] The Devil.

covered, and worm-eaten ; the white ashes of a
wood fire on a cracked hearth-stone ; and a bed.
The embroidered hangings were drawn closely
round the oaken posts, and rustled shiveringly in
the gust of fresh air which wandered round the
room.

"Draw un, Jan, if thee beest a mon,"
whispered the dame under her breath, looking
round anxiously in the direction of the gap at
which she had entered.

John screwed up all his courage, and with a
desperate hand tore down the hangings on the
side which was nearest the window.

In that dim half-light, for the night was
closing in rapidly and the shadows falling heavily,
they saw a white and grinning skull gazing
grimly at them from the hollowed pillow, and one
white and polished arm-bone lying idly on the
crimson quilt, and clutching the silken fringe
with its crooked fingers.

The dame swooned with a great cry, and her
husband, stunned and sickened, dashed to the
casement, and, swinging it back on its creaking
hinges, leant out, for the sake of a breath of
pure air.

Horror of horrors! The garden was alive
with ghastly forms ; ill-shapen, unearthly, demon-
like heads rose and fell with threatening gestures,
and mopped and mowed at him from among the
flowers of that quiet plesaunce.

Hastily raising his wife in his strong arms,
he made his way as best he could through the
welcome breach, nor did he rest that night till he
had walled up and secured, for a future generation, the terrors of the Haunted Room.

"I should love thee, Jewel, wert thou not a Zwinglian. In thy faith thou art a heretic, but in thy life thou art an angel"—in such terms did Dr John Harding address his former school-fellow at Barnstaple, but at that time his great antagonist—Bishop Jewel, whom Westcote describes, with punning enthusiasm, as "a perfect rich gem and true jewel indeed." This ornament of the English Church was born at Bowden, in the parish of Berry Narbor, which has the reputation of being about the healthiest in the country—a place where only old people die. The seventeenth-century writer, evidently a lover of puns, quotes the following epitaph on one, Nicholas Harper, who lies buried in the church :—

> "Harper, the musique of thy life,
> So sweet, so free from jarr or strife,
> To crowne thy skill hath raysed thee higher
> And placed thee in angels' quier,
> For though that death hath throwen thee down,
> In heaven thou hast thy harpe and crowne."

In Swymbridge Church, where Parson "Jack" Russell ministered so long, is a "shoppy" inscription on a monument erected to the memory of "John Rosier, Gent., one of the Attorneys of the Court of Common Pleas and an Auncient of the Honble Society of Lyons Inne, who died the 25th day of December, 1685, Ætatis suae, 57." It is as follows :—

> "Loe with a warrant sealed by God's decree
> Death his grim sergieant hath arrested mee,
> No bayle was to be given, no law could save
> My body from the prison of the grave.

Yet by the Gospell my poor soule had got
A supersedeas, and death seaz'd it not ;
And for my downe cast body, here it lyes ;
A prisoner of hope, it shall arise.
Faith doth assure mee God of his great love
In Christ will send a writ for my remove,
And set my body, as my soul is, free
With Christ in Heaven—Come, glorious Libertie ! "

Our next and last point is Combmartin,
Westcote's village—a long, straggling place,
which Miss Marie Corelli annexed for her
Mighty Atom, and another lady, whom I met at
Challacombe some years ago, designated with
pious horror as "dark"—no doubt in allusion
to the bits of folklore, which—happily, as I
think—yet linger in these rural districts. It
would be easy to cite many illustrations of
West-country "superstition," such as the fruitful
influences of the moon, which will send a man to
dig in his garden when it is covered with snow ;
but, having devoted a considerable section of my
Book of Exmoor to this fascinating topic, I will
here confine myself to the principal interest of
Combmartin—namely, its silver mines. In the
reign of Elizabeth, however, it was a great place
for hemp, and a project was formed for establishing a port at Hartland entirely on account
of this trade. As it was, the shoemakers'
thread manufactured in the neighbourhood was
sufficient to supply the whole of the western
counties.

As to the mines, Westcote states :—

" This town hath been rich and famous for
her silver mines, of the first finding of which
there are no certain records remaining. In the
time of Edward I. they were wrought, but in the

tumultuous reign of his son they might chance to
be forgotten until his nephew (?) Edward III., who
in his French conquest made good use of them,
and so did Henry V., of which there are divers
monuments, their names to this time remaining ;
as the King's mine, storehouse, blowing-house,
and refining-house."

The industry was resumed in Queen
Elizabeth's reign, but seems to have been checked
by the influx of water. However, a great
quantity of silver is said to have been raised and
refined, mainly through the enterprise of Adrian
Gilbert and Sir Beavois Bulmer, who bargained
for half the profit. Each partner realised
£10,000. The owner of the land, Richard
Roberts, who happens to have been Westcote's
father-in-law, presented William Bourchier, Earl
of Bath, with a "rich and rare" cup, bearing
the quaint inscription :—

> "In Martin's Comb long lay I hiyd,
>   Obscur'd, deprest wth grossest soyle,
> Debased much wth mixed lead,
>   Till Bulmer came, whoes skill and toyle
> Refined me so pure and cleen,
>   As rycher no wher els is seene.

> "And adding yet a farder grace,
>   By fashion he did inable
> Me worthy for to take a place
>   To serve at any Prince's table ,
> Comb Martyn gave the Oare alone,
>   Bulmer fyning and fashion."

Another cup was given to Sir Richard Martin,
Lord Mayor of London, who was also master and
manager of the Mint, the design being that it

COMBMARTIN CHURCH.

should remain in the permanent possession of the Corporation. It weighed 137 oz., and like its fellow, was engraved with naïve, and, I fear, doggerel verses.

> " When water workes in broaken wharfe
>   At first erected were,
> And Beavis Bulmer with his art
>   The waters, 'gan to reare,
> Disperced I in earth dyd lye
> Since all beginnings old,

> " In place cal'd Comb wher Martin long
>   Had hydd me in his molde.
> I did no service on the earth,
>   Nor no man set me free,
> Till Bulmer by skill and charge
>   Did frame me this to be."

The Latin appendices to the "poems" show the date of the presentations to have been the year 1593; and Blackmore seems to refer to them when he speaks of the "inaccurate tales concerning" the silver cup at Combmartin, sent to Queen Elizabeth (*Lorna Doone*, chapter lviii.). Ultimately the flooding, with which there was no means of effectually coping, put a stop to the operations; but it is possible that they were not entirely suspended, as a few years ago I saw a report in a local journal that a Combmartin half-crown of 1645 was sold in an auction room in London for the sum of £5, 12s. 6d.

In 1659 the working of the mines was brought before Parliament by a distinguished mineralogist named Bushell, but nothing was done, and, when, forty years later, an attempt was made to exploit them, it resulted in failure. Between 1796 and 1802 the experiment was renewed, and 9293 tons of ore were shipped to Wales. The mines were then closed, and so remained till 1813, when 208 tons were sent to Bristol. The cost, however, exceeded the profit, and in 1817 the mining was again abandoned.

Yet another effort was made in 1833, this time by a joint-stock company with a capital of £30,000, nearly half of which was expended in plant, the sinking of shafts, etc. However, a rich vein having been discovered, work was carried on feverishly night and day, and a large profit realised, three dividends being made to the shareholders. As the result, shares were run up to a high premium by speculators, who, in mining phraseology, "worked the eye out." In 1845 a smelting company was formed, but neither this nor the mining company, whose expenses averaged £500 a month, was destined to last. In 1848 the engines were taken down, and apart from a spasmodic and, 'tis said, unprincipled attempt at company promoting in 1850, nothing has since been done.

The levels were driven under the village; and beneath the King's Arms (or Pack of Cards, as the old manor-house of the Leys is usually designated) runs a subterranean passage, constructed for drainage purposes. The ore is exceedingly rich in silver and lead, and the opinion has been expressed that the mines, worked fairly, would have yielded a tolerable return.

There is an old saying, "Out of the world, and into Combmartin." On this odd text Miss

Annie Irwin has based the following pretty verses :—

> " ' Out of the world ' they call thee.   True,
>   Thy rounded bay of loveliest blue,
>   Thy soft hills veiled in silvery grey,
>   Where glancing lights and shadows stray ;
>
> " Thy orchards gemmed with milk-white bloom,
>   Thy whispering woodlands, grateful gloom,
>   Thy tower, whose fair proportions rise,
>   'Mid the green trees, to summer skies—
>
> " Viewed thus afar, by one just fled
>   From the vast city's restless tread,
>   He well might deem, when gazing here,
>   His footsteps pressed some lovelier sphere."

Both Combmartin and Martinhoe—Martin's vale and Martin's hill—received their name from one of William the Conqueror's ablest lieutenants, Martin of Tours.

The horrible murder which gave rise to the traditional couplet,

> " If anyone asketh who killed thee,
>   Say 'twas the Doones of Bagworthy,"

is located by Blackmore in the parish of Martinhoe, and he subjoins the following note : " The story is strictly true ; and true it is that the country-people rose, to a man, at this dastard cruelty, and did what the Government failed to do."   The term "strictly" seems to imply that Blackmore had been informed by some authority that Martinhoe was the place of the tragedy, and that murder was aggravated by abduction.   On both these points the account in *Lorna Doone* is at variance with Mr Cooper's version (quoted on p. 144), which mentions Exford as the scene of the butchery, and altogether omits the other incident. Of course, there may have been different versions floating about.

Past Lee Bay and Wooda Bay, both sweetly sylvan, the pilgrim fares to the Valley of Rocks and Lynton.

ENVOY

The most expeditious mode of returning from the precipices and cascades of Lynton is by means of the light railway to Barnstaple. The conscientious pilgrim, however, will not quit the neighbourhood without visiting Parracombe, which ought to be, in a peculiar sense, his Mecca. In the prologue, reasons have been advanced, which need not be repeated, why this is the case, and although our course has been a devious one, it will now be recognised that there was method in the madness. The spot which must have been to Blackmore the most sacred of all—except, perhaps, Teddington Churchyard, where his wife slept her last sleep—was surely Parracombe—the home of his race; and here I propose to take leave of the reader. The local traffic being small, trains do not stop at Parracombe all the year round, but at any time this courtesy will be extended to passengers desiring it.

The manor of Parracombe was formerly in the hands of the St Albans (or Albyns) family, joined by Blackmore (*Maid of Sker*, chapter lxvi.) with the Tracys and Bassets, as among the most distinguished in North Devon. About a century and a half ago their lands were sold, principally to yeomen who farmed the soil; and, as we have seen, the Blackmores belonged to this category. A representative of the clan still owns Court Place and Church Town farms; and Mr H. R. Blackmore, proprietor of the "Fox and Goose," can claim to be second cousin of the novelist.

Situated on the south-west of the river Heddon is Halwell Farm, the property of Sir Thomas Acland, where is a circular British encampment, standing, as such encampments usually do, on a height. The trenches are about fifteen feet deep. There are two or three similar remains within a short radius, but they are less conspicuous and important. It is said that cannon balls have been dug up at Halwell Castle.

Mr Page does not speak too flatteringly of the scenery, but Parracombe Common, with its scent-laden breezes, is by no means destitute of charm, for the purple eminence of Chapman Barrows, the highest point in North Devon, and the lovely valley of Trentishoe below, compose a landscape fair enough for the most exacting eye. Beyond is Heddon's Mouth, where Old Davy landed on a memorable occasion (*Maid of Sker*, chapter liii.), and on the road is that well-known and most quaint and attractive hostel, the Hunter's Inn.

This, however, is to wander away from Parracombe, which is itself a quaint old village, while Parracombe Mill, Heal, and Rowley are picturesque hamlets. The old twelfth-century church has been abandoned, since 1878, for ordinary uses, but it still stands—about half a mile from the village—and the tower has been recently in part restored.   And now, with a final reminder of East Bodley and Barton and Kinwelton (in Martinhoe parish), our pilgrimage has reached its goal.   In a few moments we shall be tumbling downhill along the surprising curves of the Lynton railway, to re-enter the world of commonplace.

NOTES

I. Mr Arthur Smyth believes that the founder of the Quartly herd was Mr Henry Quartly, who married Betty Blackmore. His mother often visited her uncle Quartly, and he tells us that he had heard her speak of the care and attention they received, and how fat they were. They were brought to perfection by his son, Mr James Quartly, of West Molland House, who was one of the judges at Smithfield. Mr John Quartly of Champson never exhibited. Mr James Quartly had no children, and on his retirement the herd was dispersed.

II. Son of the before-named John Quartly, and grandson of Henry Quartly, he had never exhibited, but kept up the reputation of the family as breeders.

A sister of John and James Quartly married her cousin, the Rev. Richard Blackmore, of Charles, and another sister married Captain William Dovell, to whom at one time the novelist's brother, Mr Turberville, bequeathed his property. Captain Dovell's mother was a Blackmore. To what branch of the family she belonged is uncertain, but it was through her that Court Barton came to the Dovells.

Mr Smyth tells an extraordinary story of this gentleman.

"Captain Dovell," he says, "was born at Killiton. He hated farming, and at last his family gave him his desire and he went to sea. He related a story of his wreck off the coast of Ireland, and how the natives fought for the wreckage. At last, as captain of an East Indiaman (his own), he took his wife and son, a boy of eight years, with him to sea. The vessel was wrecked. He never saw the boy, but he caught his wife and swam for hours ; she died in his arms from exposure. He got ashore at last, and had to read the burial service over his wife. He was never the same after that. When I knew him in the early sixties, he was a powerfully built man of the kindliest disposition. I was an invalid then, and he would sit with me for hours relating stories of his boyish scrapes or playing for hours. He married again, and settled at Barnstaple, where he died about twenty years ago. His wife survived him only about one week ; both are buried in the family vault at Parracombe churchyard."

INDEX

2-N

PRINTED BY OLIVER AND BOYD, EDINBURGH.

A SERIES OF BEAUTIFUL BOOKS IN COLOUR

BEAUTIFUL BRITAIN

LARGE SQUARE DEMY 8vo, BOARDS, WITH PICTURE IN COLOUR ON THE COVER

EACH CONTAINING 12 FULL-PAGE ILLUSTRATIONS IN COLOUR

PRICE **1/6** NET EACH

(By Post 1/10)   *(By Post 1/10)*

VOLUMES IN THE SERIES:

CANTERBURY
CAMBRIDGE
THE CHANNEL ISLANDS
THE FIRTH OF CLYDE
THE ENGLISH LAKES
THE ISLE OF MAN
THE ISLE OF WIGHT
OXFORD

STRATFORD - ON - AVON,
    LEAMINGTON AND
    WARWICK
THE THAMES
THE TROSSACHS
NORTH WALES
WESSEX
WINDSOR AND ETON

AND, UNIFORM WITH THE ABOVE

THE ROMANCE OF LONDON

NOTE

This is a new series of colour-books produced at a popular price, and they are the most inexpensive books of this character which have ever been produced. They therefore make a significant epoch in colour-printing, *bringing for the first time a high-class colour-book within the reach of all.* The illustrations are by well-known artists, and their work has been reproduced with the greatest accuracy, while the printing reaches an exceedingly high level which will satisfy the most exacting reader. The authors have been selected with great care, and are well known for the charm of their style and the accuracy of their information. Among them may be mentioned Mr Joseph E. Morris, B.A., Mr C. G. Harper, Miss G. E. Mitton, Mr Gordon Home, Mr Dixon Scott, and Mr T. H. Manners Howe.

PUBLISHED BY
ADAM & CHARLES BLACK, 4, 5 & 6 SOHO SQUARE, LONDON, W.

BLACK'S
HOME GUIDE BOOKS

BATH AND BRISTOL. 6d. net.
BELFAST AND THE NORTH OF IRE-
LAND. 1s. net.
BOURNEMOUTH. 6d. net.
BRIGHTON AND ENVIRONS. 6d. net.
BUCKINGHAMSHIRE. 1s. net.
BUXTON AND THE PEAK COUNTRY.
1s. net. [net.
CANTERBURY AND EAST KENT. 1s.
CHANNEL ISLANDS. 1s. net. Cloth,
with extra Maps, 2s. 6d. net.
CORNWALL AND SCILLY ISLANDS.
2s. 6d. net.
DERBYSHIRE. 2s. 6d. net.
DEVONSHIRE. 2s. 6d. net.
DORSETSHIRE. 2s. 6d. net.
DUBLIN AND THE EAST OF IRELAND.
1s. net.
EDINBURGH. 6d. net.
ENGLISH LAKES. 3s. 6d. net.
ENGLISH LAKES. Cheap Edition,
1s. net.
EXETER AND EAST DEVON. 1s. net.
GALWAY AND WEST OF IRELAND.
1s. net.
GLASGOW AND THE CLYDE. 6d. net.
GUERNSEY, HERM, SARK, AND
ALDERNEY. 6d. net.
HAMPSHIRE. 2s. 6d. net.
HARROGATE. 1s. net.
ILFRACOMBE AND NORTH DEVON.
6d. net.
IRELAND. 5s. net.
IRELAND. Cheap Edition. 1s. net.
ISLE OF MAN. 1s. net.
ISLE OF WIGHT. 1s. net.
JERSEY. 6d. net.
KENT. 2s. 6d. net.
KENT, EAST (CANTERBURY, MAR-
GATE, RAMSGATE, ETC.) 1s. net.
KENT, WEST (TUNBRIDGE WELLS,
MAIDSTONE, ETC.). 1s. net.

KILLARNEY AND THE SOUTH OF
IRELAND. 1s. net.
LEAMINGTON, STRATFORD, ETC.,
1s. net.
LIVERPOOL AND DISTRICT. 1s. net.
LONDON AND ENVIRONS. 1s. net.
AROUND LONDON, COMPLETE.
2s. 6d. net.
AROUND LONDON, NORTH. 6d. net.
AROUND LONDON, WEST. 6d. net.
AROUND LONDON, SOUTH. 6d. net.
MANCHESTER AND SALFORD. 1s. net.
MARGATE AND THE EAST OF KENT.
1s. net.
MATLOCK (DOVEDALE AND CENTRAL
DERBYSHIRE). 1s. net.
MOFFAT. 1s. net. [1s. net.
PLYMOUTH AND SOUTH DEVON.
SCOTLAND. 7s. 6d. net.
SCOTLAND. Cheap Edition. 1s. net.
SCOTLAND, EAST CENTRAL. 2s. 6d.
net.
SCOTLAND, NORTH. 2s. 6d. net.
SCOTLAND, WEST AND SOUTH-
WEST. 2s. 6d. net.
SCOTLAND, SOUTH-EAST. 2s. 6d. net
SHERWOOD FOREST AND THE
DUKERIES. 6d. net.
SOMERSET. 2s. 6d. net.
SURREY. 2s. 6d. net.
SUSSEX. 2s. 6d. net.
TORQUAY AND THE SOUTH HAMS.
6d. net. [1s. net.
TROSSACHS AND LOCH LOMOND.
TUNBRIDGE WELLS AND WEST
KENT. 1s. net.
WALES, NORTH. 3s. 6d. net.
WALES, SOUTH. 3s. 6d. net.
WALES. Cheap Edition. 1s. net.
WHAT TO SEE IN ENGLAND. Illus-
trated. 2s. 6d. net.
WYE, THE. 1s. net.

*A full List of Black's Home and Foreign Guide Books can be obtained
on application to the Publishers.*

PUBLISHED BY
ADAM & CHARLES BLACK, 4, 5 & 6 SOHO SQUARE, LONDON, W.

www.ingramcontent.com/pod-product-compliance
Lightning Source LLC
Chambersburg PA
CBHW072337090426
42741CB00012B/2821